more
LATIN FOR THE ILLITERATI

By the Same Author

Latin for the Illiterati: Exorcizing the Ghosts of a Dead Language

   and

The Craft of Religious Studies

A Guide to the End of the World

On the Boundaries of American Evangelicalism

Prime-Time Religion: An Encyclopedia of Religious Broadcasting

JON R. STONE

more
LATIN FOR THE ILLITERATI

A GUIDE TO EVERYDAY

MEDICAL, LEGAL, AND RELIGIOUS LATIN

ROUTLEDGE
NEW YORK AND LONDON

Published in 1999 by

Routledge
29 West 35th Street
New York, NY 10001

Published in Great Britain in 1999 by

Routledge
11 New Fetter Lane
London EC4P 4EE

Copyright © 1999 by Jon R. Stone
Printed in the United States of America
Design and Typography: Jack Donner

Library of Congress Cataloging-in-Publication Data

Stone, Jon R., 1959–
    More Latin for the illiterati : a guide to everyday medical, legal, and religious Latin / Jon R. Stone.
        p.   cm.
    Includes bibliographical references and index.
    ISBN 0–415–92210–0 (hb: alk. paper). — ISBN 0–415–92211–9 (pb: alk. paper)
        1. Latin language—Dictionaries—English.   2. Latin language—Terms and phrases.   3. Latin language—Medical Latin.   4. Latin language—Church Latin.   5. Law—Dictionaries.   I. Title.
PA2365.E5S77   1999
473'.21—dc21   98–43820
                                                                       CIP

To My Lovely Godparents,

Clyde J. and Betty F. Taylor,

*who have kept me on the straight and narrow
with patience, humor, and grace*

CONTENTS

PREFACE

These days it seems as though everyone is uttering mea culpas. From the literati to the glitterati it has become a commonplace—dare one say, all the vogue—for fallen heroes and heroines in the worlds of politics, sports, and, yes, even religion to seek public forgiveness for indiscretions past and present. This curious turn to public confession seems to have had its origins in the scandal-ridden decades of the '70s and '80s, when miscreant politicians, sportscasters, televangelists, and movie stars began making regular appearances in the nation's courts. By the 1990s, the indelible image of public confession, having become a regular feature of the nightly news, became fixed in the public mind.

Into the late 1990s, public tastes have continued to call for breast-beating and tears of contrition from fallen celebrities. Most public confessions have tended to follow the pattern set in 1988 by the remorseful Jimmy Swaggart, who, with tears streaming down his cheeks and a quiver in his voice, spoke those ancient words of repentance: *peccavi* (I have sinned). Since that time, many of our celebrated sinners, including Marv Albert and Bill Clinton, have fashioned themselves into poster children of contrition, seeking either to remove the tarnish of sin from their names or to bolster sagging polls.

With all these Swaggartesque made-for-television confessions, one might rightly begin to wonder: Can this kind of media repentance be sincere, or does this type of public ritual naturally lead to the shedding of so many *lacrimae simulatae* (crocodile tears)? And, with nearly everyone in Washington, *a maximis ad minima* (from the greatest to the least), being called before a federal grand jury for sharing a salacious tidbit or speaking an *obiter dictum* (informal remark) into a microphone, little wonder that, in our frustration and disbelief, we find ourselves exclaiming with Cicero of old: *O tempora!, O mores!* (O the times!, O the morals!).

As a culture, we have become quite accustomed to the language of culpability. Words and phrases such as *subpoena* (under penalty), *habeas corpus* (lawful detention), *quid pro quo* (a reciprocal arrangement), and *nolo contendere* (a plea of no-contest) speckle our sentences. But, even as we have become fluent in the language of guilt and shame, as a culture we have also remained conversant in the languages of healing and grace. For every *mea culpa*, there is also a corresponding *indulgentia ad omni peccato* (forgiveness from all sin). It is therefore interesting to note that whether the language we speak be that of justice, mercy, or love, we as a society have tended almost naturally to draw upon our Latin heritage.

"Latin?" one might well question; "Isn't Latin a *dead* language?" True, while we moderns might no longer read or speak Latin, we cannot help but notice how much of its influence continues to the present day. Though "dead," its ghosts lie at the foundation of Western medical, legal, commercial, philosophical, and religious knowledge. Though "dead," its use remains integral to our daily lives.

In a previous book, *Latin for the Illiterati* (1996), I set out to exorcize these ghosts by providing lay readers with a fairly comprehensive handbook of common Latin words and phrases. This present work is a companion volume that is meant as a *vade mecum* (guide) for those working in the major professions—Medicine, Religion, and Law—who encounter in their work a more specialized set of Latin words, phrases, and abbreviations. Though not a comprehensive work, *per se*, this reference text should give its readers a firmer grasp of the major terms and concepts that underlie modern Western professional life.

A reference book of this sort does not come without problems, and thus it does not come without a *caveat* or two from the author. First of all, though Latin as a spoken language died centuries ago, it did not escape subsequent corruptions in spelling, usage, and meaning. Contradictions there are many, and not only from one source to another but even within the same source. Though such discrepancies will doubtlessly frustrate the Latin master who might chance to open this book, in the end, I did not see it as my task to correct centuries upon centuries of change (indeed, I am still trying to fix all the mistakes in my last book!). I understand that in so doing I am guilty of preserving corrupted forms of spelling and usage and passing them on to the next generation of professionals, few of whom will have been educated in the so-called Classical languages. For the purposes of this book, however,

I decided that it was simply my duty as a scholar of Western religious and social history to record these words and phrases as they have been written and used in their respective professions, not as they *should* have been written and used.

A second problem (and *caveat*) has to do with the many Greek words that appear in this book. The Romans freely used Greek terms much as we freely use foreign terms. Many words and phrases listed in this book, such as *pater* (father), *mater* (mother), *sophia* (wisdom), *episcopus* (bishop), *philtrum* (love potion), and *Kyrie eleison* (Lord, have mercy on us) have Greek origins. This borrowing, while itself a type of corruption, gave to Latin a greater depth and variety of expression than it might otherwise have had were it not enamored of and influenced by Greek culture and ideas.

An additional problem (and *caveat*) relates to the authority that is often lent to arcane language. In the case of the legal maxims recorded in this book, many of them no longer carry force in American or English law—and some never did. The medieval right of *jus primae noctis* (the right of the first night) is a case in point. To list this ancient custom does not imply that it is or ought to be currently in force. As a lawful practice, *Primae noctis* was long ago abandoned by the Christian West as immoral and barbaric, though there were no doubt a few holdouts.

Also, the reader will notice that some maxims included in this book are blatantly sexist—at least to modern sensibilities. It should be noted that, in an attempt to be faithful to the sources, the inclusion of such culturally insensitive material becomes all but avoidable. Thus, while I have included some such maxims in this work, their appearance is for purposes of historical reference and the glimpse such phrases and maxims may provide into an earlier age of Western social and religious life.

Few books are written *in claustro* (in a cloister), and such is the case with this present work. Accordingly, I would like to extend my thanks and appreciation to a number of individuals who have given me encouragement and support over the years. Of the many whom I could name, I would especially like to acknowledge the following people: my parents, Robert H. and Bobbie Jean Stone; my brothers and their wives, Richard and Dawn Stone and David and Mary Stone; my nieces and nephews, Lauren, Shawna, Bethany, Christopher, Brenton, and Zachary; my lovely grandparents, Irene Timme and Curtis and Lois Stone; my dear friends and university colleagues, Brian and Maria Allen, Katherine Baker, Peter and Eileen Barker, John and Carrie Birmingham, Jeff Brodd, Tom and Karin Bryan, Mike and Leslie Burdick, Bill and Sharon Francis, Helen Harrington, Ben and Mimi Johnson, Kimberly Labor, Eric Mazur, Bill Medlen, Ken Montojo, Birger Pearson, Casey and Kathy Roberts, young Matthew and Tristan Roberts, Clark and Terry Roof, Ninian and Libushka Smart, Scott and Annelie Williams, Brian and Cybelle (Shattuck) Wilson, and Roy Zyla; I would also like to express special appreciation to Kevin Ohe, the Reference Editor at Routledge, for convincing me to undertake this second Latin project.

Last of all, I would like to express my love and profound respect for my godparents, Clyde and Betty Taylor, who, by their example, have helped instill within me a deep reverence for life and a fascination with its sacred mysteries. I dedicate this book in their honor.

Bonis Quod Bene Fit Haud Perit.

Jon R. Stone
University of California, Berkeley
September 1998

REFERENCES AND SOURCES

Anon. *Latin for Lawyers*. London: Sweet and Maxwell, 1915.

Ballentine, James A. *Ballentine's Law Dictionary* (3rd ed., edited by William S. Anderson). San Francisco: Bancroft-Whitney Co., 1969.

Beard, John Grover. *Latin for Pharmacists*. Chapel Hill, NC: The Book Exchange, 1942.

Collins, John F. *A Primer of Ecclesiastical Latin*. Washington, D.C.: The Catholic University of America Press, 1985.

Cooper, J. W., and A. C. McLaren. *Latin for Pharmaceutical Students*. London: Pitman and Sons, 1930.

Diamond, Wilfrid. *Liturgical Latin*. New York: Benziger Brothers, 1941.

Fuller, Horace J. *Latin for Pharmacy Students* (2nd rev. ed.). New Haven, CT: Published by author, 1951.

Groessel, William V. *Selections from Ecclesiastical Latin*. New York: The Bruce Publishing Co., 1931.

Howe, George, and John Grover Beard. *Latin for Pharmacists*. Philadelphia: P. Blakiston's Son, 1919.

Huber, Vincent. *Latin for Sisters*. Clyde, MO: Tabernacle and Purgatory Press, 1919 [reprinted 1931].

Lewis, James John. *The Collegiate Law Dictionary*. Brooklyn, NY: The American Law Book Co., 1925.

Longley, Elias. *Pocket Medical Lexicon*. London: Henry Kimpton, 1884.

McCullough, James A. *A Medical Greek and Latin Workbook*. Springfield, IL: Charles C. Thomas, 1962.

Nunn, H. P. V. *An Introduction to Ecclesiastical Latin*. Cambridge: Cambridge University Press, 1922.

Perkins, Mary. *Your Catholic Language: Latin from the Missal*. New York: Sheed & Ward, 1940.

Simpson, D. P. *Cassell's Latin Dictionary*. New York: Macmillan, 1977.

Spilman, Mignonette. *Medical Latin and Greek*. Ann Arbor, MI: Edward Brothers, Inc., 1949.

Stelten, Leo F. *Dictionary of Ecclesiastical Latin*. Peabody, MA: Hendrickson Publishers, 1995.

Stimson, F. J. *A Concise Law Dictionary* (rev. ed., edited by H. C. Voorhees). Boston: Little, Brown, and Co., 1911.

Stone, Jon R. *Latin for the Illiterati*. New York & London: Routledge, 1996.

Trayner, John. *Latin Phrases and Maxims*. Edinburgh: William Patterson, 1861.

Webster's New World Dictionary of the English Language. New York: World Publishing Company, 1964.

Woods, Robert S. *The Naturalist's Lexicon*. Pasadena, CA: Abbey Garden Press, 1944.

PRONUNCIATION GUIDE

Pronouncing Latin words is not as daunting as it may seem. Most Latin sounds have corresponding English sounds, following the same rules for short and long pronunciation of vowels. For example, the long *a* in *father* is the same sound as the long *a* in the Latin word *pater*. The short *a* in the English words *par* and *far* are very similar in sound to that of the Latin words *pax* and *fax*. The short *e* in *pet* is similar in sound to the Latin *et*, as is the short *i* in *twig* the same as the *i* in the Latin word *signum*. The long *o* in *Ohio* sounds very much like the *o* in the Latin word *dolor*. In the same way, the short *o* in *pot* is pronounced similarly to the short *o* in *populas*. Likewise, the Latin *u* in *runa* and *pudicus*, one long and the other short, sound the same as the long and short *u* vowels in *rude* and *put*.

With respect to Latin consonants, one should nearly always pronounce them as those in English (e.g., **b** = b, **d** = d, **f** = f, **l** = l, **m** = m, **n** = n, **p** = p, **r** = r, **s** = s, **t** = t, etc.), with the exception of **c**, **g**, **h**, **i-j**, and **v**, which are always pronounced like **k** (as in kirk), **g** (as in give, gave, and go), **h** (as in hard), **y** (as in you, yam, and use), and **w** (as in we and was) respectively.

Vowel diphthongs are another matter. Most Classical Latin linguists prefer to pronounce **ae** as if it were a long *i* (as in pine), **oe** as *oi* (as in boy), **au** as *ou* or *ow* (as in bough or now), **ei** as a long *a* (as in weight), **eu** as *eu* (as in feud), **ui** as *wee* (as in the French *oui*).

MEDICAL LATIN

A

a dextra: on the right

a latere: from the side

a sinistra: on the left

a tergo [in the rear]: behind

ab extra [from without]: from the outside

ab incunabulis [from the cradle]: from childhood

ab intra: from within; from the inside

absente febre (abs. febr.): in the absence of fever

absinthium: wormwood

absorbens: absorbent

abortus: aborted; prematurely born

absque ulla nota: without any mark

acanthulus: an instrument for removing thorns, splinters, and the like, from wounds

acephalus: without a head

acerbitas: acidity; sourness

acerbus (acerb.): sour; bitter

acetas: acetate

acetica: preparations of vinegar

acetum (acet.): vinegar

aciditas: acidity

aciditate infestante: when troubled with acidity

acidulus: sourness

acidum or acidus: acid

aconitum napellus: wolfsbane

acor: acidity in the stomach

activatus: activated

acus: needle

acutus: sharp; acute

ad aptam crassitudinem: to a suitable consistency

ad duas vices (ad 2 vic.): in two doses

ad gratam aciditatem (ad grat. acid.): to an agreeable sourness

ad gustum: according to taste

ad partes dolentes: to the painful parts

ad secundum vicem (ad 2nd vic. or ad sec. vic.): for the second time

ad syrupi densitatem evaporet: let it evaporate to a syrupy consistency

ad tempus [at the right time]: in due time; according to the circumstances

ad tertiam vicem (ad ter. vic.): to the third time

ad tres vices (ad 3 vic.): for three times

ad vivum [to the life]: lifelike

adde (ad. or add.): let there be added (i.e., add)

addendus (addend.): to be added

additum (pl. addita): something added

adeps: lard; fat

adhaesivus: adhesive

adhibendus (adhib. or adhibend.): to be used

adjuvans: an adjuvant (a strengthening agent that assists other remedies)

admove (admov.): apply

admoveatur (admov.): let it be applied

adolescens: youth

adstante febre (adst. febr.): in the presence of fever

adstrictus: confined

adstringens: astringent

adversus (adv.): against

aeger (f. aegra): sick; a patient; a medical excuse

aegrescit medendo [he grows worse with the treatment]: the remedy is worse than the disease

aegri somnia [a sick person's dreams]: hallucinations

aegrotat (pl. **aegrotant**) [he/she is ill]: a medical excuse

aequalis (aeq.): equal

aer: air

aeratus: aerated

aes: copper or brass

aestuarium: a vapor bath

aestus: heat

aetas: age

aether: ether

aethereus: ethereal

aethusa cynapium: garden hemlock (or fool's parsley)

affluxus: flowing to

aggrediente febre (aggred. febr.): on the approach of fever

agita (agit.): shake

agita ante dispensationem: shake before dispensing

agitato vase (agit. vas.): the vial being shaken

agitatus: having been shaken

albus (alb.): white

alcoholicus: alcoholic

alga: seaweed

alimentum: food

alium or **allium**: garlic

alius alias: one now, another later

alkalinus: alkaline

allevare (or **adlevare**): to alleviate

alligare (or **adligare**): to bind

allium cepa: onion plant

allium sativum: garlic plant

alpinia cardamomum: cardamom

alter ... alter ... (alt. ... alt. ...): the one ... and the other ...

alternis annis (alt. anni.): every other year

alternis diebus (alt. die.): every other day

alternis horis (alt. hor.): every other hour

alternus: alternate; one after the other

alterum tantum [as much again]: twice as much

alumen: alum

alvearium: the external opening of the ear

alveolus: a little hollow; a tray or trough

alveus: hollow area; cavity

alvo adstricta (alv. adst.): the bowels being confined or constricted

alvo soluta: with the bowels being loosened

alvus: the bowels

amarities: bitterness

amarus: bitter

ambo [two together]: both

ambrosia [food of the gods]: poison antidotes

amens: insane

amiantus: asbestos

amictus: clothed

ammonia: ammonia

ammoniatus: ammoniated

amphetamina: amphetamine

amphora: a jar

amplus (amp.): large; ample

ampulla: a small bottle

amygdala amara: bitter almond

amygdala dulcis: sweet almond

amygdalae: the tonsils

amygdalus persica: the peach

amylum: starch

ana (aa): of each

analgesicus: an analgesic

androgynus: an androgyne

anethum: dill; sweet fennel

anetus: intermittent fever

angina: sharp, constricting pain; the quinsy (i.e., tonsillitis)

angina maligna: a severe sore throat

angina parotydea: the mumps

angina pectoris: sharp pain in the chest (i.e., muscle spasms)

angina tonsillaris: tonsillitis

angina trachealis: croup
angustifolius: narrow-leaved
angustis: narrow
animalcula: a microscopic insect
animalis: (adj.) animal
animus: the mind; the life principle
anisum: anise
anno interiecto: after the interval of a year
anno vertente: in the course of the year
annos vixit (a.v.): he/she lived (so many years)
annuus: annual
anodyna: pain-relieving medicines
antacidus: antacid
ante cibum (a.c.): before meals
ante jentaculum (a.j. or ant. jentac.): before breakfast
ante lucem: before daybreak
ante meridiem (a.m. or A.M.): before noon
ante partum or **antepartum** [before birth]: before childbirth
anterior: at the front; the front part
anthelminticus: wormicidal
anthemis: chamomile
anticardium: the pit of the stomach
anticoagulans: anticoagulant
antidiphthericus: antidiphtheric
antimonialis: antimonial
antimonii vinum: wine of antinomy
antimonium: antimony
antisepticus: antiseptic
aperiens: aperient (e.g., a laxative)
apertus: opened
apex: the top; the pointed end of the heart (as opposed to **basis cordis**)
aphtha (pl. **aphthae**): ulcers in the mouth (as in thrush)
apis: a bee
apis mellifica: the honey bee
apocynum: dogbane
apotheca: a drug store
apparatus: apparatus

applicetur (applicet.): let it be applied
aqua (aq.): water
aqua aerata (aq. aerat.): carbonated water
aqua astricta (aq. astr.): frozen water (i.e., ice)
aqua bulliens (aq. bull.): boiling water
aqua caelestis [celestial water]: pure rainwater; also, a cordial
aqua camphorae: camphor water
aqua communis (aq. comm.): common water (i.e., tap water)
aqua destillata (aq. dest.): distilled water
aqua fervens (aq. ferv.): hot water
aqua fluvialis (aq. fluv.): river water
aqua fontana or **aqua fontalis** or **aqua fontis (aq. font.)**: spring water
aqua fortis (aq. fort.): nitric acid
aqua intercus: dropsy
aqua marina (aq. mar.): seawater
aqua menthae viridis: spearmint water
aqua mirabilis [wonderful water]: an aromatic cordial
aqua naphae (aq. naph.): orange-flower water
aqua nivalis (aq. niv.): snow water
aqua pluvialis (aq. pluv.): rainwater
aqua pura (aq. pur.) [pure water]: distilled water
aqua regia (aq. reg.) [royal water]: a mixture of nitric and hydrochloric acids that dissolves platinum and gold
aqua saliens (aq. sal.): a jet of water
aqua vitae (aq. vit.) [water of life]: a distilled spirit (e.g., whiskey)
aqualis: pertaining to water
aquosus: watery
arcanum (pl. **arcana**) [secret]: a medicine whose composition is closely guarded
arctium lappa: burdock (or beggar's-buttons)
ardor: a flame or the heat from a flame
ardor febrilis: feverish heat

ardor urinae: burning sensation during urination caused by inflammation of the urethra

ardor ventriculi: heartburn

arenosa urina: urine with gravel

areola: the colored area that rings the nipple

argenteus: silvery

argentum (ag. or Ag.): silver

argentum vivum: mercury

argilla: white clay

aridus [arid]: parched; dried; thirsty

armoracia: horseradish

armus: shoulder; shoulder blade

aromaticus: aromatic

ars: art; practice

arsenum or **arsenicum**: arsenic

arteria aspera: the trachea; the windpipe

arteria magna: the aorta (the artery of the body that carries blood from the heart)

arthriticus: pain in the joints of the body (i.e., arthritis)

articulorum dolor: a form of gout

articulus: knuckle

artificialis: artificial

artus: joint

asarum canadense: wild ginger

asbestus: asbestos

ascaris vermicularis: the thread worm

ascensus morbi: increase of a disease

asepticus: aseptic

assidue: constantly

astringens: astringent

attinctus: blackened

attonitus: stunned

augeatur (aug.): let it be increased

aura: a steam or subtle vapor

aura epileptica: the premonitory sensation of epilepsy sufferers, similar to the sensation of cold fluid rising to the brain

aura seminalis: the principle of attraction that drives semen up the fallopian tubes toward the ovum

aura vitalis: the life principle

aurantium amarus: bitter orange

aurantium dulcis: sweet orange

auri (pl. auribus; aur.): to or for the ear

auri lamina: gold leaf

aurinarium (aurin.): an ear cone; an ear suppository

auris: the ear

auristillae (auristill.): ear drops

aurum (au. or Au.): gold

avenae farina: oatmeal

avis: bird

axilla: armpit

axungia: lard

B

bacca (pl. baccae): berry

bacchia: pimpled condition of the face that attends heavy alcohol consumption

bacillus: rod; bacillus

baculus: a ball- or oblong-shaped lozenge

balanus: the glans penis and glans clitoridis

balneum: bath

balneum animale (baln. anima.): part of a freshly killed animal applied to a patient's body or limb

balneum arenae (B.A. or baln. aren.): a sand bath

balneum maris (B.M. or baln. mar.): a saltwater bath

balneum medicatum (baln. med.): a medicated bath

balneum siccum (baln. sicc.): a bath of dry ashes

balneum vaporis (B.V. or baln. vap.): a vapor or steam bath

balsamicus: balsamic

balsamum: balsam

barba: beard

barbitalum: barbital

barium (Ba.): barium

basis cordis: the base or rounded end of the heart (as opposed to **apex**)

belladonna: deadly nightshade

bene decessit [he died well]: he died naturally

benzosulphinidum: benzosulphinide (saccharin)

berberis: barberry

betula: sweet birch

bibe (bib.): drink

bibere: to drink

bibulus: taking up or taking in water or moisture

bicarbonas: bicarbonate

biduum: a period of two days

bifariam: in two parts

bifurcus: having two forks or prongs

bihorium: two hours

bilibra: two pounds weight

bilis: bile

bini: two at a time

bis: twice

bis bina [twice two]: two pairs

bis in die (b.i.d.): twice a day

bis terve die (b.t.d.) or **bis terve in die (b.t.i.d.)**: two or three times a day

bismuthum: bismuth

bitumen: asphalt

boletus: mushroom

bolus (bol.): a large pill

bombus: buzzing sound in the ears; gurgling sound in the intestines

borax: sodium borate

bougium: a bougie (a flexible instrument for entering the urethra, rectum, etc.)

bracchium (or brachium): the arm

brachio (brach.): to the arm

brevis: brief; short

breviter: briefly; shortly

brodium: broth; any liquid in which something is boiled

bromidum: bromide

brygmus: grinding of the teeth

bucca: cheek

buffera: buffered

buginarium (buginar.): a nasal bougie

bulbus: a plant bulb

bulla: blister caused by a burn or by scalding

bulliat (bull.): let it boil

bulliens: boiling

bullire: to boil

bursa [purse]: sac

butyrum (but.): butter

C

cacumen: tip

cadaver: a corpse

caducus: deciduous; perishable

caecitas: blindness

caecus: blind

caeruleus (caerul.): blue

caffea: coffee

caffeina: caffeine

calcaneum: heel

calcar: spur

calculus (pl. calculi): stone or gravel, found chiefly in the kidneys, bladder, and gall ducts

caldaria: a cauldron

calefacere: to warm

calefaciens: warming

calefactus: warmed

calendula: marigold

calidus: warm; hot

caligo [fog or darkness]: dimness or blindness of vision; mental darkness

caligo lentis: a cataract

calor: heat; warmth

calvaria: the human skull

calvus: bald

calx: lime; the heel

calx viva: quicklime

cambogia: gamboge

camera: a room or chamber

camphora: camphor

camphoratus: camphorated

cancrum oris: ulcer of the gums and cheek; cancer of the mouth

candidus: white; clear

caninus: canine

canius spasmus: spasms experienced by hydrophobes

cannabis indica: a type of hemp from which the narcotic hashish is derived

cannabis sativa (or cannabis): hemp

cannula: a hollow surgical instrument through which fluid is extracted from a tumor or cavity

capacitas: capacity

capiat (cap.): take

capiat aeger/aegra: let the patient take

capiendus (capiend.): to be taken

capillaris: pertaining to the hair; hairlike

capillatus: hairy

capilliculus: the minute veins of the organs

capillus: hair; head of hair

capiti (cap.): to the head

capitiluvium: a wash for the head

capsicum: cayenne pepper

capsula (cap. or caps.) [a small chest]: capsule

capsula amylacea (caps. amylac.): a cachet

capsula gelatina (caps. gelat.): a gelatin capsule

capsula vitrea (caps. vitrea): a glass capsule

captus: seized

caput (pl. capita): head

carbasus (carbas.): gauze

carbo: carbon; charcoal

carbo animalis: animal charcoal (i.e., bone-black)

carbo ligni: wood charcoal

carbo vegetabilis: in homeopathy, wood charcoal

carbolatus: carbolated

carbolicus: carbolic

carbonarius: a charcoal burner

carbonas (carb.): carbonate

carboneum: carbon

cardamomum: cardamom

cardiopalmus or cardiotromus: palpitation of the heart

caries: bone or tooth decay

caro or carnis: meat; flesh

carptus: plucked

carpus: the bones that comprise the wrist

cartilago: cartilage; gristle

carum: caraway

caruncula [small piece of flesh]: a carbuncle

caryophyllus: clove (the bud of the **caryophyllus aromaticus**)

cataplasma (cat. or catap. or cataplasm.): a poultice

catharticus: cathartic

catinum or catinus: vessel; dish

caulis: stem

causa: cause; reason

causticus: caustic

caute: carefully

cautus: careful

caveat [let him beware]: a warning or caution

cavus: hollow; concave

cedrus: cedar

celeriter: quickly

cella: storeroom

cenatus: after dinner

centrum: center; middle point

centrum commune: the solar plexis

cepa: onion

cephalagia: a headache

cera: wax

cera alba: white wax (beeswax bleached by exposure to sunlight)

cera flava: yellow wax (beeswax)

cerasus: cherry

ceratum (cerat.): cerate (i.e., wax)

ceratus: waxed

cerealis: cereal

cerebellum: the smaller portion of the brain

cerebrum: the brain

cereolum: a wax bougie

cereolus (cereol.): an urethral bougie

cerevisia: beer

cerifera myrica: bayberry (wax myrtle)

ceroma [wrestler's ointment]: a fatty tumor of the brain

cerumen: ear wax

cervix: the back of the neck or a necklike part

cetaceum: proper name for spermaceti, a substance obtained from the sperm whale

charta (chart.): paper; powder

charta bibula: blotting paper

charta cerata (chart. cerat.): waxed paper

charta exploratoria: test paper

charta exploratoria caerulea: blue litmus paper

chartula (chartul.): small paper

chirurgicalis or **chirurgicus**: surgical

chirurgus: a surgeon

chlorinatus: chlorinated

chlorum (cl.): chlorine

cholera infantus: infantile cholera

cholera morbus (or **cholera nostras**): a noninfectious form of cholera

cholericus: bilious; related to cholera

chololithus: a gallstone

chondrus crispus: Irish moss

chorda: cord; gut; suture

chordapsus: spasmatic intestinal colic

chorea scriptorum: writer's cramp

cibus (cib.): meal; food

cicatricula: a small scar

cicatrix: the scar of a healed cut or sore

cicatrix manet: the scar remains

cicuta maculata: water hemlock (used as a nonmedicinal narcotic)

cicuta virosa: poisonous water hemlock

cilia: eyelashes

cilium: the edge of the eyelid

cinereus: gray

cinnamomum: cinnamon

circa (c. or **ca.)**: about; near; around

circiter (c. or **circ.)**: about

circulus: a circle or ring

circum (c. or **circ.)**: around or about

circus: circle

cito: swiftly; quickly

cito dispensatur (cito. disp.): let it be quickly dispensed

citrus limetta: the plant from which bergamot oil is extracted

clauditas: lameness

clava: club

cnicus benedictus: blessed thistle

coagulare: to coagulate; to curdle

cocaina: cocaine

coccinus: scarlet

coccus: cochineal

cochleare (coch.): a spoonful

cochleare amplum (coch. amp. or **coch. ampl.)**: a dessertspoonful

cochleare infantis (coch. infant.): a teaspoonful

cochleare magnum (coch. mag.): a tablespoonful

cochleare magnum mensura: a measured tablespoonful

cochleare maximum (coch. max.): a tablespoonful

cochleare medium (coch. med.): a dessertspoonful

cochleare minimum (coch. min.): a teaspoonful

cochleare modicum (coch. mod.): a dessertspoonful

cochleare parvum (coch. parv.): a teaspoonful

cochleare plenum (coch. plen.): a tablespoonful

cochlearia magna duo (coch. mag. ij): two tablespoonfuls

cochlearia parva tria (coch. parv. iij): three teaspoonfuls

cochleatim: by spoonfuls; a spoonful at a time

coctilis: cooked

coctio (coct.): boiling; cooking

coctus: boiled; cooked

codeina: codeine

codex [book]: a formulary

coitus or **coetus:** sexual union

coitus interruptus [interrupted intercourse]: a method of natural birth control

cola (col.): strain

colaturae (colatur.): a strained liquid; the substance strained

colatus (colat.): strained

coleatur (colet.): let it be strained

colentur (colen.): let them be strained

colica biliosa: colic from an excess of bile in the intestines

colica calculosa: colic from calculi in the intestines

colica meconialis: colic from unexpelled meconium

colica pictorum [painter's colic]: colic from lead in the intestines

colliculus seminalis: the crest of the urethra

collodium (collod.): a collodion

colloidalis: colloidal

collum or **collus:** the neck

collunarium (collun.): a nasal douche

collutorium (collut.): a mouthwash

collyrium (coll. or **collyr):** an eyewash

colocynthis: bitter apple

color: color

coloratus: colored

colum: a sieve; a strainer

columna nasi: the dividing wall of the nose

columna oris: the uvula

columna vertebralis: the spinal column

coma: the hair of the head

comans or **comatus:** hairy

comminuere: to diminish; to reduce

comminutus: broken; crushed

commisce: mix together

commissura: a seam; a joining together

communicans: diseases that are communicable

communis: common

compos mentis [sound of mind]: in one's right mind

compositus (comp.): compounded

compressus: compressed

conarium: the pineal gland

concentratus: concentrated

concha [seashell]: the hollow portion of the external ear

conchae narium: the spongy bones of the nose

conchus: the cavities of the eyes

concisus: cut up

concusso prius vitro: the bottle having been previously shaken

concussus: shaken

condimenta: spices taken with food to promote digestion

condire: to pickle

confectio or **confectum (conf.):** a confection

congelatus: frozen; congealed

congius (c. or **cong.):** a gallon

congressus: coitus

conium maculatum: a type of hemlock, given in small doses as a sedative

conjugata diagonalis: diameter of pelvic opening

consensus: the sympathetic relation between certain organs of the body

conserva (cons.): a conserve (i.e., jam or confection); also, keep

consperge (consperg.): sprinkle; dust

conspersus: sprinkled

constrictor ani: muscles that close the anus (also, **sphincter ani**)

constrictor oris: the lip muscle (also, **orbicularis oris**)

constringentia: astringent

contactus: contact

contagio: contagion (spreading of a disease through contact)

continuantur remedia (cont. rem.): let the remedy be continued

continuetur (contin.): let it be continued

contraria contrariis curantur: opposite cures opposite

contusus (cont.): crushed; bruised

conus: cone

coque (coq.): boil

coque ad medietatis consumptionem (coq. ad med. consump.): boil to the consumption of half (i.e., render by one half)

coque in sufficiente quantitate aquae (coq. in S.Q.A.): boil in a sufficient quantity of water

coque secundum artem (coq. S.A.): boil according to pharmaceutical method or approved practice

coquere: to boil

cor: heart

cordiale: a cordial

coriandrum satirum: cilantro (or Chinese parsley)

corium: skin; hide; a leather thong

cornu [horn]: a horny kind of wart

cornutus: horned

corona veneris: syphilitic blotches around the forehead

corpori (corp.): to the body

corpus (pl. corpora): the body

corpus humanum: the human body

corrigens: a corrective (i.e., that part of a prescription meant to modify other ingredients)

corrosivus: corrosive

cortex (cort.): a peel; outer layer (e.g., bark)

corticatus: having a bark

costa: a rib

cotidianus (or cotidie): daily

coxa: hip; hip-joint

cranium: the section of the skull containing the brain

cras: tomorrow

cras mane (c.m.): tomorrow morning

cras mane sumendus (c.m.s.): to be taken tomorrow morning

cras nocte (c.n.): tomorrow night

cras nocte sumendus (c.n.s.): to be taken tomorrow night

cras vespere (c.v.): tomorrow evening

crastinus (crast.): of tomorrow; on the morrow

crassamentum: a clot of blood

cremor: cream

crepitus (crep.): discharge of wind or gas from the bowels

creta: chalk

creta praeparata: prepared or washed chalk

cribratus: sifted

cribrum: a sieve

cribrum ferreum: a wire sieve

cribrum setaceum: a hair sieve

crinis: hair

crispus: curled

crocus: the crocus; saffron (properly, **crocus sativus**)

crudus: crude

cruentus: bloodstained

cruri: to the leg

crus (pl. crura): a leg or shank; shin-bone

crux medicorum: the crux or puzzle of doctors

crystallinus: crystalline

crystallizatus: crystallized

crystallus: crystal

cubiculum: a bedroom

cubicus: cubic

cubitum: the elbow

cubitus: forearm

cucurbita [gourd]: a cupping-glass

cucurbita sicca: a glass used for dry-cupping

cujus libet: of whatever you please

cum (c̄): with

cum aqua: with water

cum duplo (c̄ dup.): with twice as much

cum parte aequale (c̄ pt. aeq.): with an equal quantity

cum penicillo (c̄ pen.): with a camel-hair brush

cum tanto (c̄ tant.): with as much

cuneus: wedge

cuprum (cu.): copper

cura: care; healing

curatio [healing]: the treatment of disease

curatus: cared for

curcuma: turmeric

cuspidatus: a pointed tooth

cutis: the skin

cutis anserina [goose flesh]: goose bumps or goose pimples

cutis capitis: the scalp

cyanidum: cyanide

cyathus [a ladle used for filling wine-glasses]: a wineglass; a wineglassful

cyathus amplus (cyath. amp.) or **cyathus magnus (cyath. mag.)**: a tumblerful

cyathus parvus (cyath. parv.) or **cyathus vinarius (cyath. vinar.)** or **cyathus vinosis (cyath. vin.)**: a wineglassful

cydonium: the quince fruit

D

da (d.): give

dandus (dand.): to be given

dare: to give

de die: while still day

de die in diem (de d. in d.): from day to day

de nocte: while still night

deaurare: to gild

deaurentur pilulae (deaur. pil.): let the pills be gilded (i.e., coated)

debilitas: weakness

debita spissitudine (deb. spiss.): of a proper consistency

decanta (dec.): pour off

deceptio visus: an optical illusion

decigramma (dg. or dgrm.): a decigram

decimillilitra (decimil.): a decimilliliter

decimus: tenth

decoctio or **decoctum (decoct.)**: a decoction

decoctum (decoct.): a decoction

decoctum hordei: barley water

decoloratus: decolorized

decoquere: to boil down

decorticatus: peeled (i.e., the bark having been removed)

decubitus (decub.): lying down

decubitus hora: (decub. hor.): at bedtime

defaecatus: refined

defectio animi (or defectum animae): fainting; a fainting spell

deflagratus: fused

deglutiatur (deglut.): let it be swallowed

dehydratus: dehydrated

deinde: then; next

delibutus: steeped

delicatus: soft; tender

deliquescens: deliquescent

deliquium: falling or fainting

delirium tremens (D.T.) [trembling delirium]: mental delusions caused by alcohol poisoning

delphinium: larkspur seed

dementia: insanity

dementia a potu [insanity from drinking]: delirium tremens

dementia praecox: a form of early insanity

demortuus: the late (i.e., deceased)

demulcens: softening; soothing

demum: at length

denigratus: blackened

denigrescens: nonstaining; stainless

dens (pl. **dentis**): a tooth

dentes cuspidati [the pointed teeth]: the eyeteeth

dentes incisores [the biting teeth]: the incisors

dentes molares [the grinding teeth]: the molars

dentes sapientia: the wisdom teeth

dentifricium: dentifrice; tooth powder

dentium cortex: the enamel coating of the teeth

dentur (d.): let them be given

dentur tales doses iv (d.t.d. iv): let four such doses be given

deodoratus: deodorized

depilatorium (depilat.): a depilatory

depurantia: medicines used to purify the blood

depuratus: purified

despumatus: skimmed; clarified

destillatus: distilled

desudatio: sweating

detannatus: tannin-free

detergens: cleansing

detritus [a rubbing away]: waste matter from washing or erosion

detur (d.): let it be given

detur talis dosis: (d.t.d. or D.T.D.): give of such a dose

dextra: the right hand

diaeta: a daily regimen; a diet

diagnosticus: diagnostic

dialysatus: dialyzed

dictus [said]: prescribed; indicated

diebus alternis (dieb. alt.): every other day

diebus tertiis (dieb. tert.): every third day

diem ex die: from day to day

dies: daytime or day

dies natalis: birthday

digestivus: digestive

digitatus: fingered

digitus [finger]: a finger's breadth (i.e., one inch)

digitus anularius: the ring finger

digitus auricularis: the little finger

digitus index: the index finger

digitus medius: the middle finger

digitus pedis: a toe

digitus pollex: the thumb or big toe

dilapsus: effloresced

dilubilis: dilutable

dilue (dil.): dilute or dissolve

dilutus (dil. or dilut.): diluted

dimidium (dimid.): half; the half

dimidius (dim.): one half

dioxidum: dioxide

diphthericus: diphtheria

directione propria (d.p. or D.P. or direc. prop.): with proper directions

dispensa (disp.): dispense

dispensatus: distributed by weight

distoma hepaticum: distoma (the fluke-worm; also, **fasciola hepatica**)

disulphidum: disulphide

diurnus: daily

diverticulum: a sac

dividatur in partes aequales (d. in p. aeq. or div. in par. aeq.): let it be divided into equal parts

divide (div.): divide

dolens: painful

dolenti parti or **dolentibus partibus (dolent. part.)**: to the painful part(s)

dolor: pain

dolor artuum: gout

dolore urgente (dol. urg.): with the onset of pain; when the pain is severe

domesticus: domestic

domi [in the house]: at home

donec (don.): until

donec perfecte coeant: until they mix perfectly

dorsum: the back

dosibus dividuis: in divided doses

dosibus exiquis: in small doses

dosibus magnis: in large doses

dosibus repetitis: in repeated doses

dosis (dos.): dose

dosis augeatur ad guttas iv (dos. aug. ad gtt. iv): let the dose be increased to four drops

drachma (dr. or drach.): drachm (one eighth of an ounce)

ductilis: plastic (able to be shaped)

ductus: duct; canal

ductus aquosi: the lymphatic ducts

ductus ejaculatorius: the duct that carries the semen into the urethra

dulcis: sweet

dulcis unda: fresh water

duo: two

duo sextarii: a quart

duodecim: a dozen

duplum (dup.): twice as much

dura mater: the external membrane of the brain

durante: during

durante dolore (dur. dolor.): the pain continuing

durus: rough; hard

dysentericus: dysentery

E

e lacte (e lact.): with milk

e paulo aquae (e paul. aq.) or e pauxillo aquae (e paux. aq.): with a little water

e quolibet vehiculo (e quol. veh.): with any vehicle

e quovis liquido (e quov. liq.): with any liquid

e vino (e vin.): with wine

eadem (ead.): the same

ebriolus: mildly intoxicated

ebrius: drunk

edulcora (ed.): sweeten

edulcoratus (ed.): edulcorated (i.e., sweetened)

edulis: edible

effervescens: effervescent

effervescentia: effervescence

efficaciter: effectively

effluvium: vaporous stench from decaying matter

ejusdem (ejusd.): of the same

egestus (pl. egesta): waste matter

elapsus: elapsed

elastica: rubber

elasticus: elastic

electuarium (elect.): an electuary (a confection)

electus: elected; chosen

elixir (elix.): an elixir

emeticus: emetic

emolliens: softening

empiricus: a physician who relies on practical rather than scientific knowledge (i.e., a quack)

emplastrum (emp.; pl. emplastra): a plaster

emplastrum lyttae: a blistering plaster

emulgens: emulsifying

emulsio or emulsum (emul. or emuls): emulsion

enema (en. or enem.; pl. enemata): an enema; a clyster

ens: being

entericus: enteric (i.e., pertaining to the intestines; intestinal)

epicranium: the scalp

epidemicus: epidemic

epigastrium: upper region of the abdomen below the sternum

epispasticus: blistering

epistomium (epistom.): a stopper

epistomium suberinum: a cork stopper

epistomium vitreum: a glass stopper

epithelium: cuticular areas of the body that differ from normal skin, such as the lips and nipples

erectus: upright

erigeron philadelphicum: fleabane

erythema: a simple skin rash

escharoticus: caustic

esculentus: edible

essentia: essence

evaporans: evaporating

ex modo praescripto (e.m.p.): after the manner prescribed

ex morbo convalescere: to recover from a disease

ex sanguis [without blood]: deathly pale

ex somnis: sleepless

ex vulnere mori: to die of wounds

excipiens: an excipient

excrementum (pl. **excrementa**): human excrement

exemplum: example

exhibeatur (exhib.): let it be exhibited

exoticus: foreign; exotic

expectorans: expectorant

expressus: expressed

exsanguis: bloodless

exsiccatus: dried

exsucidus: juiceless

extende (ext.): spread

extensus: extended; spread

extractum (ext. or **extr.)**: an extract

F

fac (f. or **F.)**: make

facies: the face

facies rubra: redness in the face

facilis: easy

factitius: artificial

faex: the dregs

farina (far.): flour

fascia: bandage; binding

fascia spiralis: a type of bandage that is wound around the limb in spiral fashion

fasciola hepatica: the fluke-worm (also **distoma hepaticum**)

fastigiatus: tapering

fauces: the throat

favus [honeycomb]: a type of pustule

febre durante (feb. dur.): the fever continuing

febricula: a slight fever

febris: a fever

febris carcerum [jail fever] or **febris castrensis** [camp fever]: typhus gravior

fecula: starch

fel: the gall bladder; bile

fel bovinum: ox gall

fel bovinum purificatum: purified ox bile

fellifluus: flowing with bile

femina (f.): female; a woman

femur: the thigh

fenestra [window]: an opening

ferax (or **fertilis**): fertile; fruitful

fere: almost; nearly; about

fermentatus: fermented

fermentum: yeast

ferratus: containing iron; iron-colored

ferreus: made of iron

ferrum (Fe. or **ferr.)**: iron

fertilis: fertile; fruitful

fertilitas: fertility

fervens (ferv.): hot; boiling

fervente die: in the heat of the day

fervidus: boiling hot

fetus or **foetus**: offspring

fiant (f. or **ft.)**: let them be made

fiant chartae (ft. chart.): let papers/powders be made

fiant pilulae (ft. pil.): let pills be made

fiant suppositoria (ft. suppos.): let suppositories be made

fiant trochisci (ft. troch.): let lozenges be made

fiat (f. or ft.) [let it be so]: let it be made

fiat cataplasma (ft. cataplasm.): let a poultice be made

fiat ceratum (ft. cerat.): let a cerate be made

fiat collyrium (ft. collyr.): let an eyewash be made

fiat confectio (ft. confec.): let a confection be made

fiat electuarium (ft. elect.): let an electuary be made

fiat emplastrum (ft. emp.): let a plaster be made

fiat emulsum (ft. emuls.): let an emulsion be made

fiat experimentum in corpore vili: let the experiment be done upon a worthless body (or object)

fiat gargarisma (ft. garg.): let a gargle be made

fiat haustus (ft. haust.): let a draught be made

fiat infusum (ft. infus.): let an infusion be made

fiat injectio (ft. inject.): let an injection be made

fiat lege artis (f.l.a. or F.L.A.): let it be made according to practice or the usual method

fiat linimentum (ft. linim.): let a liniment be made

fiat massa (ft. mas.): let a lump or a mass be made

fiat mistura (ft. mist.): let a mixture be made

fiat pulvis (ft. pulv.): let a powder be made

fiat pulvis subtilis (ft. pulv. subtil.): let a fine powder be made

fiat secundum artis regulas (f.s.a.r. or F.S.A.R.): let it be made according to the rules of practice

fiat solutio (ft. solut.): let a solution be made

fiat unguentum (ft. ung.): let an ointment be made

fibra: fiber

fictile: an earthenware container

ficus: fig

filix: a fern

filtrum: a filter

fimbria (pl. fimbriae) [fringe]: the fringe-like areas on the ends of the fallopian tubes

fimus or fimum: filth; dung

finis: the end

fistula: pipe; small tube; an internal ulcer

fistula in ano: an anal ulcer

fixus: fixed

flamma: flame

flatus: flatulence

flavus (flav.): yellow

flexibilis or flexilis: flexible; supple

flocci volitantes: a type of vision impairment in which one sees objects flying before the eyes

floccus: a tuft of wool

flos: flower

fluctus: wave

fluiddrachma: fluid drachm

fluidextractum (fldext. or fldxt.): fluid extract

fluiduncia: fluid ounce

fluidus (fl. or fld.): fluid; liquid

fluoridum: fluoride

foeniculum: fennel

foetidus: fetid

folium (fol.): a leaf

fomentum: fomentation

fontanus: from a spring

foramen: aperture; opening; hole

foramen magnum [great opening]: the passage from the cranial cavity to the spinal canal

foratus: pierced

forceps: a pair of tongs

forfex: a pair of scissors

forma: shape; form
formaldehydum: formaldehyde
formula: formula
fornax: oven; furnace
fortior: stronger
fortior vino: stronger than wine
fortis: strong
fortissimus: strongest
fossa: ditch; trench; sinus
fotus: fomentation
fovea: pit; pitfall
fractura: a break in the bone
fractus: broken
fragilis: fragile; brittle
fragilitas ossium: brittleness of the bones
fragrans: fragrant
frater: brother
fremitus: vibration
frendere: to grind
frequens: frequent; repeated
frequenter (freq.): frequently
frequentissime: very frequently
fricamentus: rubbing
fricare: to rub
frictio: friction
frigidus or **frigus**: cold; chilly
frons: forehead
frontis: front
fructus (fruct.): fruit
frumentum: corn; grain
frustillatim (frust.): in little pieces
fulmine ictus: struck by lightning
fumans: fuming
fumus: smoke
funis: cord; rope
furca: fork
fusus: molded; melted

G

galea [helmet]: a type of headache; a head bandage
gargarisma (garg.): a gargle
gaster: stomach; belly
gaultheria procumbens: wintergreen
gelasinus: a dimple (on the cheek)
gelatina: jelly
gelatinum: gelatin
gelidus: cold
gelsemium: yellow jasmine
gena (pl. **genae**): the cheek
geniculum: knee joint; kneecap
genticulatus: knotty
genu: knee
genua valga: a deformity that results in knocked knees
genus: genus; kind
geratici: a class of diseases
geraticus: old age
germen: sprout; bud; germ
gibbus: hump
gingiva (pl. **gingivae**): gum
glabella: the space between the eyebrows
glaber: smooth; hairless; bald
glacialis: icy
glacies: ice
glandula: gland; a small gland
glans clitoridis: the tip of the clitoris
glans penis: the head of the penis
globula: globule
glomus: a ball of thread or yarn; a skein
glossa: tongue
gluten: glue; gluten
gluteus maximus: the major muscle of the buttocks
glutineus: sticky
glyceritum (glyc. or **glycer.** or **glyct.)**: glycerite
glycyrrhiza: licorice
gossypium (gossyp.): cotton

gossypium absorbens: cotton wool

gradatim (grad.) [step by step]: gradually or by degrees

gradus: step; degree

gramen: grass

gramma (grm.): a gram

granulatus: granulated

granulum: granule

granum (gr. or grn.; pl. grana): grain

graveolens: strong-smelling

gravidus uterus: the condition of the uterus during gestation

gravis: grave; serious

grossus: coarse

gummi: gum

gummifer: gum-bearing

gummosus: gummy

gustus: taste

gutta (g. or gt.): a drop

guttae (gtt.): drops

guttatim (guttat.): by drops; drop by drop

guttur: throat; windpipe

gutturi (gutt.): to or for the throat

gyrus: circle

H

habeat (habt.): let him/her have

hac nocte (hac noct.): tonight; this night

haesitantia linguae: a speech impediment

halitus: exhalation; breath; vapor arising from newly drawn blood

hallex: the big toe; the thumb

halo: to exhale or breathe

hamamelis: witch hazel

hauriatur in fauces: let it be drawn into the throat

haustus (haust.): a draught

hebdomada (hebdom.): a week; a seven-day period

hebdomas: the seventh day of a disease (said to be a critical day)

helianthus annuus: the sunflower

hepar: liver

hepatarius: related to the liver

hepatolithus: calculus of the liver

herba: herb; grass

hermaphroditus: a hermaphrodite

hernia: rupture

hernia humoralis: inflammation of the testicle

hernia inguinalis: hernia at the groin

herpes circinatus: ringworm

herpes zoster capitas: shingles

hircismus [goat smell]: armpit odor

hircosus: smelling like a goat

hirsutus: bristly; prickly; hairy

hirudo (hir. or hirud.): a leech

hoc vespere (hoc vesp.): this evening

hora (H. or hor.): hour

hora decubitus (h.d. or H.D. or hor. decub.): at bedtime

hora somni (h.s. or H.S.): at the hour of sleep; at bedtime

horae quadrante (hor. quad. or hor. quadrant.): a quarter of an hour

horae unius spatio (hor. un. spat.): after one hour

hordeum: barley

hordeum decorticatum: pearl barley

horis intermediis (hor. interim.): at intermediate hours

horridus: cold shivers

humerus or **umerus**: the shoulder; the upper arm

humidus: wet

humor: any body fluid other than blood (e.g., bile)

humulus: hops (properly, **humulus lupulus**)

hydragyrum (hg. or hydr.): mercury

hydratus: hydrated

hydrocephalus: dropsy of the brain

hydrochloricus: hydrochloric

hydrogenium (H.): hydrogen
hydrops: dropsy
hydrops siccus [dry dropsy]: tympanites
hydrosus: hydrous; aqueous (i.e., watery)
hydroxidum: hydroxide
hyoscyamus: henbane
hypericum perforatum: St. John's wort
hypodermicus: hypodermic
hypogastrium: the lower part of the abdomen
hyssopus: hyssop

I

ictericus: jaundiced
icterus: jaundice
ictus solis: sunstroke
iecur (or **jecur**): the liver
ientaculum (or **jentaculum**): breakfast
ignis: fire
ignis actualis [actual fire]: cautery of the flesh by fire or heated iron
ignis sacer [sacred fire] or **ignis sancti Antonii** [St. Anthony's Fire]: erysipelas
ilium: the hip-bone
illicium anisatum: star anise
illico (illic.): immediately
illinendus (illinend.): to be smeared
imberbis or **imberbus**: beardless
immanis: huge
immaturus: unripe
immedicatus: unmedicated
impurus: impure; unclean
in actu effervescentiae: while effervescing
in articulo mortis: at the point or moment of death
in aurem dextram (in aur. dext.): into the right ear
in aurem sinistram (in aur. sinist.): into the left ear

in dies (in d.) or **indies (ind.)**: daily
in dorso: in or on the back
in dubio [in doubt]: undetermined
in extremis: at the point of death
in fauces: in or into the throat
in folio argenti: in silver leaf
in folio auri: in gold leaf
in horas: hourly
in incertum: for an indefinite period
in loco: in place of; in lieu of
in loco frigido: in a cool place
in melius mutari: to take a turn for the better
in oculum dextrum (in ocul. dext.): into the right eye
in oculum sinistrum (in ocul. sinist.): into the left eye
in partes aequales: into equal parts
in phiala: in a bottle
in scatula: in a box
in singulas aures (in sing. aur.): into each ear
in statu effervescentiae: while effervescing
in tempus [for a time]: temporarily
in utero: in the womb
in vacuo: in a vacuum
in vitro [in glass]: in a test tube or petri dish
in vivo: in the living organism
inanimus: lifeless
incide (inc.): cut
incisus: cut into pieces
incoctus [uncooked]: raw
index [a sign]: the forefinger
indicium (pl. **indicia**) [an indicating mark or sign]: a symptom
indolentia: free from pain
induratus: hardened
infans: infant
infestans: attacking; infesting
infestus: infested
infirmitas: sickness
infirmus [weak or feeble]: sickly

inflammatus: inflamed

inflatus: inflated

infricetur (infric.): let it be rubbed in

infunde (inf.): pour in

infundibulum: a funnel

infusio or **infusum (inf.** or **infus.)**: an infusion

inguen: groin

inhaletur (inhal.): let it be inhaled

injectio or **injectum (inj.** or **inject.)**: an injection

injectio hypodermica (inj. hyp.): hypodermic injection (i.e., beneath the skin)

injiciatur enema (inj. enem.): let an enema be injected

injuria: injury

innocuus or **innoxius**: harmless

inodorus: odorless

inolens: without smell

inquietus: restless

insanabilis: incurable

insipidus: tasteless

insomnia: sleeplessness

insomnis: sleepless

inspiretur (inspir.): let it be breathed (into)

inspissatus: thickened

instanter: instantly; at once

instillentur (instill.): let them be dropped in

instilletur (instill.): let it be dropped in

insufflatio (insuff.): an insufflation

inter cenam: during dinner

inter cibum or **inter cibos (i.c.)**: between meals

inter noctem (inter noct.): during the night

intercus: under the skin

interdum: now and then; sometimes

internus (int.): inward; internal

intestinum: intestines; bowels

intramuscularis: intramuscular

invicem: by turns

involve (involv.): roll

iodatus: iodized

iodinium or **iodum (iod.)**: iodine

iter a palato ad aureum [the path from the mouth to the ear]: the Eustachian tube

iterum: again; a second time

J

jam non: no more

jecur (or **iecur**): the liver

jentaculum (jent. or **jentac.)**: breakfast

jugulo (jug.): to or for the throat

jugulum (or **iugulum**): the throat

julapium or **julepus (jul.)**: a mixture; a julep

junior: younger

jus bovillum or **jus bovinum**: beef broth

jus gallinaceum: chicken broth

juventus (f. juventus): youth; adolescence; the prime of life

juxta or **iuxta (jux.** or **iux.)**: near; next to

K

kalinus: containing potassium

kalium (K.): potassium

kaolinum: kaolin

keratinum: keratin

L

labia or **labium** or **labrum**: lip; the lips

labia majora: the outer folds of the vulva

labia minora: the inner folds of the vulva

labium leporinum or **leporinum labium**: hare lip (i.e., a cleft lip)

lac: milk

lacertus: the upper arm with its muscles

lachesis: snake venom used in homeopathy

lacrima (pl. **lacrimae**): a tear

lacticinium: foods prepared with milk

lacticus: lactic

lactuca sativa: garden lettuce

lactucarium: lettuce juice (used as a sedative)

laevigatus: smoothed

laevus (laev.): left

lagena: a bottle

lamina: a thin plate or layer

lana: wool

laneus: woolen

languor: sickness

lapis calaminaris: calamine

lappa officinalis: burdock

laridum: lard

lassus: weary

lateri dolenti (lat. dol.): to the painful side

latex: milk juice; liquid

latissimus dorsi: the back muscle

latitudine (lat. or **latitud.)**: in width

latus (lat.): broad; wide; side; flank

laudanum: tincture of opium (one twenty-fifth of a gram of opium)

laurocerasus: cherry laurel

laurus: bay laurel

lavabrum: washing; a bath

lavandula: lavender

lavatio (lavat.): bathing; washing; also, a washing apparatus

laxans or **laxativus**: laxative

laxatus: loosened

laxus: loose

leni calore: with gentle heat

leniens: soothing

lenis: gentle

leniter: gently

lente: slowly

lentus: tough; resistent

leontodon taraxacum: the dandelion

levator: a lifting muscle

levis: smooth; light (in weight)

libra (lb.) [a pair of scales]: a Roman pound (i.e., 12 oz.); a U.S. pound (i.e., 16 oz.)

ligamenta subflava: the yellow ligaments that fill the spaces between the vertebrae

ligamentum: ligament; bandage

ligneus: wooden

lignum: wood

lilium candidum: white lily

limatura: filings

limon: lemon (properly, **citrus limonium**)

limpidus: clear; limpid

linctus (linct.): a soothing cough syrup

lingua: the tongue

linimentum (lin.): a liniment

linteum: linen

linteus: (adj.) linen

linum: linseed; flaxseed

liquefactus: liquified

liquidum: liquid

liquor (liq.): liquor; solution; liquid

liquor amnii: the liquid that surrounds the fetus *in utero* (i.e., amniotic fluid)

liquor pancreatis: pancreatic fluid

liquor sanguinis: the watery element of blood

lithium (Li.): lithium

lobelia inflata: Indian tobacco

lobus: ear lobe

locum tenens (pl. **locum tenentes**): a substitute or deputy, especially for a physician or a cleric

locus: place

longissimus: the longest

longitudine (long.): in length

longus: long

longus colli: the long muscle of the neck

lotio (lot.): a lotion

lotus: washed

loxophthalmus: squinting of the eyes

lubricans: lubricating

lubricus: slippery

lues: a plague (also, syphilis)

lues venerea: syphilis

lumborum (lumb.; sing. lumbus): the loins

lumbricus: worm

lupulus: hops (properly, **humulus lupulus**)

lupus [wolf]: a malignant ulcer or cancer of the face

lusus naturae: a freak of nature

lutum: clay

lux: light

lycopersicum: a type of tomato used in homeopathy

lympha: clear spring or river water

M

macera (mac.): macerate

macerare: to macerate (i.e., to soak)

macula: spot; stain; blemish

macula matricis [spot from the mother]: a prenatal skin blemish

maculatus: spotted (also, **maculis distinctus**)

madefactus: moistened

madidus: steeped

magnus (mag.): large; great

major: larger; greater

mala praxis: malpractice

malignus [hostile]: malignant

malleus: a hammer or mallet; a small bone of the inner ear

maltum: malt

malum: apple

malum medicum: a lemon

malum punicum: a pomegranate

malus: bad

mamma: the breast

mammalia: mammals

mancus: crippled; maimed

mandibula: the lower jaw bone

mane (m.): morning; in the morning

mane et nocte (m. et n.): morning and night

mane primo (m. pr. or m. prim.): early in the morning

mane sequenti (m. seq.): on the following morning

manet cicatrix: the scar remains

mania a potu [mania from drinking]: delirium tremens

manipulus: a handful

manubrium [handle]: a part of the sternum

manus: hand

margo: margin, border, edge

marrubium (also **marrabium**): horehound

marsupium: a pouch (e.g., the scrotum)

masculus (m.): male

massa (mas. or mass.): a mass

masticare: to chew

mastiche: mastic

mater: mother

materia: material

materia medica: notions and remedies used by physicians to heal patients

matrix: mother; the womb

maturus: ripe; mature

matutinus (matut.): of the morning

maxilla: jaw; upper jaw-bone

maximus: largest; greatest

meatus: a cavity; an opening; a passage

meatus urinarius: the urethra

medicamentarius: a pharmacist

medicamentum: drug; medicine

medicatus: medicated

medicina: medicine

Medicinae Doctor (M.D.): Doctor of Medicine

medicinalis: medicinal

medicinus: the art of healing

medicus: a physician (also, medical)

Medicus Veterinarius (M.V.): a veterinarian

mediocritas: moderation

medius: medium; middle-sized

medulla: pith; marrow

medulla spinalis: the spinal cord

mel: honey

mel despumatum: clarified honey

melilotus: three-leaf clover (sweet clover)

melior: better

melissa officinalis: lemon balm

membrana: membrane

membrana tympani: the membrane of the ear drum

membratim [limb by limb]: one by one; piecemeal

membrum: limb

membrum virile [the male member]: the penis

mens: mind

menses (pl.): menstruation

mensis: month

menstruum: a solvent

menstruus: monthly or month-long; menstrual

mensura (mens. or **mensur.)**: measure; by measure

mentha: mint

mentha piperita: peppermint

mentha pulegium or **pulegium**: pennyroyal

mentha viridis: spearmint

menthol: menthol

mentum: the chin

merda: excrement

meridies: noon

mesogastrium: the central area of the abdomen

metallicus: metallic

metallum: metal

metrum: meter

mica: crumb

mica panis (mic. pan.): a crumb of bread

mineralis: mineral

minimum (m. or **min.)**: a minim; a drop; a very small amount

minimus: smallest

minor: smaller

minus: less

minutum (minut.): a minute

misce (m. or **M.)**: mix

misce fiat mistura (m. ft. m.): mix to make a mixture

misce secundum artem (m.s.a.): mix according to practice

mistura (mist.): a mixture

mitigatus: mitigated (i.e., reduced in strength)

mitis: mild

mitte tales (mit. tal. or **mitt. tal.)**: send such

mixtus: mixed

modicissimus: a very little

modo praescripto (mod. praesc. or **mod. praes.)**: in the manner prescribed

modulus: a mold

modus: manner; way

moles: weight; mass

molestia or **molestus**: irksome; troublesome

mollis: soft

mollities cerebri: softening of the brain

mollities ossium: softening of the bones

mons veneris: the female pubic region

morbilli: the measles (i.e., **rubeola**)

morbillosus: pertaining to the measles

morbo corripi: racked with disease

morbus: sickness; disease

morbus caducas [falling sickness] or **morbus comitialis**: epilepsy

morbus coxarius: disease of the hip or hip-joint

morbus ingravescit: the disease grows worse

mordicus [by biting]: with the teeth

more dicto (**m.d.** or **more dict.**): as directed; in the manner directed

more solito (**m.s.** or **more sol.**): in the usual manner

moribundus: dying; on the verge of death

morphina: morphine

morrhuae oleum: codliver oil (also **oleum jecoris aselli**)

mors: death

mors immatura or **mors praematura**: an untimely death

morsus: a bite

mortarium: a mortar

mortuus: dead

motores oculorum: the nerves that move the eyes

mucilago (**muc.** or **mucil.**): mucilage

muciparus: mucus-producing

mucus: mucus

multicavus: porous

multus: much; many

muriaticus: hydrochloric

murus: wall

muscae volitantes [flying flies]: spots before the eyes

musculus: muscle

mutitas atonica: nerve defect of the tongue resulting in the inability to speak

mutitas surdorum: the inability to speak due to deafness

myrica acris: the source of bay rum

myristica: nutmeg

myrrha: myrrh (properly, **balsamodendron myrrha**)

N

naevus or **nevus**: a mole or birthmark

naevus maternus [maternal mark]: a mark on the neck of a child at birth

nanus: a dwarf

nares or **naris**: the nose (i.e., nostril)

naso: to or for the nose

nasus: nose

natrium (**Na.**): sodium

natu: by birth

naturalia: the sex organs

naturalis: natural

natus (**n.**): born

nausea: general nausea

nausea marina: seasickness

ne: lest; not

ne tradas sine nummo (**n.t.s.n.** or **ne tr. s. num.**): do not deliver unless paid (i.e., c.o.d.)

nebula: a mist or vapor; a spray

neonatus: newly born

nepeta cataria: catnip; catmint

nervus: nerve; sinew

neuter [neither]: of neither sex

neutralis: neutral

niger (**nig.**): black

nimis: very much; too much

nisus [exerting; striving]: the action of the diaphragm and abdominal muscles in expelling any matter from the body (e.g., childbirth)

nisus formativus: the vital power in the organs of the body to perform their specific functions

nitras: nitrate

nitricus: nitric

nitris: nitrite

nitroglycerinum: nitroglycerine

nitrosus: nitrous

nitrum: soda

nocte (**n.**): at night; in the night

nocte et mane (**n. et m.**) or **nocte maneque** (**n.m.**): night and morning

noctu: by night

nocturnus: by night; nocturnal

nodus: a knot; a node

non: no

non compos mentis: not of sound mind

non dolet: it does not hurt

non repetatur (non rep.): let it not be repeated (i.e., no refill)

nondum natus: unborn

nostrum: quack medicine

novus: new

nox (pl. **noctis**): night

nucleus: a pit or stone

nudatum corpus: the naked body

nudus: bare; naked

numero (**no.** or **No.**): in number

numerus: number (i.e., a measure)

nutriens: nourishing

nutrimen or **nutrimentum**: nourishment

nux: a nut

nux vomica: Quaker button (used as a heart stimulant)

nymphae: the labia minora

O

obducere: to coat

obesus: fat or swollen

obiit (ob.): he/she died

oblatum (oblat.): a cachet

obscuro loco natus: of unknown origin

obstetrix: a midwife

obturatus: stoppered; closed

occiput: the back of the head (as opposed to **sinciput**)

octarius (**o.** or **O.**): a pint

oculentum: an eye ointment

oculo (pl. **oculis**; **ocul.**): to or for the eye

oculus: the eye

oculus dexter (o.d.): the right eye

oculus sinister (o.s.): the left eye

odontalgia: a toothache

odontalgia urgente: with the toothache being troublesome

odor: a smell

odoratus: odorous

officialis: official; approved

officinalis: authorized for use in an apothecary shop

oleatus: oiled

oleosaccharum: oilsugar

oleosus: oily

oleum (ol.): oil

oleum jecoris aselli: codliver oil (also, **morrhuae oleum**)

oleum olivae (o.o. or **ol. ol.)**: olive oil

olfactus: sense of smell

olibanum: frankincense

oliva: olive

olivum: olive oil

olla: jar

omne die (o.d. or **omn. die)**: all day; every day

omni alterna hora (o. alt. h.): every other hour

omni bihora (o.b. or **omn. bih.)**: every two hours

omni hora (o.h. or **omn. hor.)**: every hour

omni mane (o.m. or **omn. man.)**: every morning

omni nocte (o.n. or **omn. noc.)**: every night

omni quadranta hora (o.q.h. or **omn. quad. hor.)**: every quarter hour

omni sexta hora (o. sext. h.): every six hours

omni singula hora (o.s.h. or **o. sing. h.)**: every single hour

omnis (omn.): all; every

ope penicilli (ope pen.): by means of a camel-hair brush

opertus: covered

ophthalmicus: ophthalmic (pertaining to the eye)

opprobrium medicorum [the reproach of physicians]: an incurable disease

orbicularis oris: the lip muscle (also, **constrictor oris**)

orbicularis palpebrarum: the muscle that shuts the eye

ordinarius: ordinary

ori: to or for the mouth

os (pl. **ora**): the mouth; an opening

os (pl. **ossa**): a bone

os externus: the mouth of the vagina

os femoris: the femur bone

os humeri: the humerus bone (i.e., upper arm)

os pectoris: the breast bone; the sternum

os tincae or **os uteri** or **os internum**: the mouth of the uterus

oscillatio: swinging to and fro

osculum: a small mouth or opening (also, a kiss)

ossa: a skeleton

ossa pubis: the pubic bone

osseus: bony

ossicula: small bones

ossium compages: the skeletal system

ostium: an opening

oticus: relating to the ear

ovi albumen (ovi alb.): the egg white

ovi vitellus (ovi vit.): the egg yolk

ovula: an ovule

ovum (ov.): an egg

oxidatus: oxidized

oxidum: oxide

oxygenium: oxygen

oxymel (ox. or **oxy.** or **oxym.)**: a mixture of honey, vinegar, and water

oxyuris vermicularis: the tapeworm

P

pabulum: food

palatum durum [hard palate]: the front of the mouth

palatum molle [soft palate]: the back part of the mouth

pallidus: pale

palma: the palm of the hand

palpebra: the eyelid

panacea [a plant believed to heal all ailments]: a cure-all

panax quinque folium: ginseng

panchrestus: good or useful for everything

pancreas: pancreas

pancreaticus: pancreatic

panniculus: a covering

pannus: cloth

papaver somniferum (or **papaver**): the poppy from which opium and morphine are derived

papilla: nipple; teat

papula: a pimple

pappus: the first soft beard on the chin

paralysis agitans: Parkinson's disease

paratus: prepared

paries (pl. **parietis**): a side or wall of a cavity

pars: part

partes aequales (P.ae. or **p.ae.** or **pt. aeq.)**: in equal parts

parti affectae or **partibus affectis (p.a.)**: to the affected part(s)

parti affectae applicandus (p.a.a.): to be applied to the affected part

parti affectae pingendus: to be painted on the affected part

partitis vicibus (part. vic.): in divided doses

partus: birth

parum profuit: (fig.) it helped too little

parviflorus: small-flowered

parvulus: very small

parvus: small

pasta: paste

pastillum or **pastillus (pas** or **pastil.)**: a small lozenge; a breath lozenge

pastinaca sativa: the parsnip

pastus: food

patella: the kneecap

pater: father

patiens: a patient

patina: a dish

paullum (paul.): a little

pauxillum (paux.): a little

pectinum: pectin

pectoralis: pectoral

pectori (pect.): to the chest or breast

pectus (pect.): chest; breast

pedetentim (pedet.): step by step; by degrees

pediculus: louse

pediculus pubis: the crab louse

pediluvium: a foot bath

pedis digitus: a toe

peior or **pejor**: worse

pellis: skin; hide

peltatus: shield-like

pelvis [a basin]: the interior cavity at the base of the body

pendens (pend.): weighing

penicillum: a small brush

peniculum camelinum (pen. cam. or **penicul. cam.)**: a camel-hair brush

peniculus: a brush; a sponge

penis [tail]: the male sex organ

penna: a feather

pepsinum: pepsin

pepticus: digestive

peptonatus: peptonized

per biduum: for two days

per cribrum trajicere: to pass through a sieve

per diem [by the day]: daily

per horam: for an hour, by the hour

per infortunium: by accident

per mensem [by the month]: monthly; for each month

per os: by mouth

per singulos dies: day by day; every day

per somnum: asleep

per tres consequentes noctes: for three consecutive nights

per triduum: for three days

perendie: on the day after tomorrow

perforatus: pierced

peroxidum: peroxide

perpolitio: a polishing

perstetur (P. or **pt.)**: let it be continued

pertussis: whooping cough (also **tussis convulsiva**)

pervigilium: inability to sleep

pes or **pedis** (pl. **pedes**): the foot

pessimus: worst

pessus (pess.): a pessary; a vaginal suppository

pestis: plague or pestilence; a contagious fever

petalum: a petal

petra: rock; stone

petrolatum: petroleum jelly

petroleum [rock oil]: petroleum oil

pharmaceuticus: pharmaceutical

pharmacopola: a druggist (also, a quack)

phellus: cork

phiala: phial; vial; bottle

phiala agitata: the bottle having been shaken

phiala bene obturata: a well-sealed bottle

phiala prius agitata (P.P.A. or **p.p.a.)**: after first shaking the bottle

phiala prius concussa: the bottle having been previously shaken

philtrum: a love potion

phosphas: phosphate

phosphorosus: phosphorous

phosphorus: phosphorus

phrenesis: madness; frenzy

physiologicus: physiological

pigmentum (pigm.): pigment; paint

pilocarpus: jaborandi (the leaves of the **pilocarpus pinnatus**)

pilorum arrectores: the tiny muscles that cause the skin hair to rise when a person is cold or frightened

pilosus: covered with hair; hairy

pilula (pl. **pilulae; pil.)**: a pill

pilulae tunicatae: coated pills

pilus: hair

pimpinella anisum: anise

pinguedo: fat

pinguis: (adj.) fat; fatty

piper: pepper

piper nigrum: black pepper

piperitus: peppery

pistillum: a pestle

pix carbonis: coal tar

pix liquida: tar; wood tar

placebo [I will please] (. . .): a prescription given to please a patient

planta: the sole of the foot

plasma: plasma (also, a nonfatty ointment)

plexus: a network of blood vessels or nerves

plica: a fold; a plait

pluma: feather

plumatus: covered with feathers

plumbum (pb. or Pb.): lead

plumbum album [white lead]: tin

plumeus: downy

pluries: frequently; often

plurimus: most

plus: more

pocillum (pocill.): a small cup

poculum (poc. or pocul.): a cup

podex: anus

podophyllum: mandrake (mandragora); may apple

pollen [fine flour]: pollen (i.e., the powder found in flowers that possesses regenerative power)

pollex (poll.): the thumb or big toe; an inch in length

pollices sex (poll. sex): six inches (i.e., half a foot)

pomeridianus: of the afternoon

pomum Adami: the Adam's apple

pondere (P.): by weight

ponderosus: heavy; weighty

pondus: weight

pone aurem (pone aur.): put behind the ear

pons (pl. **pontes**) [a bridge]: a part connecting two other parts

porrigo: dandruff; ringworm of the scalp

portio: part; portion; section

portio dura: the facial nerve

portio mollis: the auditory nerve

porus: a pore; a callus

post cibum (p.c.): after meals

post duas horas: after two hours

post meridiem (p.m. or P.M.): after noon

post mortem (p.m. or P.M.): after death

post obitum: after death

post partum: after birth

post singulas dejectiones liquidas (p.s.d.l.): after each loose bowel movement

post singulas sedes liquidas (p.s.s.l.): after each loose stool

postea: afterward

posterior: at the rear; the rear part

postridie: on the following day

potassium (K.): potassium

potestas res cognoscendi: the power of the recognition of things

potus (pot.): a drink

praecipitatus: precipitated

praecox: premature

praeparatio: preparation

praeparatus (praep.): prepared

praescriptio or prescriptio: prescription

praesentia animi: presence of mind

prandium (prand.): lunch or dinner

prelum: a press

pressus: pressure

prima luce (prim. luc.) [at first light]: early in the morning

primae viae: the primary passages of the body (e.g., the stomach and the intestines)

primipara: a mother who is pregnant with or has delivered her first child

primo mane (prim. m.): early in the morning

primus: first; foremost

prius: previous; previously

pro capillis (pro capill.): for the hair

pro dose: for a dose

pro dosi: as a dose

pro jugulo (pro jug.): for the throat

pro naso: for the nose

pro oculis (pro ocul.): for the eyes

pro oculo dextro (pro ocul. dext.): for the right eye

pro oculo laevo (pro ocul. laev.): for the left eye

pro portione: in proportion

pro ratione aetatis (p.r.a. or pro rat. aet.): according to age of the patient

pro re nata (p.r.n. or P.R.N.): whenever necessary; as needed

pro singulis oculis (pro sing. ocul.): for each eye

pro usu externo: for external use

procumbens: prostrate

profluens: running water

profundus: deep-seated

prolapsus: a collapse or protrusion

prolapsus ani: a collapse of the extremity of the anus

prolapsus uteri: a collapse of the womb

prope: near

proprius [one's own]: proper; suitable

protinus: instantly

prurigo: a skin eruption attended with itching

pruritus: excessive itching

pubescens: pubescent

pudenda muliebre: the female reproductive system

pudenda virorum: the male reproductive system

puella: a female youth; girl

puer: a male youth; boy

puerpera: a woman in labor

puerperium: chidbirth; labor

pugillus (pug.): a pinch (a small quantity; only that which can be held between the thumb and index finger)

pulegium: pennyroyal (also, **mentha pulegium**)

pulmo (pl. pulmones): a lung

pulpa: pulp

pulsus: pulse

pulsus cordis: the beat of the heart

pulveratus: pulverized

pulvereus: powdery

pulverisatus: powdered

pulvis (pulv.): dust; powder

pulvis conspersus (pulv. consper.): a dusting powder

pulvis subtillisimus (pulv. subt.): the very finest powder

pumex: pumice

pumilio or **pumilus**: a dwarf

puncta lachrymalia: the openings in the lower eyelids where the tears appear

punctum: point; prick

punctum caecum: the blind spot of the eye

punctum saliens: the first movement of the embryo after fertilization

purgans: purging

purgus: purgative

purificatus: purified

purus: pure

putris: rotten; putrid

pyorrhea alveolaris: Rigg's disease

pyxis (pyx.): a pillbox

pyxis chartacea: a powder box

Q

quadrans: a quarter

quadratus: squared

quaeque: each; every

quam maxime: as much as possible

quam multi?: how many?

quamprimum: as soon as possible

quantitas (qt.): quantity

quantitas duplex (qt. dupx. or qt. dx.): twice the quantity

quantum libet (q.l. or q. lib.) [as much as you please]: liberally

quantum placet (q. pl. or q.p.): as much as you please

quantum satis (q.s. or quant. sat.): as much as satisfies

quantum sufficit (q.s. or quant. suff.): as much as suffices

quantum vis (q.v.): as much as you will

quaque (qq. or Qq.): each; every

quaque alterna hora (q. alt. h.): every other hour

quaque hora (q.h. or qq. hor.): every hour

quaque mane (q.m. or Q.M.): every morning

quaque nocte (q.n.): every night

quaque sexta hora (q. sext. h.): every six hours

quaque singula hora (q.s.h. or q. sing. h.): every single hour

quarta pars: one quarter

quartana: a fever occurring every fourth day, as in malaria (also, **febris quartana**)

quartis horis (quart. hor.): every four hours

quartus: fourth

quater: four times

quater in die (q.i.d.) (also, **quater die**): four times a day

quaterni: four each; four at a time

quinina: quinine

quinquies: five times

quinquies vel sexies in die (quin. vel sex. in d.): five or six times a day

quintus: fifth

quisque: each; every

quoque (qq. or Qq.): also, too

quotidianus or **quotidie (quot.):** daily; everyday

quoties: as often as; whenever

quoties opus sit (q.o.s. or quot. op. sit): as often as required

quotquot: as many as

R

racemosus: clustered (i.e., having racemes)

raditicus: by the roots

ramenta: shavings; splinters; chips

rasus: shredded

ratio: ratio; proportion

raucitas: hoarseness

raucitate urgente: with hoarseness being serious

recens (rec.): fresh

recipe (℞): take

rectalis: rectal

rectificatus: rectified; refined

rectum: the lower section of the intestines

rectus: straight

rectus abdominis: the abdominal muscles

rectus femoris: the major thigh muscle surrounding the femur bone

rectus musculus or **rectus:** any of various straight muscles

redigatur in pulverem (r. in p. or **red. in pulv.):** let it be reduced to a powder

redivivus [restored to life]: resuscitated

reductus: reduced

refrigerans: cooling

regimen: guidance; direction

reliquum or **reliquus (reli.** or **reliq.):** the remainder; the remaining

remedium: remedy; cure

remedium efficacissum: a sovereign remedy (i.e., an effective cure)

remisso animo [with inactive mind]: listlessly

renes (sing. **ren):** the kidneys

repetatur (rep. or **repet.** or **rept.):** let it be repeated

residium: residue

resina: resin; rosin

restrictus: confined

rete (pl. **retia**) [a net]: plexus of nerves; vascular network

rete mucosum: the tissue below the skin that gives it its color

rheum palmatum or **rheum**: rhubarb

rheumaticus: rheumatic

rhus radicans: poison ivy (also **rhus toxicodendron**)

rigens: stiff; unbending

rigidus: rigid; stiff

rigor mortis: the stiffening of the body after death

risus sardonicus: convulsive laugther associated with tetanus

roborans: strengthening

roboratus: strengthened

rosa: rose

rosmarinus: rosemary

rostrum: beak; snout

rotula: a lozenge

rotundifolius: round-leaved

rubefaciens: blistering; reddened

rubeola: the measles

ruber: red

ructus: belching

rugosus: wrinkled

rumex crispus (or **rumex**): yellow dock (sorrel)

ruptus: burst open

S

sabal: saw palmetto

saccharatus (sacch.): sugar-coated

saccharinum: benzosulphinide (saccharin)

saccharomyces: yeast

saccharum (sacch.): sugar; cane sugar

saccharum lactis: sugar of milk

sacculus: sack; a small bag

sacer ignis [sacred fire]: erysipelas

sacer morbis [sacred sickness]: epilepsy

saepius: more often

sal: salt

sal amarus [bitter salt]: a cathartic (e.g., Epsom salt)

sal catharticus: a cathartic (e.g., Epsom salt)

sal culinarius [cooking salt]: table salt

sal gemmae: rock salt

sal prunella: potassium nitrate

sal volatile: ammonium carbonate solution used as a restorative in fainting

saliva: saliva; spittle

salix: willow

salubritas: soundness; wholesomeness

salus: health; safety

salutaris: healthful; beneficial

salvia officinalis: sage

salvo praescripto: except as directed

sanguine suffusus: bloodshot

sanguis: blood

sanies: bloodied; a discharge from ulcers

sanitas: health; wholeness; sanity

santonica: wormseed

sanus: sane; healthy

sapo: soap

sapo kalinus: potash soap

saponarius: soapy

sarcophagus: flesh-eating (also, a tomb)

sarza: sarsaparilla

satis: enough

sativus: cultivated

saturatio: saturation

saturatus: saturated

scalpellum: a small surgical knife

scalprum: a penknife

scapula (pl. **scapulae**): shoulder blade

scarlatina: scarlet fever

scatula (scat.): box

scatula pilularum: a box of pills

scissus: cut; torn

scorbutus: scurvy

scrobiculus cordis: the cavity of the heart; the pit of the stomach

scrupulus or **scrupulum** (**scr.**): a scruple

scutum: a shield

sebum: grease; tallow

secale: rye

secundis horis (**sec. hor.**): every two hours

secundum (**sec.**): according to

secundum artem (**s.a.** or **S.A.** or **sec. art.**): according to pharmaceutical practice

secundum naturam (**s.n.** or **S.N.** or **sec. nat.**): according to nature; naturally

secundus: second

sedans: a sedative

sedativus: soothing; sedating

sedes: stool

selibra: half a pound

semel: once

semel die (**s.d.** or **sem. die**) or **semel in die** (**s.i.d.** or **S.I.D.** or **sem. in die**): once a day

semen [seed]: semen

semicyathus: half a glassful

semidrachma (**semidr.**): half a drachm (dram)

semihora (**semih.**): half an hour

seminex: half-dead

semis (**ss**): half or one half

semper: always

sempervirens: evergreen

semuncia: half an ounce

senectus: old age

senior: older

sensim: gradually; by degrees

sensorium: the seat of sensation; the brain (also, **sensorium commune**)

septicus: septic

septimana: a week

septimus: seventh

septum: a barrier or partition

septum nasi: the division between the nostrils

septum scroti: the partition separating the testicles

sequens: following

sequestrum: a deposit

sera nocte: late at night

seriparus: curdling

serra: a saw

serrulatus: saw-toothed

serum: serum (i.e., the fluid part of the blood)

sesqui: one and one half

sesquihora (**sesqh.**): an hour and a half

sesuncia: one and one half ounces

sevum: suet

sexies die (**sex. d.**) or **sexies in die** (**sex. in d.**): six times a day

sextarius: a pint

sextis horis (**sext. hor.**): every six hours

sexus: sex (i.e., gender)

sexus muliebris: the female sex

sexus virilis: the male sex

si dolor urgeat (**si dol. urg.**): if the pain is severe

si non valeat (**s.n.v.** or **si n. val.**): if it does not respond

si opus sit (**s.o.s.** or **si op. sit**): if necessary

si vires permittant (**s.v.p.** or **si vir. perm.**): if strength permits

sic: thus

siccant: drying (i.e., a desiccant)

siccat: it dries

siccatus: dried

siccus: dry; desiccated

signa (**S.** or **Sig.**) [write]: that which is to be written on the label of a prescription

signare: to label

signatura: signature (also, **subscriptum**)

signetur (**s.** or **sig.**): let it be written; label

signetur nomine proprio (**s.n.p.** or **sig. nom. prop.**): label with proper name

signum: a mark; sign

similia similibus curantur: like cures like

similis: like; similar

simplex: simple

simul: together; at the same time

simulare morbum: to feign illness

sinapis (sinap.): mustard

sinapis nigra: black mustard

sinapismus: a mustard poultice

sinciput: the front of the head (as opposed to **occiput**)

sindon: muslin; cotton cloth

singulorum (sing.): of each

sine: without

sine aqua: without water

sine auxilio: unaided

sine dolore: painless

sine maculis [without stain]: spotless

singulis horis (sing. hor.): every hour

singultus: a gasp; a hiccup

sinister (sinist.): left

sipho: a syringe

sitis: thirst

smilax: sarsaparilla

solidus: solid

solitus: usual

solubilis: soluble

solutio or **solutum (sol.)**: a solution

solutus: dissolved; loosened

solve (solv.): dissolve

solve cum calore (solv. c̄ cal.): dissolve by warming

somnifera: sleep-producing

somnolentus: sleepy

somnus: sleep

sonitus: a buzzing sound in the ears

sonus: sound

sopiens: sleep-inducing

sopor: deep sleep

sorbilis: drinkable

sorbilo [by sipping]: drop by drop

soror: sister

spasmus caninus: spasms attending tetanus

spatium: space; interval

spatula: a knife for mixing medicines

species: a species

species novum (sp. nov.): a new species

specificum: specific

specimen: a sample; an example

speculum [mirror]: an instrument used for expanding natural openings to aid doctors during examinations

sphincter [bracelet]: contracting muscles that surround natural openings

sphincter ani: muscles that close the anus (also, **constrictor ani**)

sphincter oris: a muscle that closes the mouth

spicula: bone splinter

spina: spine; backbone

spiracula [air-holes]: respiratory pores of the skin

spiritus (sp. or **spr.** or **spts.)**: a spirit

spiritus vini (s.v. or **spirit. vin.)**: an alcoholic spirit

spiritus vini methylatus: a methylated spirit

spiritus vini rectificatus (s.v.r.): alcohol

spissatus: thickened

spissus: thick

spondylus: a vertebra; also, a whirlpool

spongia: sponge

sputum: spittle

squama [fish scale]: scaly condition of the skin

squamatus: scaly

squamula: a small scale from the skin

squarrosus [scaly]: covered with scales

stadium [race course]: a stage or period; the course of a disease

stagnum: a pond or marsh

stannum (Sn.): tin

statim (stat.): immediately; on the spot; at once

status: state; condition

stent: let them stand

sterilis [barren]: sterile

sterilisatus: sterilized

sterno (stern.): to the chest

sternum: chest

sternutamentum or **sternutatorium (sternut.)**: snuff

stertor [snoring]: loud and harsh respiration

stet (st.): let it stand

stibium: a type of eye salve

stigma: a mark on the skin

stillicidium: flowing drop by drop

stimulans: stimulating

stimulus: a stimulant

stomachus: the stomach

strabismus: the squinting of one or both eyes

stratum super stratum (S.S.S. or s.s.s.): layer upon layer

stria [furrow]: a mark under the skin that appears in some fevers

struma: swelling; tumor

strychnina: strychnine

stupor: drowsiness; senselessness

stypticus: styptic, (i.e., aiding in the contraction of the blood vessels)

suber: cork

suberatus: made of cork

subinde: now and then

subscriptum: signature (also, **signatura**)

subsultus: twitching

subter: under

subtilis: fine; subtle

succedaneum: a substitute medicine

succus: juice

sucidus: juicy

sudarium: a towel or handkerchief

sudator (f. **sudatrix**): causing perspiration

sudatorius: sweat-producing

sudor: sweat

sufficiens: sufficient

sugatur (sug.): let it be sucked

sulfur or **sulphur (S.)**: sulfur

sulphuricus: sulphuric

sumantur (sum.): let them be taken

sumat (sum.): let him take

sumat talem: take one such

sumatur (sum.): let it be taken

sume (sum.): take

summum bonum medicinae sanitas: the chief good of medicine is health

super gossypium (sup. gossyp.): upon cotton wool

super linteum (sup. lin.): upon linen or lint

supercilium: eyebrow

supersubstantialis: life-sustaining

supplementum: supplement

suppositorium (supp. or **suppos.)**: suppository

supra morem: more than usual

suprarenalis: suprarenal (i.e., above the kidney)

sura: calf of the leg

surditas: deafness

surdus: deaf

sus: pig; swine

suspirium: a deep breath; a sigh

synclonus bolismus: the shaking palsy

syrupus (syr.): a syrup

T

tabella (tab.): a tablet

tabes [wasting away]: decay; consumption of the body

tabletta: a small tablet

taenia: a tapeworm

taenia lata and **taenia solium**: species of tapeworm that grow to enormous lengths

talcum: talc

tales doses (tal. dos.): such doses

talis (tal.): such

talpa [mole]: a type of tumor on the head

talus: ankle; ankle-bone

tantum quantum: just as much as is required

tantus: so much; so great

taraxacum dens-leonis: the dandelion (also, **leontodon taraxacum**)

tardus: slow

tarsi oculorum: the eyelids

tarsis oculorum (tars. ocul.): to the eyelids

tarsus: the instep

taxis: an operation in which an organ is replaced to its natural position by hand

tectus: covered; concealed

tela: tissue

tempus: time; temple of the head

tendo calcaneus (or **tendo Achillis**): the Achilles tendon

tenesmus: a straining during bowel movements but without discharge

tentaculum: a feeler (i.e., an exploratory instrument)

tenuis: thin; diluted

tepidus: warm or lukewarm

ter [thrice]: three times

ter in die (t.i.d. or **T.I.D.)**: three times a day

ter in hebdomada (ter in hebdom. or **t. in hebdom.)**: three times a week

ter quaterve die (t.q.d.): three or four times a day

ter quotidie (ter quot.): three times daily

tere (ter.): rub

tere bene: rub well

tere bene simul (ter. bene sim.): rub together well

terebinthina: turpentine

terebra: a trepan; a gimlet

terra: earth

tertiis horis (tert. hor.): every three hours

tertius: third

testa: a shell; urn; also, a coating or covering

testa praeparata: powdered oyster shell

testis (pl. **testes**): a testicle

theaepoculum: a teacupful

thermae: warm springs or baths

thoraci (thorac.): to the chest

thorax: chest; the breastplate

thyroideum: the thyroid gland

thyroideus: pertaining to the thyroid

tibia: the shin-bone

tinctoreus: colored

tinctura (tinct or **t.)**: tincture

tinnitus aurium: ringing in the ears (also, **tinnitus**)

titulus: a label or inscription

tolutanus: pertaining to tolu

tomentosus: wooly

tormina: dysentery with gripping pain

torpor: numbness; lack of sensation

tostus: toasted

toties quoties (tot. quot.) [as often as]: repeatedly; on each occasion

totus: whole

totus in toto, et totus in qualibet parte: wholly complete and complete in every part (i.e., the human heart)

toxicum: poison

toxitabella: a poison tablet

tractim [in managed bits]: by degrees

translucidus: translucent; transparent

traumaticus: traumatic

tremor cordis: palpitation of the heart

tremulus: trembling

tricupis: three-pointed

triduum: a period of three days

trihorium: a period of three hours

triplex: triple

triplum: three times the amount

trismus: tetanus (i.e., lockjaw)

trismus nascentium: infantile lockjaw

trochiscus (troch.): a lozenge

trochlea: a pulley

truncus: stem; trunk

tuber: swelling; protuberance

tubercula: small hard tumors

tubulus: a small tube

tubus: pipe; tube

tum: at that time

tumidus: swollen

tumor [a swelling]: a protuberance

tunica: a covering

tunicatus (tunicat.): coated

tunicentur cum gelatino (tunic. c̄ gelat.): let them be gelatin coated

tunicentur pilulae (tunic. pil.): let the pills be coated

tunicetur (tunic.): let it be coated

tussi molesta (tuss. mol.): with the cough being troublesome

tussi urgente (tuss. urg.): when the cough is severe

tussis: cough

tussis convulsiva: whooping cough (also, **pertussis**)

tussis molestante (tuss. mol.): when the cough is troublesome

tympanum: the drum of the middle ear

typhus: typhus fever

typhus gravior: a malignant typhus, typically found in military camps **(febris castrensis)** or in prisons **(febris carcerum)**

U

ubi desinit philosophus, ibi incipit medicus: (fig.) where the philosopher ends, the physician begins

ulcus: sore; ulcer

ulmus fulva: slippery elm

ulna: elbow; arm

ultimo praescriptus (ult. praesc. or **ult praes.)**: last ordered

ultra non: no more

umbilicus: the navel

umbra: shade; shadow

umerus or **humerus**: the shoulder or upper arm

unam ter in die: one three times a day

uncia (oz. or **unc.)**: an ounce

unguentum (ung. or **ungt.)**: an ointment

unguiculus: fingernail or toenail

unguilla: an ointment box or jar

unguis or **ungula**: nail; claw; hoof; talon

unus: one

urgens: urgent

urina: urine

urtica: nettle

ustus: burnt

usus: use

ut: in order that; so that

ut dictum (ut dict.): as directed

uterus: the internal area of the womb

utilis: useful

uva ursi: bearberry

V

vaccina or **vaccinia**: cowpox, used as a vaccine against smallpox

vaccinum cholerae: cholera vaccine

vaccinum febris flavae: yellow fever vaccine

vaccinum lac (vac. lac): cow's milk

vaccinum pertussis: whooping cough vaccine

vaccinum rabies: rabies vaccine

vaccinum typhosum: typhoid vaccine

vaccinum variolae: smallpox vaccine

vacuo: in a vacuum

vacuum: vacuum

vagina [sheath]: the female sex organ

vagitus: the first cry of a newborn child

valetudinarius: valetudinarian (i.e., a sick or infirm person)

vanilla: vanilla (properly, **vanilla aromatica**)

vanillinum: vanillin

vapor: vapor; steam

varicella: chicken pox

varicosus: having varicose veins

variola: smallpox

varix: a varicose vein

varus: crooked; knock-kneed

vas (pl. **vasa**) [utensil]: a vessel or duct

vas apertum: an open or uncovered vessel

vas deferens (pl. **vasa deferentia**): the sperm duct

vas fictile: an earthenware vessel

vas vitreum: a glass vessel

vasa vasorum: small vessels that supply larger veins

vasa vorticosa: the hairlike veins of the eyes

vasculum: a small vessel

vehiculum (**vehic.**): a vehicle

velum: a veil; a screen

vena (pl. **venae**): a vein

vena basilica: the major vein of the arm

vena cava (pl. **venae cavae**): one of the large veins flowing into the heart

venaesectio (**vs.** or **venaes.**): bleeding; venesection (i.e., bloodletting)

venenosus: poisonous

venenum [venom]: drug; poison

venienti occurrite morbo: (fig.) prevention is better than cure

venificus: poisonous

venter or **ventriculus**: the belly or stomach

ventriculo jejuno: on an empty stomach

veratrum: hellebore

vermis (pl. **vermes**) or **vermiculus**: a worm

vernix: a varnish

verruca: a wart

versicolor: variegated

vertebra (pl. **vertebrae**): one of the twenty-four bones of the spinal column

vertex: the crown of the head

vertigo [whirling round]: dizziness or light-headedness

vesania: insanity

vesica: bladder

vesicans or **vesicatorius**: blistering

vesper (**vesp.**): evening

vespere or **vesperi** (**vesp.**): in the evening

veterinarius: veterinary; veterinarian

viae lachrymalis: the tear ducts

vibix (pl. **vibices**): a mark from a blow; a weal

vices (**vic.**): time; times

victus: nourishment

villosus: hairy; shaggy

vinosus: containing wine

vinum (**vin.**): wine

vinum xericum: sherry (also, **xericus**)

vinylicus: vinyl

vir: man

vires corporis: bodily strength

virginale claustrum: the hymen

viridis (**vir.** or **virid.**): green

virus: poison

vis: power; force

vis formativa: the body's own power to grow and nourish itself

vis medicatrix: healing power

vis medicatrix naturae: the healing power of nature

vis vitae: vital power; life force

viscera (sing. **viscus**): internal organs (i.e., the guts)

viscidus: sticky

vita propria: the vital power peculiar to any organ

vita: life

vitellus: an egg yolk

vitreus: glassy

vitrum: glass

vivus: living

vixit . . . annos (v.a.): he lived . . . years
volatilis: volatile
volvendus (volvend.): to be rolled
vomica: an ulcer or sore; a boil
vomicus: having emetic properties
vomitione urgente (vom. urg.): the
  vomiting becoming serious
vox (pl. voces): voice
vox abscissa: loss of voice
vulnus: injury; wound
vulpis morbus: death or loss of hair
vulva: the external area of the womb

X

xericus: sherry

Z

zincum (Zn.): zinc
zingiber: ginger
zona: a girdle, applied to the shingles

LEGAL LATIN

A

a coelo usque ad centrum: from the heavens to the center of the earth

a contrario sensu: on the other hand

a datu: from the date

a die: from that day

a fortiori: with greater force; more conclusively

a jure suo cadunt: they lose their right

a maximis ad minima: from the greatest to the least

a mensa et toro (or thoro) [from table and bed]: a limited divorce

a minori ad majus: from the lesser to the greater

a pari: equally; in like manner

a posse ad esse: from possibility to realization

a posteriori [from after]: reasoning from specific instances to general conclusions (i.e., inductive or empirical knowledge)

a primo: from the first

a principio: from the beginning

a priori [from before]: reasoning from premise to logical conclusions (i.e., deductive or presumptive knowledge)

a pueris or a puero: from boyhood

a quo: from which (opposite of ad quem)

a rubro ad nigrum [from the red to the black]: from title to text (i.e., the entire statute has legal force)

a sociis: by its associates

a sursum usque deorsum: from top to bottom

a teneris annis [from tender years]: from childhood or youth

a tergo [in the rear]: behind

a verbis ad verbera: from words to blows

a verbis legis non est recedendum: from the words of the law there is no retreat

a vinculo: from the bond or tie

a vinculo matrimonii [from the bond of marriage]: an absolute divorce

ab absurdo: from the absurd

ab abusu ad usum non valet consequentia: the usefulness of something is not invalidated by the consequences of its abuse

ab actu ad posse valet illatio: it is possible to infer the future from the past

ab ante: in advance; beforehand

ab epistulis [of letters]: secretarial matters

ab extra [from without]: from the outside

ab inconvenienti: from the inconvenience involved (referring to a law that should not be passed because of certain hardships or inconveniences such a law would create)

ab incunabulis [from the cradle]: from childhood

ab initio (ab init.): from the beginning; from the start

ab intestato: from a person dying intestate (i.e., without a will)

ab intra [from within]: from the inside

ab invito: unwillingly

ab irato [from an angry man]: in a fit of anger (i.e., not to be taken too seriously)

ab olim: formerly; in times past

ab omni parte: from every side

ab origine [from the origin]: from the beginning

ab ovo [from the egg]: from the beginning

ab uno ad omnes: from one to all

ab uno disce omnes [from one learn all]: from one sample we judge the rest

abest (pl. **absunt**): he/she is absent

abinde: from thence; thenceforth

abortivus: abortive

abscissio infiniti [cutting the infinite]: in logic, the process by which the true conclusion is reached by a systematic comparison and rejection of hypotheses

abscondita: hidden places

absente reo (**abs. re.**): the defendant being absent

absit invidia [let there be no ill will]: no offense intended

absque hoc: without this

absque injuria: without injury

absque paucis casibus: except for a few cases

absque tali causa: without such cause

absque ulla nota: without any mark

abundans cautela non nocet: abundant caution does no harm

abusus non tollit usum [abuse does not take away use]: abuse is no argument against use

ac etiam or **acetiam**: and also

accedas ad curiam [you may approach the court]: a common-law writ to remove a case to a higher court

accepta: receipts; credits

accidere: to happen; to befall

accusare nemo se debet: no one is compelled to accuse him/herself

acervatim [in heaps]: summarily

acta diurna: daily records

acta exteriora indicant interiora secreta: external actions indicate internal secrets

acta publica: matters of public concern

actio: a legal action

actio bonae fidei: an action in good faith

actio empti: an action of the buyer to compel delivery of a purchased item

actio familiae erciscundae: an action to divide an inheritance among the heirs

actio finium regundorum: an action reestablishing the boundaries between adjoining lands

actio non accrevit infra sex annos: the action did not accrue within six years (i.e., the action was not brought within the statute of limitations)

actio personalis moritur cum persona: a personal right dies with the person

actio redhibitoria: an action to return a damaged or defective purchase and to receive a refund of the purchase price

actio venditi: an action of the seller to receive payment

actionem non habere (**actio. non**): a denial of a plaintiff's charge

actiones penales: penal actions

actiones populares: public actions

actiones rei persecutoriae: actions for the recovery of something belonging to the one bringing the action

actiones stricti juris: actions of strict law

actor: a plaintiff

actor sequitur forum rei: a plaintiff follows the court of the defender

actori incumbit onus probandi: the burden of proof falls to the plaintiff

actum agere: to do what has already been done

actum et tractatum: done and transacted

actus (pl. **acta**): an action or an actuality

actus animi [an act of the mind]: an intention

actus Dei nemini nocet: acts of God bring injury to no one

actus legitimus: a legal act

actus non facit reum, nisi mens sit rea: an act does not make one guilty, unless the mind is guilty

actus reus: a criminal act

ad absurdum [to what is absurd]: an argument which demonstrates the absurdity of an opponent's proposition

ad alium diem: at another day

ad amussim [according to a rule]: accurately or exactly

ad annum: a year from now

ad arbitrium: at will

ad baculum [to the rod]: an argument or appeal which resorts to force rather than reason

ad captandum: an argument or appeal which is presented for the sake of pleasing the audience

ad captandum lucrum: for the purpose of making money

ad captum vulgi [to the common understanding]: easily understood

ad certum diem: at a certain day

ad civilem effectum: as to the civil effect

ad colligendum: for collecting

ad commune nocumentum: to the common nuisance

ad communem legem: at common law

ad convincendam conscientiam judicis: sufficient to satisfy the conscience of the judge

ad crumenam [to the purse]: an argument or appeal to one's personal interests

ad curiam: at court

ad damnum: to the damage

ad diem: at the day

ad eundem gradum (ad eund.): to the same degree or standing

ad exiguum tempus: for a short time

ad extremum [to the extreme]: to the last; to the end

ad factum praestandum: for the performance of a certain act

ad filum aquae: to the center of the stream

ad filum viae: to the middle of the way

ad finem (ad fin.) [to or at the end]: finally

ad fontes: at or to the source

ad hanc vocem (a.h.v.): at this word

ad hoc [to this]: an action taken for a specific purpose, case, or situation

ad hominem [at the man]: an argument that appeals to personal prejudice or emotions rather than to reason

ad horam compositam: at the agreed hour

ad hunc locum (a.h.l.): at this place

ad idem: to the same point

ad ignorantiam [to ignorance]: an argument or appeal that is ignorant of the needed facts

ad infinitum (ad inf. or ad infin.) [to infinity]: endless; limitless; forever

ad initium (ad init.): at the beginning

ad instantiam: at the instance

ad instantiam partio: at the instance of a party

ad instar [after the fashion of]: like

ad interim (ad int. or ad inter.): in the meantime; temporarily

ad internecionem: to the point of extermination

ad invidiam [to envy]: an argument that appeals to prejudice or envy

ad judicium [to judgment]: an argument that appeals to common sense

ad largum: at large (also, **ire ad largum**)

ad levandam conscientiam: for the purpose of easing the conscience

ad libitum (ad lib.) [at pleasure]: to improvise

ad limina [to the threshold]: to the highest authority

ad litem: to or for the suit or action

ad literam or **ad litteram** [to the letter]: literally

ad locum (ad loc.): to or at the place

ad longum: at length

ad lunam: by moonlight

ad melius inquirendum: a writ directing a coroner to hold a second inquest

ad misericordiam [to pity]: an argument that appeals to pity

ad modum [in or after the manner of]: like

ad multus annos: for many years

ad nauseam [to nausea]: to the point of disgust

ad ostium ecclesiae [at the church door]: at the marriage

ad pares casus: to similar cases

ad pensam: by weight

ad perpetuam rei memoriam: for a perpetual record of the matter

ad perpetuam remanentiam: to remain forever

ad perpetuitatem: forever

ad populum [to the people]: an argument that appeals to popular prejudices or passions

ad postremum: lastly; for the last time

ad pristinum statum: to the former condition

ad punctum temporis: at the point in time

ad quem: to which (opposite of **a quo**)

ad quod damnum: to what damage

ad referendum [for reference]: for further consideration; for the approval of a superior

ad rem [to the matter]: a term denoting something relevant to the point at issue

ad respondendum: to answer

ad rimandam veritatem: for the purpose of investigating the truth

ad sectam (**ads.** or **adsm.**; also **ats.**): at the suit of

ad similes casus: to similar cases

ad summam [on the whole]: in general; in short

ad tempus [at the right time]: in due time; according to the circumstances

ad tunc et ibidem: at the very time and in the same place

ad ultimum: to the last

ad unum omnes [all to a one]: everyone without exception (i.e., unanimous)

ad usum (**ad us.**): according to custom

ad valorem (**ad val.**): according to the value

ad verbum [word for word]: literally; to the letter

ad verecundiam [to modesty]: an argument that appeals to modesty

ad vicem: in place of; instead of

ad vindictam publicam: for the defense of public interest

ad vitam: for life

ad vitam aeternam [for eternal life]: for all time

ad vitam aut culpam [for life or until fault]: until death or delinquency removes one from the office; held for life

ad vitandum perjurium: for avoiding perjury

ad vivum [to the life]: lifelike

adde huc (or **adde eo**) [add to this]: consider this as well

addendum (pl. **addenda**): an attachment to the end of a manuscript indicating the words to be added or the corrections to be made

additum (pl. **addita**): something added

additur: it is added (i.e., an increase in the amount for damages awarded by the jury)

ademptio: a revocation of a legacy

adhuc sub judice lis est: the case is still before the court

adiratus: lost; strayed

aditus: a public road or access

adjudicata: decided; settled

adscripti glebae: joined to the land

adsumptio: in logic, the minor premise of a syllogism

adversa fortuna: ill fortune

adversus (**adv.**): against; opposed to

adversus bonos mores: contrary to good morals

adversus solem ne loquitor [neither speak against the sun]: do not dispute what is obvious

advisare: to advise or consider

aedificatum solo, solo cedit: the thing built on the land goes with the land

aegis [a shield]: sponsorship; protection

aequalitas: equality

aequitas: equity

aequitas est quasi equalitas: equity is as it were equality

aequitas sequitur legem: equity follows the law

aequum est: it is just

aequus: equal; equitable

aes alienum [money belonging to another]: debt or debts

aetatis (aet. or **aetat.)**: of the age; of one's lifetime

aetatis suae (A.S.): of his/her age; of his/her lifetime

affectio: a condition; an influence

affinitas affinitatis [affinity of affinity]: related by affinity of marriage but not by law or by blood (e.g., the brother of a husband is related by affinity of marriage to the sister of his brother's wife)

affirmanti incumbit probatio: proof is incumbent upon the one who alleges a fact (i.e., the one who makes the allegation)

affirmanti non neganti incumbit probatio: the proof does not lie with the one who denies the charge

agendum est: the matter to be treated is . . .

ager: land; a field; also, an acre

ager limitatus (pl. **agri limitati**): lands or property limited by natural boundaries or by the lines of government survey

ager publicus: public land

agricola: a farmer

aio et nego: I say yes and I say no

album: record

alia de causa: for another reason

alias: otherwise; on other occasions

alias dictus [otherwise called]: an alias

alibi: elsewhere; at another place

alieni juris: subject to the authority of another

alio intuitu: from another point of view

alio pacto: in another way

alioquin: otherwise

aliqua ex parte: in some respect

aliquando: at times; sometimes

aliquis: someone; something

aliquo: somewhere

aliter: otherwise

alitur vitium vivitque tegendo [the crime is nourished and lives by being concealed]: vice lives and thrives by secrecy

aliud est celare, aliud tacere: it is one thing to conceal, another to be silent

aliud est possidere, aliud esse in possessione: it is one thing to possess, another to be in possession

aliunde [otherwise]: from another source

alius: other; another

alius aliter: in different ways

allegatio falsi: a false statement

alta proditio: high treason

alta via: a highway

alter: other; another

alter ego [one's other self] or **alter idem** [another of the same kind]: a second self

alternis annis: every other year

alternis diebus: every other day

alternis vicibus: alternately; by turns

alterum non laedere: to injure no one

alteruter: one or the other

altius non tollendi: of not raising higher (a reference to codes regulating the height of tenement buildings)

altum mare: the high sea

alvei mutatio: a change in the course of a stream

alveus: a riverbed

ambidexter: an attorney who receives pay from both sides; a bribed juror

ambigendi locus: room for doubt

ambiguitas contra stipulatorem est: an ambiguity is interpreted against the drafter

ambiguitas latens: a latent ambiguity

ambiguitas patens: a patent ambiguity

ambiguum pactum contra venditorem interpretandum est: an ambiguous contract is interpreted against the seller

ambitiosus: ambitious

ambo [two together]: both

amiciter: in a friendly way

amicus curiae [a friend of the court]: a disinterested advisor

anguis in herba [a snake in the grass]: an unsuspected danger

animal rationale: a reasoning person

animo: with intention or design

animo defamandi: with the intention of defaming

animo differendi: with the intention of obtaining delay

animo donandi: with the intention of making a donation

animo et corpore: with intent and act

animo et facto: in intention and fact

animo felonico: with felonious intent

animo furandi: with the intention to steal

animo obligandi: with the intention of entering into an obligation

animo remanendi: with the intention of remaining abroad

animo revertendi: with the intention of returning

animo testandi: with the intention of making a will

animus: will; intention

animus cancellandi: the intention of cancelling

animus capiendi: the intention of taking

animus contrahendi: the intention of entering into a contractual agreement

animus defamandi: the intention of defaming

animus delinquendi: the intention of abandoning

animus derelinquendi: the intention of leaving or disowning

animus donandi: the intention of giving

animus et factus: intention and act

animus furandi: the intention of stealing

animus hominis est anima scripti: the intention of the person is the intention of the written instrument

animus injuriandi: the intention of injurying

animus lucrandi: the intention of gaining

animus manendi: the intention of remaining

animus possidendi: the intention of possessing

animus quo: the intention with which (i.e., the motive behind an action)

animus recipiendi: the intention of receiving

animus recuperandi: the intention of recovering

animus republicandi: the intention of republishing

animus residendi: the intention of residing or establishing a residence

animus restituendi: the intention of restoring

animus revertendi: the intention of returning

animus revocandi: the intention of revoking

animus testandi: the intention of making a will

annales (ann.): records; chronicles

anni continui: successive years (i.e., continuing without interruption)

anni et tempora [years and times]: annals; yearbooks

anni utiles: the years during which a right may be exercised

anniculus: a one-year-old child

anno aetatis suae (A.A.S.): in the year of his/her age

anno interiecto: after the interval of a year

anno regni (A.R.): in the year of the reign

anno vertente: in the course of the year

annona: yearly crop

annos vixit (a.v.): he/she lived (so many years)

annua pecunia: an annuity

annus (pl. anni): year

annus bisextus: leap year

annus deliberandi: the year for deliberating (i.e., a reference to succession or inheritance)

annus et dies: a year and a day

annus inceptus pro completo habetur: a year begun is held as completed

annus reditus: an annuity; a yearly rent

ante: before

ante bellum: before the war

ante diem (a.d.): before the day

ante exhibitionem billae: before the showing of the bill

ante factum: a previous act or fact

ante juramentum (or **ante-juramentum**): an oath taken before the suit is tried

ante litem motam: before litigation has begun

ante lucem: before daybreak

ante mortem: before death

ante natus or **antenatus**: born before a person, time, or event

ante omnia [before all things]: in the first place

ante partum or **antepartum** [before birth]: before childbirth

antehac [before this time]: formerly

antiqua custuma: ancient customs

antiqua et nova: old and new rights

antiqua statuta: ancient statutes

apex juris: a rule or doctrine of law carried to either extreme

appendita: appendages; appurtenances

aptus: suitable

apud [according to]: in the writings of

apud acta: among the acts (i.e., among the recorded proceedings)

aqua cedit solo: the water goes with the land

aqua currit et debere ut currere solebat: water runs and should run as it is accustomed

aquae ductus (or **aquaeductus**): the right to pipe or convey water over or through the property of another (e.g., drainage)

aquae haustus (or **aquaehaustus**): a right to water cattle or livestock at any stream or pond

arbitrio suo: under his/her own control

arbitrium est judicium: an award is a judgment

arbor infelix [unhappy tree]: the gallows

arcana imperii: state secrets

arena [sand]: ground; arena

arguendo (arg.): in arguing; in the course of arguing

argumentum: an argument; a proof

argumentum a contrario: argument from the opposite [viewpoint]

argumentum a simili valet in lege: argument by analogy governs in law

argumentum ab auctoritate: a proof derived from authority

argumentum ab inconvenienti: an appeal to hardship or inconvenience

argumentum ad absurdum: an argument to prove the absurdity of an opponent's argument

argumentum ad baculum: an appeal to force or the threat of force

argumentum ad captandum: an appeal made by arousing popular passions

argumentum ad crumenam: an appeal to a person's interests

argumentum ad hominem: an evasive argument relying on attack of an opponent's character

argumentum ad ignorantiam: an argument based on an opponent's ignorance of the facts or on his or her inability to prove the opposite

argumentum ad invidiam: an appeal to prejudices or base passions

argumentum ad judicium: an appeal to judgment or common sense

argumentum ad misericordiam: an appeal to pity

argumentum ad populum: an appeal to people's lower nature rather than to their intellect

argumentum ad rem: a proper argument that bears on the real point of the issue at hand

argumentum ad verecundiam [also **ipse dixit**, argument from authority]: an appeal to modesty or a person's sense of reverence (e.g., a reliance on the prestige of a great or respected person rather than on the independent consideration of the question itself)

argumentum baculinum: an appeal to force or the threat of force

argumentum ex concesso: an argument based on points already held by one's opponent

arma in armatos sumere jura sinunt: the law allows persons to take up arms against the armed (i.e., the right to defend one's self)

assensio mentium [a meeting of the minds]: mutual consent

assignatus utitur jure auctoris: the assignee is possessed of the rights of the one he/she represents

assumpsit [he/she undertook]: a suit to recover damages for breach of a contract or actionable promise, whether expressed or implied

asylum (pl. **asyla**): a sanctuary; a place of refuge

auctor: author

auctor ignotus: an unknown author

auctor in rem suam: one who acts on his/her own behalf

audi alteram partem: hear the other side (i.e., the right of the defendant to answer a charge or to speak in his or her own defense)

audita querela [the complaint having been heard]: a common-law writ giving the defendant opportunity to appeal

auxilium curiae: a request by one party for another party to appear in court

avia: grandmother

avus: grandfather

B

ballium or **balium**: bail

Bancus Communium Placitorum (or simply, **Bancus**): Court of Common Pleas

Bancus Reginae: the court of the Queen's Bench

Bancus Regis: the court of the King's Bench

bannitus: a banished or outlawed person

bannum: a notice of prohibition

basilica: an abridgment of the Corpus Juris Civilis of the Roman Emperor Justinian, published in the ninth century C.E.

beati possidentes [happy are those who possess]: possession is nine tenths of the law

belli: at war

belli denuntiatio: a declaration of war

bellum: war

bellum atrocissimum: a war of atrocities

bellum inter duos [war between two]: a duel

bene exeat [let him/her go forth well]: a certificate of good character

bene facta: good deeds

biennium: a period of two years

billa cassetur: let the bill be set aside or tabled

billa vera: true bill (i.e., a bill of indictment containing sufficient evidence to warrant a trial)

bona: property; goods

bona confiscata: confiscated goods

bona fide [in good faith]: sincerely; genuinely

bona fides [good faith]: honest intention

bona fiscalia: fiscal or public property

bona forisfacta: forfeited goods

bona mobilia: movable goods

bona notabilia: noteworthy things

bona paraphernalia: the separate property of the wife (or simply, **paraphernalia**)

bona peritura: perishable goods

bona vacantia: unclaimed goods

boni judicis est lites dirimere: a good judge is one who prevents litigation

bonis nocet quisquis pepercerit malis: whoever spares the bad injures the good

bonum publicum (b.p. or **bon. pub.)**: the common good

bonum vacans: unowned property which belongs to whomever makes the first claim to it

bovata terrae: as much land as one ox can plow

breve (pl. brevia): a writ

breve de recto: a writ of right

breve originale: an original writ

brevi manu [with a short hand]: offhand; summarily

brevia anticipantia: writs of prevention

brevia de cursu: writs of course

brevia judicialia: judicial writs

brevitatis causa: for the sake of brevity

brutum fulmen (pl. bruta fulmina) [a harmless thunderbolt]: an empty threat

brutus: irrational

C

cadit quaestio [the question falls on the ground]: the discussion has come to an end

caeteris tacentibus [the others being silent]: the other judges expressing no formal opinion

calefagium: a right to take fuel yearly

calendarium: calendar; account book

calumniae jus jurandum: an oath against calumny

cambiparticeps: a champertor

camera: a judge's chambers

Camera Stellata [Star Chamber]: a tribunal or inquisitorial council (fig., a severe and arbitrary court)

canfara: trial by hot iron

capax doli: capable of committing crime

capias [you may seize]: a writ issued for the arrest of a person who has been accused of committing a crime

capias ad respondendum (ca. ad re. or **ca. re.** or **ca. resp.)**: a writ of arrest intended to keep the defendant safely in custody until trial

capias ad satisfaciendum (ca. sa.): a writ of arrest to hold the defendant and present him/her in court to satisfy a plaintiff's complaint

capita [heads]: persons individually considered

capitatim: by the head

Capitula de Judaeis: historically, a register of mortgages made to the Jews

caput lupinum [wolf's head]: an outlaw; a fugitive from the law

caput mortuum: a matter of no legal validity (i.e., a thing void to all persons and for all purposes)

carcer: prison

carnifex: an executioner; a hangman

carta: charter; deed (also, **charta**)

cassetur billa: let the bill be set aside or tabled

cassis tutissima virtus [virtue is the safest helmet]: an honest person need not fear a thing

casus [a falling or fall]: an occasion; an event; an occurrence

casus amissionis: the circumstances of the loss

casus conscientiae: a case of conscience

casus foederis [a case of the treaty]: a case within the stipulations of a treaty

casus fortuitus (cas. fortuit.) [a case of fortune]: a chance happening; an accident; a loss happening despite a person's best preparation and effort

casus omissus: a case omitted or unprovided for

causa: a cause; a case

causa causans: the immediate cause; the cause of an action

causa cognita: the facts being known

causa debendi: the cause of debt

causa mali [an evil cause]: a cause of mischief

causa mortis: in anticipation of death

causa privata: a civil case

causa publica: a criminal case

causa secunda: secondary cause

causa sine qua non: an indispensible condition without which the injury would not have taken place (also, **sine qua non**)

cautio: security; bond; bail

cautio fidejussoria: a bond or security paid by a third party

cautio juratoria: a bond or security given by oath

cautio pignoratitia: a bond or security given by deposit of goods

cautio pro expensis: a bond or security for costs or expenses

cautum: concern

cave canem: beware of the dog

caveat [let him beware]: a warning or caution

caveat actor: let the doer beware

caveat emptor: let the buyer beware

caveat venditor: let the seller beware

caveat viator: let the traveler beware

censor morum: a censor of morals

centum (C. or cent.): a hundred

cepi: I have taken

cepi corpus (c.c.) [I have taken a body]: the official reply by the sheriff after fulfilling a **capias** writ

cepit: he/she has taken

cera impressa: a wax seal

certiorari [to be certified]: a writ calling up the records of a lower court

certo [certainly]: yes

cessante causa, cessat effectus: when the cause ceases, the effect ceases

cessante ratione legis, cessat ipsa lex: when the reason for a law ceases, that law itself ceases

cessio bonorum: a surrender of goods

cetera desunt or **caetera desunt (c.d. or cet. d.)**: the rest is lacking

ceteris paribus or **caeteris paribus (cet. par.)**: other things being equal

ceteris rebus: as regards the rest

charta: charter; deed (also, **carta**)

charta chyrographata: a charter of indenture

chirographum [handwritten]: a handwritten document of debt

chirographum apud debitorem repertum praesumitur solutum: a bond in the custody of the debtor is assumed to have been paid

circa (c. or ca.): about; near; around

circiter (c. or circ.): about

circuitus verborum [a circuit of words]: circumlocution

circulus vitiosus [a vicious circle]: circular reasoning

circum (c. or circ.): around or about

circus: a circular enclosure

citatio ad reassumendam causam: a citation issued, at the death of the plaintiff or defendant in a pending suit, for or against the heir of either

citra causae cognitionem: without investigating the cause

civiliter: civilly (as opposed to **criminaliter**)

civiliter mortuus [civilly dead]: an outlaw

civis: a citizen

civis bonus: a good citizen; a patriot

civitas: a city

civitatis amissio: loss of citizenship

clam: secretly; covertly

clare constat: it clearly appears

clausula derogativa: a clause in a will invalidating subsequent wills

clausulae inconsuetae semper inducunt suspicionem: unusual clauses always lead to suspicion

clausura: an enclosure

clementia: clemency

codex: a code; a collection of laws

cogitationis poenam nemo meretur: no one deserves punishment for a thought

cognati [connected by blood]: relations on the mother's side

cognatus: related by birth

cognomen: a surname; a family name

cognovit or **cognovit actionem** [he has acknowledged the action]: the defendant's acknowledgment of the plaintiff's claim

cohaeres or **coheres**: a joint heir

cojudex (pl. **cojudices**): an associate justice

collegialiter: in a corporate capacity

collegium (pl. **collegia**): a corporate body; a guild

collistrigium: the pillory

colloquium [conversation]: the allegation of spreading defamatory statements to a third party

colluvies vitiorum (**coll. vit.**) [a collection of vices]: a den of iniquity

colore officii: by color of office

combustio: the ancient practice of burning persons as punishment for apostasy or treason

combustio domorum: the burning of houses

combustio pecuniae: the practice of testing the purity of coins by melting them down upon receipt

comes: a companion; an associate

comes stabuli: a constable or sheriff

comitas inter gentes [comity of nations]: civility among peaceful nations

comitatus: a county or shire

commeatus: supplies

commercia belli: an armistice between warring nations; contracts made between persons of warring countries

comminatorium: a clause admonishing the sheriff to be faithful in carrying out his or her duties

commorientes: persons who perish at the same time and place as a result of the same calamity

commune bonum: the common good

commune forum [the common forum]: a court of session

commune placitum: a common plea

commune vinculum: a common bond

communi consensu: by common consent

communibus annis: on a yearly average

communio bonorum: a community of goods

communis annis [in ordinary years]: on the annual average

communis error [common error]: an opinion or practice that is commonly held but is not adequately founded in the law

communis error facit jus: sometimes common error makes law

communis observantia non est recedendum: there must be no departure from common practice

communis opinio: common opinion

communis scriptura: a writing common to both parties; a chirograph

communis stirpes: common stock; a common ancestor

comparatio literarum: a comparison of handwritings

compendium: an abridgment

compensatio criminum or **criminis**: in divorce, the doctrine of recrimination in which the defendant may contest the charge of the plaintiff on the grounds of equal guilt

complementum justi: full justice

componere lites: to settle disputes

compos mentis [sound of mind]: in one's right mind

compos sui [master of himself]: having use of one's limbs or the power of bodily motion

compromissarii sunt judices: arbitrators are judges

compromissarius: an arbitrator

conatus: an attempt

concedo [I admit]: I grant (i.e., a concession made in an argument)

concessi: I have granted

concessio: a grant

concessit or **concessum**: granted; allowed

concilium: a council

condictio: a summons; a personal action

conditio sine qua non: an indispensible condition (also, **sine qua non**)

confer (cf.): compare

confiscare: to confiscate

confusio: blending; mixing; merging

confusio bonorum [confusion of goods]: the mixing of private property of different owners

confusio jurium: the merging of the rights of debtor and creditor in the same person

conjudex (pl. **conjudices**): an associate judge

conjugium: marriage

conjuncta: things joined together (as opposed to **disjuncta**)

conjunctim: jointly

conjunctim et divisim: jointly and severally

conjunx or **conjux (con.** or **conj.)**: a marriage partner

connubium: marriage; intermarriage

consanguineus: related by blood

consanguinitas: relation by blood

conscientia mala: a bad conscience

conscientia mille testes: conscience is as a thousand witnesses

conscientia recta: a good conscience

consensus: agreement; consent

consensus audacium [agreement of the rash]: a conspiracy

consensus facit legem: consent makes law

consensus gentium: consent of the nations

consensus omnium: universal consent

consensus tollit errorem: consent takes away error

considerabitur pro querente: judgment shall be given for the plaintiff

consideratio curiae: the judgment of the court, given after deliberation and study

consideratum est per curiam: it is the judgment of the court

consideratur: it is the judgment

consiliarius: a counselor

consilium [counsel]: the day appointed to hear the counsel of both parties

consobrini: first cousins, in general terms

consociatio: an association

consortium: a company or partnership

consortium vitae: cohabitation

constabularius: a constable

constat: it is clear or evident

constat de persona: it is clear as to the person meant

consuetudo: custom; usage

consuetudo amatoria: courtship

consuetudo curiae: the custom or practice of the court

consuetudo mercatorum: the custom or practice of merchants (also, **lex mercatoria**)

consuetudo pro lege servatur [custom is held as law]: where there are no specific laws, the issue should be decided by custom

consuetudo universa: universal custom

contemptibiliter: contemptuously

conterminus: bordering upon; adjacent

continens: joined together

continentia: a continuance

contra (con. or cont.) [opposite]: against; on the opposite side (i.e., on the contrary)

contra bonos mores (cont. bon. mor.): contrary to good morals

contra formam statuti [against the form of the statute]: against the letter of the law

contra jus belli: against the law of war

contra jus commune: against or contrary to common law

contra jus fasque: against all law, human and divine

contra jus gentium: against the law of nations

contra legem: against the law

contra legem terrae: against the law of the land

contra omnes gentes: against all the people

contra pacem: against the peace

contra placitum: a counter plea

contra rem publicam: to the disadvantage of the state

contradictio in adjecto: a contradiction in terms

contratenere: to withhold

contravenire: to contravene; to violate

controversia: a legal dispute

controversiosus: strongly disputed

controversus: disputed

contumax: an accused person who refuses to appear and answer to a charge; an outlaw

contumelia: physical violence; a verbal insult

contumeliosus: abusive; insulting

conveniens: convenient; suitable

convenit: it is agreed

convicium: censure

convictio domini: the belief that one rightfully owns a thing that one possesses

copia vera: a true copy

coram: [before]: face to face; in the presence of

coram judice: before a judge

coram nobis [before us]: in the court of King's Bench

coram non judice [before a judge without jurisdiction]: before one who is not the proper judge

coram paribus [before equals]: before one's peers

coram populo [in public]: in the sight of spectators

corona [crown]: the Crown

coronator: a coroner

corpore et animo: by physical act and mental intent

corpus [body or corpse]: a body or collection of writings

corpus comitatus [the body of the county]: the inhabitants of a county

corpus corporatum: a corporation

corpus delicti [the body of the crime]: the substance or fundamental facts of a crime

corpus juris [body of law]: a collection of laws of a country or jurisdiction

corpus juris canonici: the body of canon laws

corpus juris civilis: the body of civil laws

corpus pro corpore: body for body

correi credendi: joint creditors

corrigendum (pl. **corrigenda**) [to be corrected]: corrections to be made in a manuscript before its publication

corruptio optimi pessima: the corruption of the best is the worst

corruptissima re publica plurimae leges: in the most corrupt state exist the most laws

cras: tomorrow

crassa ignorantia: gross ignorance

crassa neglegentia or **crassa negligentia**: gross negligence

crastium or **crastino**: tomorrow; the next day

creditum: a loan

cretio: the period of deliberation allowed for an heir to decide whether to take an inheritance

crimen (pl. **crimina**): crime; guilt

crimen falsi: the crime or charge of perjury (also, **falsi crimen**)

crimen furti: the crime of larceny

crimen incendii: an incendiary crime

crimen laesae majestatis: the crime or charge of high treason

crimen majestatis: crime against the Crown (i.e., treason)

crimen raptus: the crime of rape

crimen roberiae: the crime of robbery

crimina mala in se: acts which are evil or immoral in themselves

crimina morte extinguuntur: crimes are extinguished by the death of the criminal

criminaliter: criminally (as opposed to **civiliter**)

criminosus: criminal

cui: to whom

cui bono? or **cui bono fuisset?** [for whose advantage?]: to what end?

cui fuisset bono?: for whose advantage?

cui malo?: whom will it harm?

cuius or **cujus** (**cuj.**): of which or whose

cujus est dare, ejus est disponere: whose it is to give, his it is to dispose

culpa: fault; negligence

culpa lata: gross negligence

culpa levis [a slight fault]: excusable negligence

culpabilis (**cul.**): culpable; guilty

culpam poena premit comes: punishment presses hard upon the heels of crime

cum domibus et aedificiis: with houses and buildings

cum effectu: with effect

cum grano salis [with a grain of salt]: with reservation

cum multis aliis (**c.m.a.**): with many others

cum nota [with a mark]: with reservation

cum omni causa: with every advantage

cum onere: with the burden of proof

cum onere debitorum defuncti: under burden of the debts of the deceased

cum pertinentiis: with the appurtenances (i.e., with additional rights)

cum suo onere: with its burden

cum tacent, clamant [when they are silent they cry loudest]: silence speaks louder than words

cum telo: armed

cum testamento annexo: with the will annexed

cum uxoribus et liberis: with wife and child

cumulatus (or **cumulativus**): cumulative; accruing

cura: care; custody

curator (f. **curatrix**): a curator

curator ad hoc: a specially appointed curator

curator ad litem: a person appointed to represent a ward in litigation

curator bonis: a curator of property

curia (**cur.**): a court of justice

curia advisari vult (**cur. adv. vult** or **c.a.v.**): the court wishes to be advised or to consider the matter

curia claudenda: historically, a court order compelling a plaintiff's neighbor to erect a wall or fence between their adjoining lands

curia regis: the King's court

currit quatuor pedibus [it runs on four feet]: the cases are similar and thus governed by the same law

currit tempus contra desides: time runs against those who are slow

cursus curiae est lex curiae: the practice of the court is the law of the court

custa (sing. **custum**) or **custantia**: costs

custodes pacis: guardians of the peace

custodia legis: in the custody of the law

custodia libera: house arrest

custodiae causa: for the purpose of preserving

custos ferarum: a game warden

custos morum: a custodian of morals

custos rotulorum (C.R.) [custodian of rolls]: principal justice of the peace in an English county

custos sigilli: keeper of the seal

custos terrae: guardian of the land

D

damnatus [damned]: declared guilty; condemned; sentenced

damnosa haereditas [a damaging inheritance]: an inheritance that entails loss

damnum (pl. **damna**) [damage]: physical harm; material loss

damnum absque injuria [loss without injury]: loss due to lawful competition

damnum et injuria: loss and injury

damnum et interesse: loss plus interest

damnum fatale: acts of God

damnum infectum: threatened loss

damnum sentit dominus: the master suffers the loss

damnum sine injuria esse potest: loss without injury is deemed possible

dare cervices [give the neck]: submit to the executioner

data et accepta [things given and received]: expenditures and receipts

datio [giving]: the right of alienation

datus: the date of giving

de auditu: from hearsay

de bene esse: provisionally

de bonis asportatis: of goods carried away

de bonis non administratis: of the goods not administered

de bonis non amovendis: a writ for not removing goods

de bonis propriis [out of his own goods]: out of one's own pocket

de bono et malo [of good and bad]: for better or for worse

de causa in causam: from one cause to another

de claro die: by the light of day

de cursu: of course

de die: while still day

de die in diem (**de d. in d.**): from day to day

de facto [in fact]: in reality or actuality

de fide et officio judicis non recipitur quaestio: concerning the good faith and duty of the judge, no question can be allowed

de fideli administratione: of faithful administration

de futuro: regarding the future

de gratia: by favor

de gustibus non est disputandum (or **de gustibus non disputandum**): there is no disputing about tastes

de incremento: of increase; in addition

de industria: intentionally

de injuria: of wrong

de jactura evitanda: for avoiding a loss

de jure [by right]: rightful or rightfully; according to law

de latere: collaterally

de lunatico inquirendo: a writ to inquire into the sanity of a person

de me: of me

de minimis: of trifling matters; trifles

de minimis non curat lex: the law does not concern itself with trifles

de minimis non curat praetor: a magistrate does not concern himself with trifles

de more: habitually

de morte hominis nulla est cunctatio longa: no delay is long when it concerns the death of a man

de nocte: while still night

de novo: freshly; anew; a second time

de novodamus: we give anew

de plano [with ease]: easily; in a summary manner

de praesenti or **de presenti**: at present

de praxi: according to practice

de recenti: recent; recently

de similibus idem est judicium: in similar cases, the judgment is the same

de tenero ungui: from childhood

de venter inspiciendo (or **venter inspiciendo**): examining the womb (historically, a writ commanding a sheriff to examine a woman, in the presence of twelve male jurors and twelve women, to determine if she truly is with child and, if so, when the child is likely to be born)

de verbo in verbum or **de verbo** [word for word]: literally

debet: he/she owes

debile fundamentum fallit opus: a weak foundation destroys the work

debita fundi: debts attached to the soil or secured on land

debita sequuntur personam debitoris: debts follow the person of the debtor

debito tempore: in due time

debitor: debtor

debitum (pl. **debita**): a debt

debitum subesse: that the debt is due

decem tales [ten of such]: a summons to fill vacancies on a jury

decessit sine prole (**d.s.p.**): died without issue

decollatio: beheading

decollatus: beheaded

decretum (**d.**): a decree; an ordinance

dedimus or **dedimus potestatem**: a commission to take depositions

dedititii: in Roman law, criminals who were marked permanently on the face or body with fire or a firebrand

deductis debitis: the debts being deducted

defectus: weakness; defect

defectus discretionis judicii: lack of judicial discretion

defectus sanguinis: failure of issue

defunctus: dead; the deceased

degeneres animos timor arguit: fear betrays ignoble souls

Dei judicium [judgment of God]: trial by ordeal

delatio: a charge or accusation of crime; a denunciation

delator: a spy; an informer

delegatus non potest delegare: a delegate cannot delegate

delenda: things to be deleted

deliberabundus: deliberating; carefully considering

deliberatio: deliberation; consideration

delictum (pl. **delicta**) [a fault or crime]: an offense or misdemeanor; a tort

delineavit (**del.**): he/she drew it

demens [out of one's mind]: one who has lost his/her mind through illness or some other cause

dementia: insanity

deminutio capitis: loss of civil rights

demortuus: the late (i.e., deceased)

denuntiatio: a public notice or summons

derivativa potestas non potest esse major primitiva: the power derived cannot be greater than that from which it is derived

despitus: a despicable person

desunt caetera or **desunt cetera (d.c.** or **d. cet.**): the rest is wanting (e.g., the missing part of a quotation)

dextras dare [to give right hands]: to shake hands as a pledge of good faith

dicis causa: for the sake of form

dicitur [it is said]: they say

dictum (pl. **dicta**) [a word or speech]: something that has been said; a truism; a witty saying

dictum de dicto [report upon hearsay]: a secondhand story

dictum factum: said and done

Dies Dominicus non est juridicus: the Lord's Day is not a day for legal proceedings

dies: day; daytime

dies a quo: the day from which

dies ad quem: the day to which

dies communes in banco: regular days for appearance in court

dies datus [a day given]: a day appointed for hearing a lawsuit

dies datus partibus: a continuance

dies gratiae: day of grace

dies juridicus: a day on which the court sits

dies non juridicus or **dies non**: a day on which the court does not sit

dies utiles: days available

dieta: a day's journey; a day's work; a day's expenses

dijudicatio: a decision or judgment between two parties

disjecta membra: scattered parts or remains (i.e., fragments)

disjuncta: things disjoined or separated (as opposed to **conjuncta**)

disputatio fori: argument in court

diu: for a long time

diutius: longer

divinatio: the selection of a prosecutor by the court

dixi: I have spoken

do ut des: I give that you may give

do ut facias: I give that you may do

doli capax [capable of deceit]: capable of distinguishing right from wrong

doli incapax [incapable of deceit]: incapable of distinguishing right from wrong

dolosus versatur in generalibus: a deceiver deals in general terms

dolus: fraud; deceit

dolus bonus: permissible deceit

dolus malus: unlawful deceit (i.e., fraud)

domi [in the house]: at home

dominium directum: ownership as distinguished from enjoyment

dominium directum et utile: ownership and enjoyment of a property

dominium utile: a beneficial ownership (i.e., use or enjoyment of one's own property)

domo carens: homeless

domo profugus: (fig.) a refugee

domo reparanda: a suit brought against a neighbor asking that neighbor to repair his/her house before it falls and damages one's own house or property

domus: house

donatio causa mortis: a gift by one who is dying

donatio inter vivos: a gift between living persons

donatio non praesumitur: a donation is not presumed

dono dedit (d.d.): given as a gift

donum or **donatio**: a gift

dos: a dower or dowry

dubii juris [of doubtful right]: an unsettled legal point

duces tecum [bring with you]: a subpoena (also, **subpoena duces tecum**)

duellum: a judicial contest

dum [while]: on the condition that

dum casta (or **castus**) **vixerit**: for as long as he/she lives chaste; until the supported spouse remarries

dum sola (or **solus**) [while alone]: while unmarried

duodena [the twelve]: a jury of twelve members

duplicatio: the defendant's second answer to the plaintiff

duplicatum jus: a double right (i.e., a droit droit)

duplus [twice as much]: a double penalty

dura lex, sed lex: the law is hard, but it is the law

durante absentia: during absence

durante beneplacito [during our good pleasure]: appointments made and unmade at the pleasure of the magistrate

durante minore aetate: during minority

durante viduitate: during widowhood

durante virginitate: during virginity

durante vita: during life

duritia: duress

E

e contra: on the contrary

e converso: conversely; on the contrary

e pluribus unum: from many one (a motto of the United States)

e re nata [under the present circumstances]: as matters stand

e re publica or **e republica** [in the public interest]: for the benefit of the state

e verbo [in word]: literally

eat inde sine die [that he may go thence without a day]: a full acquittal

ecce signum [behold the sign]: here is the proof

edictum (pl. **edicta**): a decree

editicius judices: jurors chosen by a plaintiff

editio tribuum: a proposal by a plaintiff for the choice of a jury

efforcialiter: forcibly

effractor: one who commits burglary

ego: I

ego ipse: I myself

einetia: the share of the eldest-born son

einetius: the firstborn son

ejectum: that which is thrown up by the sea

ejus est nolle qui potest velle: he who can consent can refuse

ejus modi [of this kind]: in that manner

ejusdem: the like

ejusdem generis: of the same genus or species

ejusdem negotii: part of the same transaction

electio est creditoris: the creditor has the choice

electio est debitoris: the debtor has the choice

elogium: an epitaph on a tombstone; a codicil to a will

emenda: amends

emendatio: improvement; amendment

emeritus (fem., **emerita**) [veteran]: a title of honor denoting long and distinguished service

emporium: a place of wholesale trade; a market

emptio et venditio: buying and selling

emptor: a buyer

emunctae naris [of wiped nose]: of matured judgment

ens: being; existence

ens legis: a being created by law

eo animo: with that intention

eo instante: at that moment

eo ipso [by that itself]: by that fact

eo loci: at that very place

eo nomine [by that name]: on this account

epistula: a letter

ergo: therefore

errare humanum est: to err is human

erratum (pl. **errata**): an error; a mistake

error qui non resistitur approbatur: an error that is not resisted is approved

errore lapsus: a mistake through error

et adjournatur: and it is adjourned

et alibi (**et al.**): and elsewhere

et alii (f., **aliae**; **et al.**): and others

et allocatur: and it is allowed/allocated

et cetera (**etc.**): and so forth

et conjunx (**et conj.**): and spouse (either husband or wife)

et hoc paratus est verificare: and this he/she is prepared to verify

et non allocatur: and it is not allocated

et non: and not

et sequens (**et seq.**): and the following

et sequentes (**et seq.**): and what follows

et sequentes paginae (**et seq. pag.**): and the following pages

et sequentia (**et seqq.**) or **et sequitur** (**et seq.**): and what follows

et sic: and thus; and so

et sic ulterius: and so on; and so forth

et similia: and the like

et uxor (**et ux.**): and wife

etiam in articulo mortis: even at the point of death

eundo, morando, et redeundo [going, remaining, and returning]: a protection from arrest while attending to official business

eventum or **eventus**: event; issue; consequence

eversio: ruin

evidens: clear; evident

ex abrupto [abruptly]: without preparation

ex abundanti: more than sufficient

ex abundanti cautela: out of abundant caution

ex adverso [from the opposite side]: in opposition

ex aequitate: according to equity

ex aequo: on equal terms

ex aequo et bono: [according to what is right and good]: justly and equitably

ex altera parte: of the other part

ex animo [from the heart]: sincerely

ex arbitrio judicis: at or upon the discretion of the judge

ex auditu: by hearsay

ex bona fide [in good faith]: on one's honor; sincerely

ex capite [out of the head]: from memory

ex certa scientia: for certain knowledge

ex comitate: out of courtesy

ex commodatio: from a loan

ex commodo: conveniently

ex comparatione scriptorum [by comparison of writings]: by comparing handwritings

ex concesso [out of concession]: from what has been granted

ex consuetudine mea: according to my custom

ex consulto: from deliberation

ex continentia: immediately (i.e., without an interval of time)

ex contractu: arising from a contract

ex contrario: on the contrary

ex curia: out of court

ex debito justitiae: as a matter of right

ex delicto [from offense]: by reason of an actionable wrong or a criminal deed

ex demissione (**ex dem.**): on the demise

ex desuetudine amittuntur privilegia: it is out of disuse that rights are lost

ex directo: directly

ex dolo malo: out of fraud or deceit

ex dono: as a gift

ex eadem causa: from the same cause

ex empto: from purchase

ex facie [on the face]: evidently

ex facili: easily

ex facto: in consequence of an act or a thing done

ex facto jus oritur: the law goes into effect after the fact

ex fictione juris: by fiction of law

ex gratia [by grace]: in absence of legal right

ex hypothesi: by hypothesis

ex incontinenti: without delay

ex industria: with a deliberate design or purpose

ex instituto: according to traditional usage

ex integro: anew

ex justa causa: from a just or lawful cause

ex justitia: justly; according to justice

ex latere: from the side; collaterally

ex lege [arising from the law]: as a matter of law

ex legibus: according to the laws

ex longinquo: from a distance

ex longo: for long; for a long time

ex maleficio: from misconduct or malfeasance

ex malis moribus bonae leges natae sunt: from bad morals, good laws have sprung

ex mandato: according to the mandate

ex memoria [from memory]: by heart

ex mero motu [of a mere impulse]: of one's own accord

ex mora [from delay]: in consequence of delay

ex mora debitoris: on account of the delay of the debtor

ex more [according to custom]: habitually

ex natura rei: from the very nature of the thing

ex necessitate: of necessity

ex necessitate legis: from the necessity of law

ex necessitate rei: from the necessity of the case

ex officio (e.o.): by virtue of one's office

ex parte [from one party]: in the interests of one side only; in part

ex parte materna: on the mother's side

ex parte paterna: on the father's side

ex paucis: from a few words or a few things

ex pede Herculem [from the foot, Hercules]: from a part one may divine the whole

ex post facto: after the fact (i.e., after the deed is done)

ex propriis: from one's own resources

ex proprio motu: of its own motion; of its own accord

ex proprio vigore: by its own force

ex pueris: from childhood

ex quo [from which time]: since

ex quo tempore: since that time

ex quocunque capite: for whatever reason

ex re et ex tempore: according to time and circumstance

ex relatione: from relation

ex statuto: by statute

ex stricto jure: according to strict law

ex summa necessitate: from the greatest necessity

ex tacito: tacitly

ex tempore: on the spur of the moment; because of time considerations; temporarily

ex testamento [from a testament]: under a will

ex tota materia: from the whole matter

ex toto: on the whole

ex uno disce omnes [from one learn all]: from one we judge the rest

ex usu [of use]: useful; advantageous; expedient

ex utraque parte: on either side

ex vi aut metu: on account of force or fear

ex vi termini: by force of the term, limit, or restriction

ex visceribus: from the vital part (i.e., the very essence of a thing)

ex voto: according to one's vow

excambium: an exchange

exceptio probat regulam: the exception establishes the rule (i.e., gives greater definition)

exceptio semper ultima ponenda est: an exception is always to be put last

exceptis excipiendis: due exceptions or objections being made

excudit (exc.): he/she fashioned it

excursus: a digression

excusatio: an excuse

excusatus: excused

executor (f. executrix): an executor

exempli causa: for instance

exempli gratia (e.g.) [for the sake of example]: for example

exemplum (pl. exempla): a sample or copy; an example

exilium or **exsilium**: exile; banishment

exitus: an export duty; rents or profits from landholdings; offspring

exlex: outside the law

expedit mihi: it is in my interest or to my advantage

expeditio brevis: the service of a writ

expertus: an experienced person; an expert

expressio falsi: a false statement

expressio unius est exclusio alterius: the express mention of the one is the exclusion of the other

extra consuetudinem: besides the usual custom

extra curtem domini: beyond the jurisdiction of his/her superior

extra judicium: out of court

extra jus: beyond the law

extra legem: outside the protection of the law

extra legem positus est civiliter mortuus: an outlaw is civilly dead

extra muros: beyond the walls

extra ordinem: out of the ordinary manner (i.e., a judgment pronounced at the discretion of the judge)

extra quatuor maria: beyond the seas

extra regnum: outside the kingdom

extra territorium judicis: beyond the jurisdiction of the judge

extra viam: out of the way

extra vires: beyond the powers of

F

facere sacramentum: to swear an oath

facias: that you may do

facio ut des: I do that you may give

facio ut facias: I do that you may do

factum: an act or a deed

factum est: it is done

factum probandum: a fact to be proved

facultas probationum non est angustanda: the opportunity of proof is not to be narrowed

facultas: possession

faex populi: the dregs of society

falsi crimen (also crimen falsi): the crime of perjury

falsonarius: a forger

falsus in uno, falsus in omnibus: false in one thing, false in everything

fama [fame]: character; reputation; rumor

fama fert [rumor runs away]: the story goes

fama nihil est celerius: nothing is swifter than rumor

famulatus: slavery; servitude; service

famulus: a slave or attendant

fas est [it is allowed]: it is lawful

fatetur facinus qui judicium fugit: to flee the law is to confess one's guilt

favorem vitae: favor of life

fecerunt (ff.) [they made it]: appended to the artists' names on a painting

fecit (fec.) [he/she made it]: appended to an artist's name on a painting

felo-de-se: suicide; also, an illegal act that results in the death of the felon

femina (f.): a woman; female

femininum (f.): feminine

fenestra [a window]: a loophole

ferae bestiae: wild beasts

ferae naturae [of a wild nature]: untamed; undomesticated

ferea via: a railroad

ferus [a wild animal]: wild; uncivilized

fessa aetas: old age

feudum antiquum: land acquired through succession (as opposed to **feudum novum**)

feudum novum: land acquired through conquest (as opposed to **feudum antiquum**)

fiat justitia, ruat coelum: let justice be done, though the heavens fall

fiat ut petitur: let it be done as asked

fictio cedit veritati: fiction yields to truth

fide mea: on my word of honor

fide, sed cui vide: trust, but be careful whom

fides publica: a promise of protection or of safe conduct

fieri facias (fi. fa.): cause it to be done (a writ commanding the sheriff to execute a judgment)

fieri feci (fi. fe.): I have caused it to be done (the sheriff's official reply to a writ of **fieri facias**)

filia: daughter

filius: son

filius familias or **filiusfamilias**: a son still under the power of his father

filius mulieratus: the first legitimate son born to a woman who has had a child by her husband before their marriage

filius nullius [a son of nobody]: an illegitimate son

filius populi [a son of the people]: a bastard

filum aquae [a thread of water]: the middle of a river or thread of a stream

filum forestae: the border of the forest

filum viae: the middle line of the way

finalis concordia: a decisive or final argument

finem facere: to impose a fine; to pay a fine

finem respice [look to the end]: consider the outcome

finis: the end

finis finem litibus imponit: the end puts an end to litigation

finis unius diei est principium alternis: the end of one day is the beginning of another

finium regundorum actio: an action for regulating boundaries

flagrante crimine: in the act or immediately after the act of committing the crime

flagrante delicto [while the crime is blazing]: in the very act of the crime

flamma fumo est proxima [flame is near smoke]: where there is smoke, there is fire

floruit (fl. or flor.): flourished

foedata: polluted; violated

forisfactum: forfeited

forisfactura plena: the complete forfeiture of a person's property

forisfactus: a person who has forfeited his or her life through commission of a capital offense

forisjudicatio: a judgment resulting in the forfeiture of property

forisjudicatus: deprived of a thing by judgment of the court

forisjurare: to forswear; to abandon

formalis: formal

formaliter: formally

forum [an open place]: a court of justice

forum competens: a competent court

forum conscientiae: the conscience

forum contentiosum: a court

forum contractus: the place where the contract is made

forum domesticum: a domestic court

forum ecclesiasticum: an ecclesiastical court

forum non conveniens: an inconvenient location for judicial undertaking

forum rei gestae: place of transaction

forum rei sitae: place where a thing is situated

forum seculare: a secular court

fossa [ditch]: a ditch full of water where women felons were executed by drowning

frater (pl. **fratres**): a brother

frater consanguineus: a brother born from the same father, though the mother may differ

frater nutricius: a bastard brother

frater uterinus: a brother born of the same mother, but not the same father

fratres: brothers and sisters

fratres conjurati: brothers (or companions) sworn to the same purpose

fraus est celare fraudem: it is fraud to conceal fraud

fronti nulla fides: there is no trusting appearances

fructus naturales: the fruits of nature produced by the power of nature alone

fulmen brutum [a harmless thunderbolt]: an empty threat

functus officio [having performed the office]: no longer useful; no longer functioning in its previous capacity

fundo annexa: things annexed or attached to the soil

fur: thief

furca [a pitchfork]: a gallows

furca et flagellum [gallows and whip]: service for life or limb

furca et fossa [gallows and pit]: legal authority to punish felons, the men by hanging and the women by drowning

furiosi absentis loco est: a madman is like a man who is absent

furiosi nulla voluntas est: a madman has no free will

furiosi solo furore punitur: a madman is to be punished by his madness alone

furiosus: a lunatic

furor: madness

furtim: by stealth

furtum: robbery; theft

furtum grave: aggravated theft

furtum manifesto [open theft]: caught in the act of stealing

G

gardia: custody

gener: a son-in-law

generale nihil certi implicat: a general expression implies nothing certain

generalia verba sunt generaliter intelligenda: general words are to be taken generally

generalis regula generaliter est intelligenda: a general rule is to be understood generally

germanus: of the same parents

gradus: step; degree

grammatica falsa non vitiat chartam: grammatical error does not invalidate a charter

gratis: free of cost; without reward

gratis dictum: a mere assertion

gravissimum est imperium consuetudinis: the power of custom is most weighty

gravitas: seriousness; weightiness; severity

gubernator (f. **gubernatrix**): a governor; a pilot of a ship

H

habeas corpus ad subjiciendum or **habeas corpus (hab. corp.)** [that you have the body]: a writ requiring that officials bring a detained individual before a court to decide the legality of that individual's detention or imprisonment

habemus confitentem reum: we have an accused person who pleads guilty

habendum et tenedum: to have and to hold

habentes homines [the men who have]: the rich

habilis: suitable

habitatio: dwelling; habitation

habitus: habit; dress

hac die: on this day

hac lege [with this law]: with this proviso

hac mercede placet: I accept the terms

haec contra: in answer to this

haec est conventio: this is an agreement

haec est finalis concordia: this is the final agreement

haeredes or **heredes proximi**: the children or direct descendants of a deceased person

haeredes or **heredes remotiores**: the kinsfolk of a deceased person, other than children or descendants

haeredes nati et facti: heirs born and made

haereditarius or **hereditarius**: inherited; hereditary

haereditas or **hereditas**: inheritance

haeredium or **heredium**: patrimony

haeres or **heres** (pl. **haeredes**; **haer.** or **her.**): an heir

haeres or **heres ex asse**: a sole heir

haeres or **heres ex besse**: heir to two thirds of the property

haeres or **heres ex dodrante**: heir to three quarters of the estate

haeres or **heres natus**: an heir by descent

haeres or **heres rectus**: a right heir

haeres est nomen juris, filius est nomen naturae: "heir" is a name given by law, "son" is a name given by nature

heri: yesterday

hesternus: of yesterday

hic casus non dignus est quem consideremus: this case is not worth considering

hic et nunc: here and now

hic iacet or **hic jacet (H.I.)**: here lies

hic iacet sepultus (H.I.S.): here lies buried

hic sepultus (H.S.): here [lies] buried

hiis testibus: these being witnesses

hinc atque illinc: on this side and on that

hoc anno (h.a.): in this year

hoc indictum volo [I wish this unsaid]: I withdraw the statement

hoc loco (h.l.): in this place

hoc mense (h.m.): in this month

hoc nomine (h.n.): in this name

hoc ordine (h.o.): in this order

hoc quaere (h.q.): look for this

hoc sensu (h.s.): in this sense

hoc tempore (h.t.): at this time

hoc titulo (h.t.): under this title

hoc voce (h.v.): under this word or phrase

hodie: today

homicidium: murder

homicidium in rixa: homicide committed during a quarrel

homine replegiando: a writ to bail a person out of prison

hominis iussu: with the sanction of a person

homo (pl. **homines**): human being; man

homo exercitalis: a soldier

homo feodalis: a vassal or tenant

homo francus: a freeperson

homo homini lupus: man is a wolf to man

homo ingenuus: a free and lawful person; a yeoman

homo liber: a freeperson

homo ligius: a subject or vassal

homo regius: a king's vassal

homo reus: an accused or guilty person

homo trium literarum [a man of three letters]: a thief (i.e., **fur**, a thief)

honeste vivere: to live respectably

honorarium: monetary compensation given to a professional who is not otherwise permitted to receive a salary for his/her services

honoris causa [for the sake of honor]: as a mark of honor (e.g., an honorary degree)

honoris gratia: honorary

horae judiciae: the hours in which a court sits to decide judicial matters

hortatus: advised

hostellagium: the ancient right of lords to receive entertainment and lodging in the houses of their tenants

hostia: a victim

hujusmodi: of this kind

humanum est errare: to err is human

humi: on the ground

hunc in modum: in this way

hypomnema: a note or memo

hypotheses non fingo: I frame no hypothesis (i.e., I deal entirely with the facts)

I

ibi: there and then

ibidem (ib. or ibid.): in the same place (e.g., in a book)

id est (i.e.) [that is]: that is to say

id ipsum: that very thing

idem (id.) [the same]: the same as above

idem quod (i.q.): the same as

idem sonans: sounding the same

identidem: repeatedly

ideo consideratum est: therefore it is considered

idonea cautio: sufficient security

idonea paries: a wall sufficient or able to bear the weight

idoneus: sufficient; adequate; fit

idoneus homo: a fit and capable person

ignis judicium: trial by fire

ignitegium: the curfew bell

ignoramus [we are ignorant]: the reply of a grand jury when it finds the evidence insufficient to try the defendant

ignorantia elenchi [ignorant reasoning]: the fallacy of refutation by indirection (i.e., by arguing an irrelevant point)

ignorantia facti: ignorance of fact

ignorantia judicis est calamitas innocentis: the ignorance of a judge is calamitous to an accused person

ignorantia juris non excusat: ignorance of the law does not excuse

ignorantia legis neminem excusat: ignorance of the law excuses no one

ignotus (ign.): unknown

illicite: unlawfully

illiterati: the unlettered

illicitus: illegal

illustratio: example

immobila situm sequuntur: immovable objects remain with the site

immunis: exempt

imparatus: unprepared

impedimentum: a hindrance

imperium [the right to command]: the right to use the force of the state to enforce its laws

imperium in imperio: a government within a government

imperpetuum: forever

impervius: impassable

impetus: attack; assault

impignorata: pledged; mortgaged

impossibilium nulla obligatio est: there is no obligation to do the impossible (or impossible things)

imprimis: first of all; in the first place

imprudencia temeraria: reckless negligence

impugnatio: an attack

impunitas: impunity; exemption from punishment

impunitas semper ad deteriora invitat: impunity is always an invitation to a greater crime

in absentia (i.a.): in absence

in acquirenda possessione: in the course of taking possession

in actu: in the very act

in adversum: against an unwilling party

in aequa manu or **in aequali manu** [in equal hand]: held equally by both parties

in aequali jure: in equal right

in aequo: on equal terms

in alieno solo: in another's land

in alio loco: in another place

in ante: from this day forth

in aqua scribis [you are writing in water]: it is without effect

in arbitrio alieno: according to the judgment of another

in arbitrio judicis: in the decision of the judge

in arcta et salva custodia: in close and safe custody

in armis [in arms]: under arms

in articulo: at the moment; immediately

in articulo mortis: at the point or moment of death

in auditu: within the hearing

in autea: in the future

in banco: in full court

in bello: in time of war

in bonis: in or among the goods or property; in actual possession

in bonis defuncti: among the goods of the deceased

in camera [in chamber]: at chambers (i.e., in private, not in open court); a meeting that is held in secret

in campo: in the field

in capita [to or by the heads]: to take equal shares of an inheritance

in capite [in chief]: rights bestowed by a feudal lord

in carcerem: in prison

in cauda venenum [in the tail is poison]: beware of danger

in circuitu: around

in clientelam recipere: to receive under protection

in colloquio: in a discourse

in commendam: in trust

in communi: in common

in consideratione legis: in consideration of law

in consimili casu: in a like case

in conspectu ejus: in his view

in continenti: immediately; without any interval

in contumaciam: in contempt of court

in crastino: on the morrow

in cujus rei testimonium: in witness or testimony whereof

in curia: in open court

in cursu rebellionis: in the course of rebellion

in custodia legis: in the custody of the law

in custodiam: in prison

in damno vitando: in attempting to avoid injury or damage

in delicto: in fault

in deposito [on deposit]: as a pledge

in diem: for a day

in dorso: on the back

in dorso recordi: on the back of the record

in dubio (pl. **in dubiis**): in doubt; in a doubtful case

in duplo (or **duplo**): in double

in eadem causa: in the same state or condition

in emulationem vicini: in hatred or envy of a neighbor

in equilibrio: in even balance; in equilibrium

in esse: in being; in existence

in essentialibus: in the essential parts

in eventu: in the event

in excambio: in exchange

in exilium: in exile

in extenso: at full length (i.e., unabridged)

in extremis: at the point of death

in facie curiae: in the presence of or before the court

in faciendo: in doing

in facto: in fact

in facto dicit: in fact says

in favorem libertatis: in favor of liberty

in favorem vitae: in favor of life

in felicitate viri: for the husband's happiness

in fieri [in being made]: in course of completion

in fine: toward the conclusion

in flagrante delicto [while the crime is blazing]: in the very act

in forma pauperis [as a poor man]: not liable for costs

in forma praedicta: in the form aforesaid

in foro [in a forum]: in court

in foro conscientiae: in the court of conscience

in foro contentioso: in a court of litigation

in foro domestico: in a domestic court (as opposed to a foreign court)

in fraudem creditorum: with intent to defraud creditors

in fraudem legis: in fraud of the law

in fructu: among the fruits

in furto vel latrocinio: in theft or larceny

in futuro: at a future time (as opposed to **in praesenti**)

in generalibus latet error: in generalities lies error

in genere: generally speaking

in gremio legis [in the bosom of the law]: under the protection of the law

in hac parte: on this side

in haec verba: in these words; in the same words

in hoc statu: in this position; in the present state of matters

in hunc modum: after this manner

in incertum: for an indefinite period

in infinitum: without limit; forever

in initialibus: in the preliminaries

in initio: in or at the beginning

in initio litis: at the outset of the suit

in integrum: in the original condition

in invidiam [in ill will]: to excite prejudice

in invitum [against the unwilling]: compulsory

in ipsis faucibus: in the very jaws; in the entrance way

in ipso termino: at the very end; on the last day

in itinere: on the way

in jure: according to the law

in jure alterius: in another's right; on another's behalf

in jure omnis definitio periculosa est: in every law definition is dangerous

in jure proprio: in one's own right; on one's own behalf

in jus vocare: to summon to court

in lecto: in bed

in lecto mortali: on the deathbed

in limine (**in lim.**) [on the threshold]: in the beginning

in limine judicii: at the outset of the suit

in linea recta: in the direct line

in litem: to or for the suit

in loco: in lieu of; in place of

in loco citato (loc. cit.): in the place cited

in loco haeredis: in place of the heir

in loco parentis: in the place of a parent

in majorem cautelam: for greater security

in mala fide: in bad faith

in maleficio: in wickedness

in manibus [hand to hand]: on hand

in manu [in hand]: in possession

in materia: in the matter; in the cause

in maxima potentia, minima licentia: in the greatest power exists the least liberty

in medias res [in the midst of the thing]: in the meat of the matter or into the heart of the matter

in medio: in the middle; intermediate

in meditatione fugae: in contemplation of flight

in memoriam [in memory]: in memory of

in modum poene: by way of penalty or fine

in modum probationis: by way of proof

in mora [in delay]: in default

in mortua manu [in a dead hand]: property held by a religious society

in naturalibus [in a state of nature]: in the nude

in nocte consilium [in the night is counsel]: sleep on it

in nomine: in the name of

in notis: in the notes

in nubibus [in the clouds]: in abeyance

in nuce: in a nutshell

in nullius bonis: in the goods of no one

in nullo est erratum [in nothing is there error]: no error has been committed

in obliquo: obliquely; indirectly (as opposed to **in recto**)

in octavis: in eight (days)

in oculis civium [in the eyes of citizens]: in public view

in odium: in hatred or detestation

in omnes partes: in all directions

in omnibus [in all things]: in all respects; on all points

in ovo [in the egg]: undeveloped

in pari causa: in a similar case; in similar conditions

in pari delicto: two equally at fault

in pari jure: in equal right

in pari materia [in the same matter]: in an analogous case

in pari passu: on equal footing

in partes: between parts; between parties

in patiendo: in permitting; in tolerating

in pectore [in the breast]: in secret; in reserve

in pectore judicis: in the heart of the judge

in pejorem partem: on the worst side

in pendente or **in pendenti**: in suspension; in abeyance

in perpetuam rei memoriam: for the perpetual memory of the thing

in perpetuum: forever

in perpetuum rei testimonium [in perpetual testimony of the matter]: for the purpose of settling the matter forever

in persona: in person

in personam [in the person]: against a particular person as distinguished from a particular thing (**in rem**)

in pios usus: for religious purposes

in plena vita: in full life

in pleno [in full]: in full court

in pleno comitatu: in full county court

in poenam: as a penalty

in populis: among the people

in posse [in possibility]: potentially (as opposed to **in esse**)

in posterum [for the next day]: for the future

in potentia: in possibility; potentially

in potestate parentis: in the power of a parent

in praemissis: in the premises

in praesens: for the moment

in praesenti: at the present time; immediately effective (as opposed to **in futuro**)

in prejudicium: in prejudice

in primis: in the first place

in privato: in private

in promptu [in readiness]: at a moment's notice

in propria causa: in one's own suit

in propria persona: in one's own person

in proximo gradu: in the nearest degree

in publica custodia: in the public custody

in publico: in public

in quantum: insofar as

in re [in the matter of]: concerning

in re propria: in one's own affairs

in rebus: in things, cases, or matters

in recto: directly (as opposed to **in obliquo**)

in rei exemplum: by way of example

in rem [in a thing]: against a particular thing as distinguished from a particular person (**in personam**)

in rerum natura: in the nature of things

in rigore juris: in strictness of law

in rixa: in a quarrel or fight

in situ [in its place]: in proper position

in solido: as a whole

in solidum: for the whole; jointly; as a whole

in solo: in the soil; on the ground

in solutum: in payment

in spe: in hope or expectation

in specie: in the same form

in statu quo: in the state in which it was before

in stirpes: according to lineage

in stricto jure: in strict right

in subsidium: in aid

in substantialibus: in substance

in summa: on the whole

in suspenso: in suspense

in tam amplo modo: in as ample a manner

in tantum: in so much; so far

in tempus [for a time]: temporarily

in tenebris [in the dark]: in the night

in terminis terminantibus: in express terms

in terrorem: in fear; as a threat

in testimonium: in witness

in totidem verbis: in just so many words

in toto [on the whole]: altogether

in transitu (in trans.) [in transit]: on the way

in tuto: in safety

in ultima voluntate: in the last will

in universum [on the whole]: universal or universally

in usu: in use; at the moment of usage

in utero: in the womb

in utraque re: in both cases

in utroque jure: under both laws (i.e., civil and canon)

in vadio: in pledge

in valorem: according to the value

in vinculis [in chains]: in prison

in vino veritas [in wine is truth]: under wine's influence, the truth is told

in virtute [in virtue of]: by reason of

in vita: in life

in vita testatoris: in the testator's lifetime

incerti temporis: of uncertain time or date

incerto patre: from an uncertain father

incidenter: incidentally

incognita causa: without examination

incommodo tuo: to your disadvantage

incommodum non servit argumentum: inconvenience does not serve as an argument

incrementa: additions

indebitatus: indebted

indefensus [undefended]: one sued who has nothing to answer

index animi sermo est: speech is an indicator of thought

indicta causa: without a hearing

indictus: unsaid; not said

indigena: a native-born inhabitant

indoctus: untrained; unskilled

indoneus: suitable; fitting

ineditus: not published

inemptus: unbought

inest de jure: it is implied in the right

infantiae proximus: next to infancy (i.e., under seven years of age)

infidelis: unfaithful

infinitum: without end; unlimited

infra: below; beneath; within

infra aetatem: under age; within age

infra annos nubiles: not of marriageable age

infra annum: within a year

infra annum luctus: within the year of mourning

infra civitatem: within the state

infra comitatum vel extra: within the country or without

infra corpus comitatus: within the body of a county

infra curtem: within the court

infra dignitatem curiae: beneath the dignity of the court

infra furorem: while in a state of insanity

infra gildam: within a guild

infra hospitium: within an inn or hospice

infra jurisdictionem: within the jurisdiction

infra libertates vel extra: within liberties or without

infra metas: within the limits

infra metas et divisas: within the limits and bounds

infra praesidia [under protection]: within a place of safe custody

infra quatuor maria: within the four seas

infra quatuor parietes: within the four walls

infra regnum: within the realm

infra sex annos: within six years

infra summonitium justiciorum: within the summons of the justices

infra tempus semestre: within six months

infra triduum: within three days

inhumatus: unburied

inimicus: a public enemy

injuria [injury]: an actionable wrong; a tort offense

injuria absque damno: injury without damage

injuria non excusat injuriam: one wrong does not justify another

injuria non praesumitur: injury is not to be presumed

injuria servi dominum pertingit: a servant's unlawful actions extend to his master

injuria sine damno: injury without damage

injustus: unjust

inlex: lawless

inlicitus: illegal

inops consilii: without counsel; deprived of counsel

inquirendo [by inquiring]: authority to inquire into something for the Crown

inquit: he or she says

inquiunt: they say

insanus omnis furere credit ceteros: every madman thinks all others insane

insidiae: an ambush; a plot

inspectio corporis: inspection of the body

inspeximus: we have observed

instanter [forthwith]: within twenty-four hours

instar: like; resembling

instar dentium [resembling teeth]: indented; indenture

instar omnium: equal to all

intentio caeca mala: a hidden intention is an evil one

inter absentes: between or among persons who are absent

inter alia: among other things

inter alios: among other persons

inter amicos: between or among friends

inter arma leges silent: in time of war, the laws are silent

inter brachia: between arms

inter caeteros: between or among others

inter conjuges: between husband and wife

inter eosdem: between the same persons

inter nos [between ourselves]: mutually

inter pares: among equals

inter partes: between parties

inter quatuor parietes: within the four walls

inter rusticos: among the unlearned

inter se: among themselves

inter terrorem: by way of threat

inter terrorem populi: to the terror of the people

inter virum et uxorem: between husband and wife

inter vivos [among the living]: between or among living persons

interdictum: a prohibition

interdum vulgus rectum videt: sometimes the common folk see correctly

interea: in the meantime

intra anni spatium: within the space of a year

intra fidem: within belief (i.e., credible)

intra fines: inside the boundaries

intra legem: within the law (i.e., legal)

intra luctus tempus: within the time of mourning

intra parietes [within the walls]: among friends

intra praesidia: within the defenses

intra quatuor maria: within the four seas

intra verba peccare: to offend in words only

intra vires: within the powers (of)

intuitu matrimonii: in the prospect of marriage

intuitu mortis: in the prospect of death

invenit (inv.): he/she designed it

inveteratus: established

invito debitore: without the consent of the debtor

invito superiore: without the consent of the superior

invitus [unwilling]: without the consent

ipse [he himself]: he/she alone

ipse dixit (also **argumentum ad verecundiam**): he/she alone has said it

ipsissima verba: the very words

ipsissimis verbis: in the very words

ipso facto [by the fact itself]: by that very fact

ipso jure: by the law itself; by that very law

ira furor brevis est: anger is a brief madness

ira motus: excited by anger or passion

ire ad largum: to go at large (also, **ad largum**)

irrevocabile verbum: an irrevocably spoken word

ita est: so it is

ita lex scripta est [thus the law is written]: such is the law

ita quod: so that

ita te Deus adjuvet: so help you God

iudex or **judex**: a judge

iudicatio or **judicatio**: a legal judgment or opinion

iuratus or **juratus**: under oath

iure or **jure**: by right or by law; rightly

iuris consultus or **iurisconsultus**: a lawyer

iuris peritus or **iurisperitus**: an expert in the law

iurisdictio or **jurisdictio**: judicial authority

ius or **jus** (pl. **jures**): law; a legal right

iusiurandum or **jusjurandum** (pl. **iusiuranda**): an oath

iussu or **jussu**: by order; by command

iustitia or **justitia**: justice

iustus or **justus**: just; equitable

iuxta or **juxta** (**lux.** or **jux.**): near; close by; according to

J

januis clausis [with closed doors]: in secret

judex or **iudex**: a judge

judex a quo: the judge from whom

judex ad quem: the judge to whom

judex damnatur cum nocens absolvitur: the judge is condemned when the guilty are acquitted

judex est lex loquens: a judge is the law speaking

judex incorruptus: an impartial judge

judicatio or **iudicatio**: a legal judgment or opinion

judicis: a panel of jurors

judicis est jus dicere non jus dare: it is the place of the judge or jury to declare the law, not to make it

judicium: a trial; a legal decision

judicium aquae [the judgment of water]: trial by water ordeal

judicium capitale: capital punishment

judicium Dei [the judgment of God]: trial by ordeal

judicium parium [judgment of peers]: trial by jury

judicium perversum: a miscarriage of justice

jura: rights; laws

jura ad rem: rights to a thing (as opposed to **jura in rem**)

jura fixa: a fixed right

jura in rem: rights in a thing (as opposed to **jura ad rem**)

jura naturae sunt immutabilia: the laws of nature are immutable

jura personarum: the rights of persons

jura publica anteferenda privatis: public rights are to be preferred before private rights

jura regalia [royal rights]: royal prerogatives

juramentae corporales: corporal oaths (e.g., to swear on the Bible)

juramento: by oath

jurare est Deum in testem vocare: to swear is to call God to witness

jurare in verba magistri [to swear the words of the master]: a confession

jurat [sworn]: a certificate attached to an affidavit declaring that it has been properly sworn

jurata: a jury of twelve persons

juratores: jurors

juratus or **iuratus**: under oath

jure belli: by the law of war

jure civili: by the civil law

jure coronae: by right of crown

jure divino: by divine right

jure gentium: by the law of nations

jure humano [by human law]: by the will of the people

jure mariti: by the right of the husband; by the right of marriage

jure naturae: according to the law of nature

jure non dono: by right, not by gift

jure propinquitatis: by right of relationship

jure representationis: by the right of representation

jure sanguinis: by right of blood

jure uxoris: by the right of the wife

Juris Doctor [J.D.]: doctor of law (a professional degree)

Juris Utriusque Doctor [J.U.D.]: doctor of both Canon and Civil laws

juris consultus or **jurisconsultus**: a lawyer

juris divini: of divine right

juris ecclesiae: by the right of the church; by ecclesiastical law

juris et de jure: of right and by law

juris peritus or **jurisperitus**: an expert in the law

juris privati: of private right

juris publici: according to common or public use

jurisdictio or **iurisdictio**: judicial authority

jus or **ius** (pl. **jures**): law; a legal right

jus accrescendi: the right of survivorship

jus ad rem: a right to a thing; a personal right

jus aequum: equitable law

jus aesneciae: the right of primogeniture (i.e., the right of the firstborn)

jus antiquum: the old law

jus aquaeductus: the right of drainage

jus aquam ducendi: the right to pipe water over another's property

jus bellum dicendi: the right to declare war

jus civile: civil law

jus commune: common law

jus coronae: the right of the crown

jus dare: to make law

jus deliberandi: the right of deliberating

jus dicere: to declare the law

jus disponendi: the right of disposing

jus est ars boni et aequi: law is the art of the good and the just

jus et norma loquendi [the law and rule of speech]: ordinary usage

jus gentium [law of nations]: international law

jus gladii [law of the sword]: supreme or executive jurisdiction

jus haereditatis: the right of inheritance

jus in re: a real right

jus incognitum: an unknown law

jus individuum: an individual or indivisible right

jus mariti: the right of a husband

jus naturae (or **jus naturale**): natural law

jus navigandi: the right of navigation

jus non sacrum: secular law

jus non scriptum: unwritten law

jus novum: the new law

jus nullum: absence of justice

jus pascendi: the right of grazing

jus personarum: the right of persons

jus pignoris: the right of pledge

jus portus: the right of port or harbor

jus possessionis [right of possession]: hypothecation

jus postliminii: law of postliminium (i.e., restoration or repatriation of goods or persons captured during war)

jus precarium: a precarious right

jus primae noctis: the right of the first night (i.e., the right of the lord to "deflower" the new bride of one of his vassals)

jus proprietatis: the right of property

jus publicum: public law

jus quaesitum: the right to recover

jus regium: the right of royalty

jus relictae or **jus relicti**: the right of the widow to her deceased husband's goods

jus rerum: the right of things

jus sanguinis: the law of consanguinity (i.e., the citizenship of the parents determines the citizenship of the child)

jus scriptum: written law

jus sibi dicere: to take the law into one's own hands

jus soli: the law of the soil (i.e, the place of birth determines the citizenship of the child)

jus strictum: strict law

jus summum saepe summa malitia est: extreme law is often extreme wrong

jus tertii: the right or interest of a third party

jus tripertitum: a threefold right

jus utendi: the right to use

jus venandi et piscandi: the right of hunting and fishing

jus vetus: the old law

jusjurandum or **iusiurandum** (pl. **jusjuranda**): an oath

jussu or **iussu**: by order; by command

justitia or **iustitia**: justice

justitia nemini neganda est: justice is to be denied no one

justitia omnibus: justice for all

justus or **iustus**: just; equitable

juvenilis: youthful

juxta or **iuxta (jux.** or **iux.)**: near; close by; according to

juxta conventionem: according to the covenant

juxta formam statuti: according to the form of the statute

juxta ratam: according to the rate

L

lacrimae simulatae [simulated tears]: crocodile tears

laesa majestas [injured majesty]: high treason

lapsus bonis: in straitened circumstances

lapsus linguae: a slip of the tongue

lapsus memoriae: a lapse of memory

lata culpa: gross neglect

lato sensu: in a broad sense (as opposed to **stricto sensu)**

latrocinium: larceny

legalis homo [a lawful person]: a person with full legal rights

legatum: a legacy

legatus [legate]: a deputy; a delegate

legem facere: to make law

legem habere: to be capable of giving evidence under oath

legem promulgare: to publish the law

legenda: things to be read

leges mori serviunt: laws are subservient to custom

leges non scriptae: unwritten laws

leges nullae [lawlessness]: anarchy

legis pacis: conditions of peace

legitimus: lawful

Legum Baccalaureus (LL.B.): Bachelor of Laws

Legum Doctor (LL.D.): Doctor of Laws

leonina societas: a leonine partnership (a legally invalid partnership in which the partner shares in the losses but not in the profits)

levis culpa: ordinary fault or neglect

levissima culpa: slight fault or neglect

lex (pl. **leges**): a law or statute

lex agraria: agrarian law

lex apostata: a thing contrary to the law

lex apparens: trial by battle or duel

lex canonica: canon law

lex communis: common law

lex contractus: the law of the contract

lex dilationes semper exhorret: the law always abhors delays

lex domicilii [law of the domicile]: laws pertaining to the person and to personal rights

lex fori: the law of the court

lex irrita est: a law is invalid

lex loci: the law of the place

lex loci contractus: the law of the place where the contract is drawn up or fulfilled

lex loci delicti: the law of the place where the injury or crime is committed

lex manifesta: trial by duel or by ordeal

lex mercatoria or **mercatorum:** mercantile law (also, **consuetudo mercatorum**)

lex non a rege est violanda: the law is not to be violated by the king

lex non curat de minimis: the law does not care about trifling matters

lex non scripta [unwritten law]: common law

lex patriae: the law of one's country

lex prospicit, non respicit: the law looks forward, not backward

lex punit mendacium: the law punishes a lie

lex rata est: a law is valid

lex reprobat moram: the law dislikes delay

lex salica [law of the Salian Franks]: the ancient law denying the French monarchy to women

lex scripta (pl. **leges scriptae**) [written law]: statute law

lex talionis: the law of retaliation (e.g., an eye for an eye)

lex terrae: the law of the land

lex uno ore omnes alloquitur: the law speaks to all with the same mouth

libellus: a letter or petition; a bill

liber (pl. **libri; L.** or **lib.**): a book; also (pl. **liberi**) a free person

liber et legalis homo: a free and lawful person

liber judiciarum [book of judgment]: the English Domesday book

liberatio: acquittal

liberis nascituris: to children yet to be born

libertas: liberty; freedom

libertas in legibus: liberty under the laws

libertus (f. **liberta,** pl. **liberti**): a freeman or freewoman

liberum arbitrium [free will]: free choice

liberum servitium: free service

licentia: excessive liberty or license

licet [it is permitted]: it is legal

licet saepius requisitus: although often requested or demanded

licitus: lawful; permitted

linea recta [a perpendicular line]: direct line of ascent and descent

linea transversalis: a transverse line

lingua: speech; language

liquet: it is apparent; it appears

lis: legal action; a suit

lis litem generat: strife begets strife

lis mota [a controversy begun]: the commencement of a suit or action

lis pendens: a pending lawsuit

lis sub judice: a lawsuit before a judge that has yet to be been decided

lite pendente [pending the suit]: during the trial

litera (pl. **literae**): a letter; a record

litis aestimatio: an estimate of damages

littera (pl. **litterae**): letter (of the alphabet)

littera scripta manet: the written letter remains

litterae clausae: letters or papers under seal

litterae mortuae [dead letters]: empty or superfluous words

litterae patentes: letters or papers not under seal

litterae sigillatae: sealed letters

litura: an erasure; a correction

locatio [a letting]: leasing; a lease

locatio operis: the hiring of labor and services

locatio rei: the hiring of a thing

loco citato (loc. cit. or **l.c.**): in the place cited

loco laudato (loc. laud.): in the place cited with approval

loco parentis: in place of a parent (properly, **in loco parentis**)

loco supra citato (l.s.c.): in the place cited before

loco tutoris: in place of a guardian

locum tenens (pl. locum tenentes) [a placeholder]: a substitute or deputy, especially for a physician or a cleric

locus citatus: the quoted passage

locus communis (pl. loci communes) [a common place]: a public place; a place of the dead

locus contractus: the place of the contract

locus criminis: the scene of the crime

locus delicti: the scene of the crime

locus in quo: the place in which; the place where

locus poenitentiae: the place of repentance (i.e., the chance to withdraw from a contract before it is signed)

locus regit actum: an act is governed by the laws of the place where it is committed

locus rei sitae: the place where a thing is situated

locus sigilli (L.S.): the place of the seal

locus standi [a place of standing]: recognized position; right to appear before a court (i.e., the right to be heard by a judge)

locutus: spoken

loquitur (loq.): he/she speaks

luce clarius: clearer than light

luce meridiana clariores: clearer than the light at midday (also, **luce clarius**)

lucidus ordo: a clear arrangement

lucri causa: for the sake of gain

lucrum: profit

lucrum cessans: a cessation of gain

luxus: luxury; excess

M

Magna Carta: the Great Charter signed at Runnymede by King John in 1215 C.E., granting certain civil and political liberties to nobles and, symbolically, to the English people

magna ex parte: in a great degree

magnetophonicus: a tape recording

magno cum detrimento: with great loss (of life)

major jus: a greater right

major pars: the majority

mala creditus: bad credit

mala fide [in bad faith]: false or falsely; treacherously (opposite of **bona fide**)

mala fides: bad faith

mala grammatica non vitiat chartam: grammatical error does not invalidate the charter

mala praxis: malpractice

mala prohibita: things prohibited by law

maleficium: injury; damage

malesuada fames: hunger that impels the crime

malevolentia: ill will; malice

mali exempli [of bad example]: of bad precedent

malitia praecogitata: malice aforethought

malitia supplet aetatem: malice supplies the place of age (a reference to crimes committed by minors)

malo animo: with intent to do evil

malo grato: unwillingly; in spite

malum: evil; bad

malum in se [a thing evil in itself]: a thing unlawful in itself, regardless of statute

malum non praesumitur: evil is not presumed

malum prohibitum (pl. mala prohibita) [a prohibited evil]: an act that is unlawful because it is forbidden by law (i.e., a legal crime though not necessarily a moral crime)

manas mediae: inferior persons

mandamus: we command (i.e., a writ requiring that a specified action be done)

mandatum: a message or commission

manica [manicles]: handcuffs

manu aliena: by the hand of another

manu brevi [with short hand]: briefly

manu forti [with a strong hand]: by force

manu propria: with one's own hand

manumissio: emancipation from slavery

mare clausum [closed sea]: a sea within the jurisdiction of a particular country

mare liberum [open sea]: a sea open to all

mater: mother

matrimonialiter: in the way of marriage

maxim: an established principle

me absente: in my absence

me auctore: by my advice

me duce: under my leadership or direction

me indicente: without my saying a word

me invito: against my will

me judice: in my opinion

me libente: with my pleasure or goodwill

me paenitet [I regret it]: I'm sorry

me vivo: in my lifetime

mea culpa [my fault]: by my own fault

media sententia: a middle view or opinion

medio tempore: in the meantime

meditatio fugae: contemplation of flight

medius fidius: so help me God

melior: better

melior res: the better thing

memorandum: a memo

memoriter [from memory]: by heart

mendacem memorem esse oportet: a liar should have a good memory

mendacium: a lie

mens legis: the spirit of the law

mens rea: a guilty intent; a guilty mind

mens sana in corpore sano: a sound mind in a healthy body

mens sibi conscia recti [a mind conscious of its own uprightness]: a good conscience

mensa: a table

mensis: month

menstruus: monthly; month-long

meo judicio: in my judgment

meo periculo [by my peril]: at my own risk

mercator: a merchant

mercatum: a market; a contract of sale

mercatus: a business or trade

merces: wages; salary

meridies (**M.** or **m.**) [midday]: noon

merx: goods; merchandise

metus causa: through fear

meum et tuum: mine and thine (i.e., a phrase expressing rights of property)

minatur innocentibus qui parcit nocentibus: he who spares the guilty threatens the innocent

minima de malis [the least of evils]: choose the lesser of two evils

minor jurare non potest: a minor cannot swear (i.e., serve on a jury)

minutia (pl. **minutiae**): a trifle

minutio [diminution]: a deduction

mitiori sensu: in a milder sense

mittimus [we send]: a warrant of commitment to prison; a writ to remove records from one court to another; a dismissal or a discharge

mobile vulgus (**mob.**)[the fickle masses]: the mob

mobilia sequuntur personam: movables follow the person

mobilis: movable

modo et forma: in manner and form

modus (pl. **modi**): a mode; method; manner

modus operandi: a mode of operating

modus vivendi: manner of living

molliter manus imposuit: he laid his hands on gently (i.e., a justification for the commiting of a wrong in order to prevent the perpetration of a greater wrong)

mora: hindrance; delay

morandae solutionis causa: for the purpose of delaying payment

more [after the manner of]: in the fashion of

mores (pl. of **mos**) [customs; habits]: customary usages; unwritten laws

mors dicitur ultimum supplicium: death is reserved for ultimate punishment

mors omnia solvit: death dissolves all things

mortis causa: by reason of impending death

mortui non mordant [the dead do not bite]: dead men tell no tales

mortuo leoni et lepores insultant: even hares insult a dead lion

mortuum vadium: a mortgage

mortuus: dead

mortuus sasit vivum: the dead ancestor invests the living heir

mos majorum: ancestral custom

mos pravus: a bad custom

mos pro lege [custom for law]: usage has the force of law

motu proprio [by one's own motion]: of one's own accord

mulcta: a fine or penalty

mulier: a woman

multifariam: in many places

multis de causis: for many reasons

multis post annis: after many years

mundus vult decipi: the world wishes to be deceived

munera publica: public offices

munus: gift; service

murus aeneus conscientia sana: a sound conscience is a wall of brass

mutanda: things to be altered

mutatis mutandis (m.m.): the necessary changes being made

mutato nomine: the name having been changed

mutua petitio: a counter claim

mutus et surdus: dumb and deaf

mutuus consensus: mutual consent

N

nam: for (i.e., because; therefore)

narratio (narr.): a narrative

nasciturus: yet to be born

natale solum: native soil

natio: nation

natis et nascituris: to children born and yet to be born

natu: by birth

naturae vis maxima: the highest force is that of nature

ne admittas: do not admit

ne exeat regno or **ne exeat** [let him not go out of the realm]: a writ of restraint forbidding a person from leaving a jurisdiction

ne fronti crede: trust not to appearances

ne multa: in brief

ne recipiatur: that it not be received

nec manifestum: not manifest

necessitas culpabilis: culpable necessity

necessitas non habet legem: necessity knows no law

necessitas publica major est quam privata: public necessity is greater than private

necessitate juris: by necessity of law

nefas: unlawful

negatum: denied

negligentia semper habet infortuniam comitem: negligence always has misfortune for a companion

negligiens: negligent

negotia publica: public affairs

nemine contradicente: no one contradicting

nemine dissentiente: no one dissenting

nemo agit in se ipsum: no one sues him/herself

nemo bis punitur pro eodem delicto: no one is punished twice for the same crime

nemo cogitationis poenam patitur: no one should suffer punishment on account of his/her thoughts

nemo debet ex aliena jactura lucrari: no one ought to gain by another person's loss

nemo est haeres viventis: no one is an heir of the living

nemo est supra leges: no one is above the law

nemo non [not no one]: everyone

nemo presumitur malus: no one is presumed to be bad (i.e., guilty)

nemo punitur pro alieno delicto: no one is punished for the crime of another

nemo repente fuit turpissimus [no one ever was suddenly base]: no one ever became a villain all at once

nemo tenetur divinare: no one is bound to foretell

nemo tenetur seipsum accusare: no one is bound to accuse him/herself

nepos: a nephew; a grandson

neptis: a granddaughter

nequiter: wickedly

nescit vox missa reverti: the word once spoken can never be recalled

neuter [neither]: of neither sex; in neither direction

nexus: tie; connection

nihil: nothing

nihil ad rem [nothing to the point]: beside the point (i.e., irrelevant)

nihil dat qui non habet: he gives nothing who has nothing

nihil debet or **nil debet** [he/she owes nothing]: a plea denying a debt

nihil dicit or **nil dicit** [he/she says nothing]: a judgment by default (i.e., when the defendant declines to enter a plea or to answer a charge)

nihil habet: he/she has nothing

nihil non [not nothing]: everything

nihil obstat: there is no objection

nihil tua refert: (fig.) it is not your business

nil: nothing

nil consuetudine majus: nothing is greater than custom

nil novi sub sole: there is nothing new under the sun

nimis: too much

nisi: unless; except

nisi aliud convenerit: unless it has been otherwise agreed

nisi prius [unless before]: a civil trial held before a judge and a jury

nocet empta dolore voluptas: pleasure bought by pain is injurious

nolens volens [whether willing or not]: willy-nilly

nolle prosequi (nol. pros.): to be unwilling to prosecute

nolo contendere (nol. contend.): a plea of "no contest" to criminal charges by the defendant without admitting guilt

nomen (nom.; pl. nomina): name

nomen collectivum: a collective name or term

nomen juris [legal name]: a technical legal term

nomina sunt mutabilia, res autem immobiles: names are mutable but things are immutable

nominandus: to be named

nominatim: by name

nomine damni [in name of damage]: on account of loss

nomine meo [in my name]: on my behalf

nomine poenae: in the nature of a penalty

non acceptavit: he/she did not accept

non accrevit infra sex annos [it did not accrue within six years]: it is beyond the statute of limitations

non assumpsit [he/she did not undertake]: a general denial in an action of assumpsit

non bis in idem [not twice for the same thing]: the legal principle of double jeopardy

non cepit: he/she did not take

non cepit modo et forma: he/she did not take in manner and form

non compos mentis: not of sound mind

non concessit: he/she did not grant

non constat [it does not appear]: the evidence is not before the court

non culpabilis: not guilty

non damnificatus: not injured

non datur tertium [no third is given]: there is no third choice

non ens (pl. **non entia**)[the nonexistent]: a nonentity

non est: he/she/it is not

non est factum [it is not done]: he/she did not do it

non est inventus or **non est**: he/she has not been found (a statement by a sheriff on return of a writ of arrest when the defendant is not to be found)

non est meus actus: it is not my act

non est vivere, sed valere, vita: life is not mere living, but rather the enjoyment of health

non fecit: he/she did not make it

non impedivit: he/she did not impede or hinder

non infregit conventionem: he/she did not break the contract

non interfui: I was not present

non juridicus: nonjuridical; not legal

non laccessitus: unprovoked

non legitimus: unconstitutional

non libet: it is not pleasing

non licet (**n.l.** or **non lic.**): it is not permitted

non liquet (**n.l.** or **non liq.**) [it is not clear]: the case is not proven

non memini: I do not remember

non numeratae pecuniae: of monies not paid

non obstante (**non obs.**): notwithstanding

non obstante veredicto: notwithstanding the verdict (a verdict for the plaintiff setting aside a verdict for the defendant)

non olet: it does not have a bad smell (i.e., money, no matter its source)

non omittas: do not omit

non omne licitum honestum or **non omne quod licet honestum**: not every lawful thing is honorable

non placet [it does not please]: a negative vote

non possumus [we cannot]: a statement expressing inability to act in a matter

non prosequitur (**non pros.**): he does not prosecute (i.e., a judgment entered when the plaintiff fails to appear)

non sequitur (**non seq.**): it does not follow

non sine causa [not without cause]: with good reason

non submissit: he/she did not submit

non sui juris: not one's own master

non sum informatus: I am not informed

non tenent insimul: they do not hold together

non utendo: by nonusage

nondum editus: unpublished

nondum natus: unborn

norma: pattern; rule

nosce te ipsum or **nosce teipsum**: know thyself

noscitur a sociis: he is known by his companions

nostro periculo: at our own risk

nostrum: ours

nota: a note; a charter or deed

nota bene (N.B. or n.b.) [note well]: take notice

notitia: a notice

nova debita: newly contracted debts

novae tabulae [new ledgers]: a cancellation of debts

novalis: a cultivated field

novissima verba: a person's last words

novitas: newness; novelty

novus homo [a new man]: a person newly pardoned of a crime

novus rex, nova lex: new king, new law

nuda possessio: mere possession

nudis verbis: in plain words

nudum pactum [a nude pact]: an invalid pact

nudus: naked

nulla bona [no goods]: no effects

nulla persona: no person

nulli secundus: second to none

nullius filius [nobody's son]: an illegitimate son

nullum arbitrium: no award

nullus: no; no person

nullus juris: of no legal force

numerata pecunia [money counted]: money paid by count (as opposed to being weighed)

numerus clausus [closed number]: a quota

nummus: money (i.e., coin)

nunc pro tunc [now for then]: retroactive (i.e., designating a delayed action which takes effect as if it were done at the proper time)

nuncius or **nuntius**: a messenger

nunquam: never

nunquam indebitatus [never indebted]: a plea denying indebtedness to the plaintiff

nuper obiit: lately deceased

nupta: married

nuptiae: marriage

nuptiae secundae: a second marriage

nuptiales tabulae: a marriage contract

nurus: a daughter-in-law

O

ob: for; on account of

ob contingentiam: by reason of relationship or connection

ob contingentiam delicti: by reason of connection to the crime

ob rem: with advantage; for gain

ob turpem causam: on account of a base or immoral cause

obiit or **obit (ob.)**: he/she died

obiit sine prole (ob. s.p.): he/she died without issue

obiter (ob.) [by the way]: incidentally; in passing

obiter dictum (ob. dict.; pl. **obiter dicta)** [an incidental remark]: an unofficial expression of opinion

obligatio [an obligation]: liable

obligatio contractu: liable per a contractual obligation

obligatio ex delicto: liable as the result of an offense

obscenus: impure; indecent; obscene

obscuro loco natus: of unknown origin

obscurum per obscurius: explaining an obscure thing by something more obscure

observandum (pl. **observanda**): a thing to be observed

obsignator: a witness to a will

obsoletus [worn out]: out of date

obtorto collo [by the throat]: compelled to appear in court

occasio furem facit: opportunity makes the thief

occupans: an occupant

occupatus: busy; engaged

octo tales [eight of such]: a summons to fill vacancies on a jury

oculatus testis: an eyewitness

odium: hatred; dislike

odor lucri [the smell of profit]: the expectation of gain

offensio: offense

officium [sense of duty]: an office; a dutiful act

omissis omnibus aliis negotiis: laying aside all other business

omne or **omnis**: every; all; everything

omne quod in se erat [all that one had in his/her power]: he/she did everything that he/she could do

omne testamentum morte consummatum est: every will is consummated by death

omnem movere lapidem: to leave no stone unturned

omnes ad unum [all to a person]: unanimous

omni ex parte: from every point of view

omni exceptiones majores: beyond all exception; beyond all criticism

omnia performavit: he/she has done all

omnibus rebus: in every respect

omnium bonorum: of all goods or effects

onera realia: real burdens

onerari non: ought not to be burdened

oneris ferendi: of bearing a burden

onus probandi: the burden of proof

ope et consilio: with aid and counsel (i.e., an accessory to the crime)

ope exceptionis: by force of exception

opere citato (**op. cit.** or **o.c.**): in the work cited

oportet [it behooves]: it is necessary

opposuit natura [nature has opposed]: it is contrary to nature

optato: according to one's wish

optima fide: in the best faith

optima legum interpres est consuetudo: custom is the best interpreter of the law

optime: very well

optimi consiliarii mortui: the best counselors are the dead

optimo jure: with full right

optimus: the best

optimus interpres rerum usus: the best interpreter of things is usage

oratio obliqua [a secondhand report]: hearsay

ordinandi lex: procedural law

ordinatum est [it is ordered]: so ordered

ordine [in turn]: in due order

ore tenus: verbally; by word of mouth

ostiatim: from door to door

P

pacta conventa [the conditions agreed upon]: a diplomatic agreement

pactum (**pact.**; pl. **pacta**) [pact]: a contract or agreement

pactum de non petendo: an agreement not to seek

pactum donationis: an agreement to give in donation

pactum illicitum: an unlawful or illegal contract or agreement

pactum vestitum: an enforceable contract or agreement

par: equal

par in parem imperium non habet: an equal has no authority over an equal

parabilis: procurable

paragium: equality

paraphernalia: the separate property of the wife (properly, **bona paraphernalia**)

paratum habeo [I have him ready]: the defendant is ready to bring to court

parens: a parent

pares: one's peers

pares cum paribus: equals with equals

pari delicto: in a similar crime or offense

pari materia [of the same matter]: on the same subject

pari passu: without partiality

pari ratione: neither is acceptable (i.e., an impasse)

paribus sententiis reus absolvitur: where opinions are equal, a defendant is absolved

parium judicium [the judgment of equals]: the right of trial by a jury of one's peers

pars: a part; a party

pars adversa: the opposite party

pars contractus: part of the contract

pars ejusdem negotii: part of the same business transaction

pars fundi: part of the ground or soil (also, **partes soli**)

pars gravata: an aggrieved party

pars judicis: the duty of the judge

pars pro toto: a part for the whole

parte inaudita: one side being unheard

parte non comparente: a party not having appeared

partes aequales (p.ae.): in equal parts

partes soli: parts of the ground or soil (also, **pars fundi**)

particeps criminis: an accomplice to the crime

particeps fraudis: a partner in fraud

partim (p.): in part

partus sequitur ventrem: the offspring follows its mother

passim (pass.) [here and there]: throughout (as in references found throughout the pages of a book)

pater: father

pater patriae: father of the nation

paterfamilias [father of a family]: head of a household

patria: native land; country

patrimonium: inherited property

patrinus: a godfather

paucus: few

pax [peace]: peace established by law

peccata contra naturam sunt gravissima: crimes against nature are the gravest

pecunia: wealth

pecunia mutua: a loan

pecunia non olet: money does not smell

pecunia numerata: money given in payment of a debt

pecunia obediunt omnia: all things are obedient to money

pedes: going by foot

pedibus [by foot]: by land

pedis possessio: actual possession

pendente lite: pending the suit

pendere filo: to hang by a thread

pendulus [hanging]: undecided

pene or **paene**: almost

penuria testium: a scarcity of witnesses

per accidens [by accident]: by chance

per alluvionem: by alluvion

per ambages: in a secret manner; by evasion

per annum (p.a.) [by the year]: annually

per aversionem: by bulk (i.e., without counting or measuring)

per capita [by heads]: for each individual

per centum (per cent. or **p.c.** or **pct.)**: by the hundred

per consequens: by consequence; consequently

per contra: on the contrary

per corpus: by the body

per curiam: by the entire court

per defaltam: by default

per diem [by the day]: daily

per eundem: by the same [judge]

per expressum: expressly; in direct terms

per extensum: at length

per formam doni: by the form of the gift

per fraudem: by fraud

per hominen stare: occurring through the fault of someone

per incuriam: through carelessness or neglect

per infortunium: by accident

per interim: in the meantime

per jocum: in jest

per legem terrae [by law of the land]: by due process of law

per membra curiae: by members of the court

per mensem (per mens.): by the month; monthly; for each month

per metas et bundas: by metes and bounds

per mille (per mil.): by the thousand

per minas: by threats

per modum exceptionis: by way of exception

per modum gratiae: by an act of favor

per modum justitiae: by way of justice

per modum poenae: by way of punishment (i.e., as a penalty)

per nomen: by name

per omnes (per omn.): by all; by all the judges

per pares: by one's peers

per plegium [by pledge]: on bail

per procurationem (p.p. or per. pro.): by proxy

per quod [through which]: by which

per saltum [by a leap]: passing over certain proceedings

per sceptrum [by the scepter]: by the sword

per se [by or in itself]: intrinsically

per stirpes (per stirp.): by families; by representation

per subsequens matrimonium: by subsequent marriage

per tacitam reconventionem: by a tacit renewal of the contract

per testes: by witnesses

per totam curiam (per tot. cur.): by the entire court (i.e., unanimously)

per universitatem: by the whole; in its entirety

per vadium: by pledge

per verba de futuro: by words of the future tense

per verba de praesenti: by words of the present tense

per viam: by way of

per vices: by retaliation; reciprocally

per visum juratorum: by the viewing of the jury

percepti sed non consumpti: fruits gathered but not consumed

periculum: peril; risk; danger

periculum in mora: there is danger in delay

permissu: by permission

persona [a mask worn by stage players]: a person or personality

persona dignior: the more worthy or suitable person

persona ficta: a fictitious person

persona grata (p.g.): an acceptable person; a welcome person

persona non grata (p.n.g.): an unacceptable person; an unwelcome person

persona proposita: the person proposed

personae miserabiles: poor and destitute persons

personali exceptione: by personal exception

personali objectione: by personal objection

personaliter: personally; in person

pessima fides: the worst faith

pessimi exempli: of the worst example

pignus: a pledge

pinxit (pinx. or pxt.): he/she painted it

placet [it seems good]: it is agreed

placita communia: common pleas

placitum (pl. placita) [a decree]: a decision

plaustrum: wagon; cart

plebs: people

plena aetas: of full age

plene administravit: he/she has fully administered

plene administravit praeter: he/she has fully administered except

plene computavit: he/she has fully accounted

pleno jure: with full right or authority

plenum dominium: the right of the owner to use his/her property as he/she deems fit

pluralis (pl.): plural

pluris petitio: a claim for more than is due

poena corporalis: corporal punishment

poena extraordinaria: unusual punishment (i.e., set at the discretion of the judge)

poena ordinaria: usual punishment (i.e., attached to specified crimes)

poena pecuniaria: a pecuniary punishment (i.e., a fine)

poenalis: penal

pondere, numero, et mensura: by weight, number, and measure

popularis: popular (i.e., belonging to the people)

portorium circumvectionis: port customs; transit duties

posse [possibility]: to be able; to be possible

posse comitatus [the power of the county]: a sheriff's posse

possessio bona fide: possession in good faith

possessio mala fide: possession in bad faith

possessio pedis: possession by occupation

possumus: we can; we are able

post causam cognitam: after the cause has been made known (through inquiry)

post contractum debitum: after debt has been contracted

post diem: after the appointed day

post facto: after the fact

post factum nullum consilium: counsel is of no effect after the fact

post hoc ergo propter hoc [after this, therefore on account of this]: a fallacy of cause and effect

post litem motam: after litigation began

post meridiem (P.M.): after noon

post mortem: after death

post natus: born after

post postscriptum (PPS): an additional postscript

post tantum tempus: after so long a time

postea: afterward; thereafter

postpartor: an heir

postscriptum (PS): a postscript

postulatus: a legal complaint or suit

potestas: power

potestas gladii: the power of the sword

potestas maritalis: powers vested by virtue of marriage

potior est conditio defendentis: the position of the defendant is stronger (i.e., to be preferred)

potior est conditio masculi: the position of the husband is stronger (i.e., to be preferred)

potior est conditio possidentis: the position of the one who possesses is stronger (i.e., to be preferred)

praecipe quod reddat: command him/her to return

praeclarus: famous

praeda bellica: booty (i.e., goods or property seized during war)

praedictus: aforementioned

praefatus: aforesaid

praedium [land]: landed property; an estate

praedium rusticum: a country estate

praedium urbanum: an urban tenement

praejudicium: an objection

praemium: a reward

praenomen or prenomen: first name

praescriptis verbis: in the words written above

praesens: present; the present time

praesentia animi: presence of mind

praeter dotem: over and above the dowry

praeter intentionem: beyond the intention

praeter jus: beyond the law

praeteritus: former

precludi non debet: he/she ought not to be barred

presumendum est pro libertate: the presumption is in favor of liberty

presumptio juris: a legal presumption

pretermit: to disregard or omit

pretium: a price

pretium affectionis [the price of affection]: the sentimental value of a thing, as distinct from its market value

pretium periculi: an insurance premium

pretium puellae [the price of a maiden]: the marriage price demanded by a young woman's guardian

pridie: on the previous day

prima: first

prima facie [at first appearance]: a judgment based on the first impression

prima luce (prim. luc.) [at first light]: early in the morning

primae impressionis: of the first impression

primo [in the first place]: first

primo fronte: at first sight

primo intuiti: at the first glance

primo loco: in the first place

primo venienti: to the person who comes first

primogenitus: the firstborn

principatus: public office

principia: principles; maxims

prior tempore, potior jure [first in time, stronger in right]: the person first in time holds the stronger legal claim

privatim [privately]: in private life

privatum commodum publico cedit: private convenience must yield to the public good

privilegium clericale: the privilege of clerics

pro bono publico [for the public good]: without charge (also known as **pro bono**)

pro confesso [for the confession]: as if confessed

pro consilio impenso: for counsel given

pro convicto: as convicted

pro defectu justitiae: for want of justice

pro defendente (pro def.): for the defendant

pro donato: as a gift

pro dote: as a dowry

pro et contra: for and against

pro et durante: for and during

pro forma: as a matter of form

pro hac vice (p.h.v.): for this occasion only

pro illa vice: for that turn or occasion

pro indefenso: as undefended (i.e., making no defense)

pro indiviso: as undivided (i.e., in common)

pro interesse suo: to the extent of his/her interest

pro laesione fidei: for breach of faith

pro loco et tempore: for the place and time

pro mea parte [for my part]: to the best of my ability

pro mutuum: as if a loan

pro non scripto: as though not written

pro nunc: for now

pro veritate: for the truth; as true

pro parte: partly; in part

pro patria: for one's country

pro posse suo: to the extent of his/her own power or ability

pro privato commodo: for private convenience

pro querente (pro quer.): for plaintiff

pro rata [according to rate]: in proportion; proportionally

pro rata itineris: for the proportion of the voyage or journey

pro re: according to circumstance

pro re nata (p.r.n.): according to the circumstances of the moment

pro se: in person

pro socio: on behalf of a partner

pro solido: for the whole; as one

pro sua parte: to the best of one's ability

pro suo: for one's own

pro tanto: to that extent

pro tempore (p.t. or pro tem.): temporarily; for the time being

pro tribunali: before the judge

pro verbo [according to the word]: literally

pro veritate: for the truth; as true

pro virili: for one's own share (properly, **pro parte virili**)

proavia: a great-grandmother

proavus: a great-grandfather

probabilis causa litigandi: a probable ground for action

probatio mortua [dead proof]: proof by writings, deeds, objects, etc.

probatio plena: full proof (proof by two or more witnesses)

probatio probata: a proven proof (i.e., a proof not open to later debate)

probatio semi-plena: half proof (proof by one witness only)

probatio viva: proof by living witnesses

probatum est: it has been proven

probi et legales homines: good and lawful men (i.e., persons competent to serve on a jury)

probum non poenitet: the honest man does not repent

propositum: resolution

propria manu (pl. propriis manibus): by one's own hand

propria persona: in his/her own person

proprietas: property

proprio jure: by one's own right

proprio motu: by one's own initiative

proprio nomine: in one's own name

proprio vigore: by its own power or force

proprius: one's own

propter affectum: a challenge to a juror who is suspected of bias

propter curam et culturam: for care and cultivation

propter defectum: on account of some defect

propter delictum: on account of a crime

propter majorem securitatem: for the sake of greater security

protestando: protesting

provisione legis: by provision of the law

provocatio: an appeal to a higher court

proximo (prox.): in the following month

proximo mense (prox. m.): in the following month

proximus: neighbor; neighboring

proximus pubertati: nearing puberty

puberes: minors having attained the age of puberty

publica vindicta: the defense of the public

publice: publicly

publicum juris: of the public right

publicus: public

puella: a female youth; girl

puer: a male youth; boy

pugna: a fight

punctatim: point for point

punctum (pl. puncta): a point or spot

punctum temporis: a point of time; the shortest space of time

pusillus: puny; petty

Q

qua: as

quae est eadem: which is the same

quae fuerunt vitia mores sunt: what were once vices are now customs

quae plura: what more

quae sequuntur personam: which follow the person

quae vide (qq.v.): (pl.) which see

quaere (qu.): a question or query

quaeritur [it is sought]: the question arises

quaestio facti: a question of fact

quaestio juris: a question of law

quaestio vexata (pl. **quaestiones vexatae**): a vexing question

quaestiones perpetuae: standing courts of justice

quaestus [acquisition]: profit; gain

qualis pater, talis filius: like father, like son

quamdiu: as long as; so long as

quamdiu se bene gesserit: during good behavior

quamprimum [forthwith]: as soon as possible

quandocunque: at whatever time; at any time

quandocunque defecerit: at whatever time he/she died

quanti minoris: an action to reduce retroactively the price of a thing sold that was found to be somehow defective

quantum: of what size or amount

quantum damnificatus: how much damage?

quantum et quale: how much and of what kind (i.e., the extent and quality)

quantum meruit: as much as it is worth (i.e., the amount deserved)

quantum nunc valent: how much are they now worth (e.g., lands; properties)

quantum scio: as far as I know

quantum sufficit (q.s. or **quant. suff.)** [as much as suffices]: a sufficient quantity

quantum valebant: as much as they were worth

quantus: how much; as much as

quare clausum fregit (q.c.f.) [because he/she broke the close]: the charge of trespassing

quare executionem non (q.e.n.): wherefore execution should not be issued

quare impedit?: why does he/she hinder? (or because he/she hinders)

quare obstruxit?: why does he/she obstruct? (or because he/she obstructs)

quarto die post: the fourth day after

quasi [as it were; as if]: almost; a sort of

quasi dicat (q.d.): as if one should say

quasi dictum (q.d.): as if said

quasi dixisset: as if he had said

quatenus: insofar as

quatuor pedibus currit [it runs upon four feet]: it is an analogous case (i.e., the principle applies here as well)

querela (pl. **querelae**) [bill of complaint]: a court action

quaestio voluntatis: a question of intention

qui approbat non reprobat: one who accepts cannot also reject

qui facit per alium facit per se: a man is responsible for the deeds he does through another

qui nimium probat nihil probat: he who proves too much proves nothing

qui non improbat, approbat: the one who does not disapprove, approves

qui peccat ebrius luat sobrius: let him who sins when drunk be punished when sober

qui tacet consentire videtur: the one who is silent appears to consent (i.e., silence implies consent)

qui tacet consentit: the one who is silent consents

qui tam (q.t.) [who as well]: an action to recover (brought by an informer in conjunction with the state)

quia ita lex scripta est: because the law is written thus

quia timet: because he/she fears

quid actum est: what has been done

quid faciendum: what is to be done

quid juratum est: what has been sworn

quid juris?: what is the law?

quid leges sine moribus vanae proficiunt?: what good are laws when there are no morals?

quid pro quo [this for that]: something given in return for a favor

quid valet nunc: what it is now worth

quidam [somebody]: a person known, though unnamed

quieta non movere [not to move quiet things]: (fig.) let sleeping dogs lie

quilibet: whoever will

quis custodiet ipsos custodes?: who shall guard the guards?

quisque: every; everyone

quisque sibi proximus: everyone is nearest to himself

quisque suos patimur manes: everyone suffers from the spirits of his/her own past

quivus: any; anyone

quo animo?: with what spirit or intention?

quo jure?: by what right?

quo modo? or **quomodo?**: by what means?; in what way?

quoad hoc [as to this]: as regards this particular matter; as far as this goes

quoad maritum: as concerns the husband

quoad minus: as to the lesser matter

quoad mobilia: as concerns the movables

quoad potest: to the extent of one's powers

quoad reliquum: as regards the remainder (i.e., the balance)

quoad valet seipsum [as regards its real value]: so far as it is worth

quoad valorem [as regards the value]: to the extent of the value

quod curia concessit: which the court granted

quod erat demonstrandum (Q.E.D.): which was to be demonstrated or shown

quod erat faciendum (Q.E.F.): which was to be done

quod est (q.e.): which is

quod necessitas cogit, defendit: what necessity forces, it justifies

quod nota (q.n.): which note; which mark

quod per me non possum, nec per alium: what I cannot do in person, I cannot do by proxy

quod recuperet: that the plaintiff recover

quod sciam: as far as I know

quod tibi fieri non vis, alteri ne feceris: what you do not want done to you, do it not to another

quod vide (q.v.): which see

quodlibet [what you please]: a subtle or debatable point

quondam [former]: formerly; at times

quota: share; proportion

quotidianus (or **quotidie**): daily

quousque: how long; how far

quovis modo: in whatever manner

R

rapina: robbery

raptus: rape

rata [rate]: an individual share

ratio decidendi: the reason for the decision

ratio est legis anima: reason is the spirit and soul of the law

ratio pertinens: a reason pertaining to the question

ratione contractus: on account of the contract

ratione delicti: on account of the crime

ratione domicilii: by reason of domicile

ratione privilegii: on account of privilege

ratione soli: by reason of the soil or land

ratione suspecti judicis: on account of the judge being suspected

ratum: deemed as valid

re: regarding; concerning

re infecta: the business being unfinished

re vera or **revera**: in truth; in fact

rebus ipsis et factis: by the facts and circumstances themselves

rectus in curia [upright in court]: blameless

redemptiones: ransom; redemption; heavy fines

reditus or **redditus** [a thing rendered]: rent; payment

reditus albi [white rents]: rent payable in money

reditus nigri [black rents]: rent payable in service or in kind

reductio ad absurdum [reduction to the absurd]: to point out the falsity of an opponent's argument by showing the absurdity of its logical conclusions

regalis or **regius**: royal

regina (R.): a queen

registrarius: a notary public

regium donum: a royal gift or grant

rei: of a thing

rei publicae causa: for political reasons

relicta verificatione: his/her plea being abandoned

reliqua: a balance of account

reliquum or **reliquus (reli.** or **reliq.)**: the remainder

remittitur: it is remitted (i.e., sent back)

remotis testibus: the witness being absent

reo absente: the defendant being absent

reo praesente: the defendant being present

res (pl. res): a thing, matter, or circumstance; a cause or action

res adjudicata [a matter already settled]: a decided case

res aliena: the property of another

res alienae [things belonging to others]: debt

res communes: things held for public use

res corporales [corporeal things]: tangible things

res discrepat: nonagreement

res expedit: it is useful, expedient, or advantageous

res familiaris: inheritance

res fessae: distress

res gestae [things done]: deeds; transactions; the attendant circumstances; exploits in war

res hereditaria: an heirloom

res in cardine est [the matter is on the hinge]: the matter is hanging in the balances

res incorporales [things incorporeal]: nontangible things

res integra [an untouched matter]: a case or matter without precedent

res integra est: the matter is still undecided

res inter alios: a matter between others

res ipsa loquitur: the matter speaks for itself

res judicata [a matter already settled]: a decided case

res judicata pro veritate accipitur: a case decided is accepted as just

res mancipi: things that might be sold

res mobiles: movable things

res nova: a new case or matter; a question not before decided

res nullius: things which are the property of no one

res periit domino: the thing is lost to the owner

res perit suo domino: the loss falls upon its owner (a reference to acts of God)

res privitae: privately held property

res publica: the state

res publicae: public property

res quotidianae: everyday matters

res repetundae: extortion

res sua: one's own property

res universitatis (or **universatis**): things belonging to municipalities or municipal corporations

respice finem [look to the end]: consider the result

respice, adspice, prospice: examine the past, examine the present, examine the future

respondeat: let him/her respond

respondeat superior [let the superior answer]: let the principal answer for the actions of his/her agent

respondere non debet [ought not to answer]: a claim of privilege by a defendant

responsa prudentum: the opinions of legal experts

responsalis: a proctor; an attorney

responsio or **responsum** or **responsura**: answer; response

respublica: a commonwealth; a republic

respublica forum: public life

retenta possessione: possession being retained

reus [an accused person]: a defendant

revocatur [it is revoked or set aside]: the annulment of a judgment because of an error in fact

rex (R.): a king

rex non potest peccare: the king can do no wrong

rogatio testium: a calling upon of the witnesses to testify

rubrica [red earth]: a law with its title written or printed in red ink

rudera [rubbish]: debris

rustica et urbana: rural and urban

S

saccularii: pickpockets

sacramentum: an oath or pledge

salus populi est suprema lex (or **salus populi suprema lex est**): the welfare of the people is the supreme law

salus ubi multi consiliarii: there is safety in many advisors

salva conscientia [with safety to one's conscience]: without compromising one's conscience

salva dignitate [with safety to one's dignity]: without compromising one's dignity

salva fide [with safety to one's faith]: without breaking one's word

salva res est: the matter is safe

salvo jure: without prejudice; without infraction of law

salvo pudore: without offense to modesty

salvo sensu: without violation of sense

salvus plegius: a safe-pledge (e.g., bail)

sanae mentis: of sound mind

sanctio: a sanction (i.e., a clause in a law defining the penalty for breach)

sanguinarius: bloodthirsty

scandalum magnatum (scan. mag.; pl. **scandala magnatum)**: defamation or slander of notable or high-ranking persons

scelus: an evil deed; a crime

sciendum est: it is to be known or understood

sciens et prudens [knowing and intending]: wittingly; in full knowledge

scienter: knowingly; willfully

scientia est potentia: knowledge is power

scilicet (sc. or ss.) [that is to say]: namely; to wit

scintilla: particle of fire, a spark

scire facias (sci. fa.) [cause it to be known]: a writ to enforce, annul, or vacate a judgment, patent, charter, or other matter of record

scire feci: I have given notice

scire fieri: a writ of inquiry

scribere est agere: to write is to act

scripsit: he/she wrote (it)

scripto: by written documents

scripto vel juramento: by writ or oath

sculpsit (sc. or sculpt.): he/she sculpted it

se defendendo: in defending one's self; in self-defense

secundum (sec.): according to

secundum allegata et probata: according to the things alleged and proved

secundum artem (sec. art.): according to practice; scientifically; artificially

secundum bonum et aequum: according to what is good and equitable

secundum formam statuti: according to the form of the statute

secundum legem (sec. leg.): according to law

secundum legem communem: according to common law

secundum naturam (sec. nat.) [according to nature]: naturally

secundum ordinem [according to order]: in an orderly manner

secundum quid [according to some one thing]: with limitations

secundum regulam (sec. reg.): according to rule

secundum subjectam materiam: according to the subject matter

secundum usum: according to usage

secundum veritatem [according to truth]: universally true

securitate pacis: security of the peace

sed non allocatur: but it is not allowed

sed per curiam: but by the court (it was held)

sedato animo: with settled purpose

semper paratus: always ready

senior: older

sensu bono: in a good sense

sensu lato (s.l. or sen. lat.): in a broad sense

sensu malo: in a bad sense

sensu stricto (s.s. or sen. str.): in a strict sense

sententia: opinion

sententiae judicum: the finding of the jury

separaliter or separtim: separately; apart from anything already pleaded

separatio a mensa et toro (or thoro) [separation from room and board]: legal separation

separatio a vinculo matrimonii [separation from the bond of marriage]: divorce

sequens (seq.): the following

sequentia (seqq.): the following things

sequitur (seq.): it follows; a logical inference

seriatim: in a series; severally

servatis servandis: the necessary service being rendered

servus (f. serva): a servant; a slave

si: if; supposing that

si aliquid sapit: if he/she knows anything

si deprehendatur: if apprehended

si ita est: if it is so

si prius: if before

si sic omnes: if all did thus

si sine liberis decesserit: if he shall have died without children

si sit legitimae aetatis: if he/she is of lawful age

sic: thus (usually found in brackets following a doubtful word in a quotation to indicate that the original passage is being followed verbatim)

sic hic: thus here

sic in originali: thus in the originals

sic passim [thus throughout]: here and there

sicut: as; as it were

sicut alias: as at another time; heretofore

sicut me Deus adjuvet: so help me God

sigillum: a seal

signator: a witness to a will or other legal document

signatura: signature (also, **subscriptio** or **subscriptum**)

signum: a signet or seal

silent leges inter arma: the laws are silent during war

silva caedua [the wood being cut]: every type of wood that can be cut down and that will grow back within a year

simplex commendatio non obligat: a simple recommendation does not infer an obligation

simpliciter [absolutely]: without reservation or reserve

simul [at once]: at the same time

simul cum: together with

simul et semel: at one and the same time

sine: without

sine animo remanendi: without the intention of remaining

sine animo revertendi: without the intention of returning

sine anno (s.a.): without date

sine auxilio: unaided

sine consideratione curiae: without the consideration of the court

sine controversia: indisputably

sine cura: without care (i.e., all the benefits of office without all the responsibilities)

sine cura et cultura: without care or culture (i.e., natural)

sine decreto: without a decree

sine die (s.d.): without a day (i.e., without fixing a day for future action or meeting)

sine dubio: without doubt

sine fraude: without deceit; without harm

sine hoc: without this

sine joco [without jesting]: seriously

sine judico [without judgment]: without a judicial sentence

sine legitima prole (s.l.p.): without legitimate issue

sine loco (s.l.): without place

sine loco, anno, vel nomine (s.l.a.n.): without place, year, or name

sine loco et anno (s.l.a.): without place and year

sine mascula prole (s.m.p.): without male issue

sine mora: without delay

sine nomine (s.n.) [without name]: anonymous

sine numero: without number

sine pacto: without an agreement

sine prole (s.p.): without issue

sine prole supersite (s.p.s.): without surviving issue

sine qua non [without which not]: something essential; an indispensible condition

sine quo non: an indispensible person (i.e., a person without whom nothing can be done)

sine vi aut dolo: without force or fraud

singularis (sg. or sing.): singular

singuli in solidum: each for the whole

sinister (sinist.): left

situs: situation; location; position

socer: father-in-law

societas: a partnership or association

socii: partners; associates

socii mei socius meus socius non est: the partner of my partner is not my partner

socius criminis: an associate in crime

sodalis: a companion; a member of a secret society

sola vestura: an exclusive right of pasturage

solacium or **solatium** [solace]: compensation for loss of pleasure or comfort

solo animo: by mere intention or design

solo cedit quod solo implantatur: what is planted in the soil belongs to the soil

solum: land; soil

solus: by oneself

solutio: payment; settlement

solventur risu tabulae [the bills of indictments are dismissed with a laugh]: the case breaks down and you are laughed out of court

solvere poenas: to pay the penalty

solvit ad diem: he/she paid at the day

solvit post diem: he/she paid after the day

solvit vel non: whether he/she has paid or not

soror: a sister

sparsium [scattered about]: here and there

speciali gratia: by special favor

spectemur agendo: let us be judged by our actions

splendide mendax [nobly mendacious]: untruthful for a good purpose

spondeo: I promise

sponsio: a solemn promise; an engagement

sponsus (f. **sponsa**): a spouse

sponte: spontaneously

sponte sua or **sua sponte** [of one's own accord]: unsolicited

sportula (pl. **sportulae**) [a small basket]: a present; a gratuity; largess

spreta authoritate judicis: despite the authority of the judge

stare decisis: to abide by precedent

stare in judico: to appear before a tribunal (either as plaintiff or defendant)

statim (**stat.**): immediately; on the spot; at once

statu quo: as things were before

statua: a statute

status: position; condition

status quo or **status in quo** [the state in which]: an existing condition or unchanged position

stet (**st.**): let it stand

stirpes [the root or stem]: the person from whom a family is descended

stricti juris: according to strict law

strictissimi juris: to be interpreted and applied in the strictest manner

stricto sensu: in a strict sense (as opposed to **lato sensu**)

strictum juris: the rigor of the law

strictum jus [strict law]: the strict letter of the law

sua cuique sunt vitia: everyone has his/her own vices

sua sponte or **sponte sua**: of one's own accord; unsolicited; voluntarily

suae potestatis: a person free from any restraint

sub audi or **subaudi** (**sub.**): to read between the lines

sub colore juris: under color of law

sub conditione: upon condition

sub cura mariti: under the care of her husband

sub curia: under the court; under the law

sub disjunctione: in the alternative

sub idem tempus: about the same time

sub judice [before the judge]: under judicial consideration

sub modo: in a qualified sense

sub nomine: under the name

sub pede sigilli [under foot of seal]: under seal

sub poena [under penalty]: a subpoena (a writ summoning a person to appear in court, with penalty for failure to appear)

sub potestate: under the power of another

sub rosa [under the rose]: confidentially

sub sigillo [under seal]: in the strictest confidence

sub silentio [in silence]: privately

sub spe rati: in the hope of a decision

sub verbo (**s.v.**, pl. **s.vv.**): look under the word

sub vino: under the influence of wine

sub voce (**s.v.**, pl. **s.vv.**): look under the word

subito: suddenly

subpoena duces tecum [bring with you under penalty]: a subpoena, with the understanding that the person will provide documents or other tangible evidence (also, **duces tecum**)

subscriptio or **subscriptum** [a writing beneath]: a signature (also, **signatura**)

sufficit (pl. **sufficiunt**): it is enough

suffragium [a voting tablet]: the right to vote

suggestio falsi [suggestion of a falsehood]: an indirect lie or misrepresentation

sui generis [of its own kind]: unique; one of a kind; something in a class by itself

sui juris [in one's own right]: of full legal capacity

summa injuria: the greatest injury

summa vitae: life span (also, **vitae summa**)

summum jus: the highest law

summum jus, summa injuria [extreme law, extreme injury]: (fig.) the law, strictly interpreted, may be the greatest of injustices

summus: the greatest; the highest

sumptibus publicis (or **sumptu publico**): at the public expense

suo jure: in one's own right

suo loco: in its proper place

suo nomine: in one's own name

suo periculo: at one's own peril or risk

super aliquam partem fundi: upon any part of the land

super altum mare: upon the high seas

super eisdem deductis: upon the same grounds

super visum corpore: upon view of the body

superflua non nocent: superfluities do not injure

supersedeas: a setting aside (a stay of execution of judgment issued while a ruling is under appeal)

supra (**sup.**): over; above; on the top

supra vires: beyond one's powers

suppressio veri: the suppression of the truth; a concealment of facts

suppressio veri suggestio falsi: suppression of the truth is the suggestion of falsehood

suspendatur per collum (**sus. per col.**) [let him/her be hanged by the neck]: the sentence of death by hanging

suspensio per collum [hanging by the neck]: execution by hanging

suus: one's own

T

tabula: a record book; a register

tabulae: written documents (e.g., contracts or wills); bills of indictment

tabulae publicae: public archives

tabularius: a notary

tacitus [silent]: unspoken; implied

tales de circumstantibus: a sufficient number of persons present to supply a deficiency in a panel of jurors

talis qualis (**tal. qual.**): such as it is

taliter: in such a manner

tam facti quam animi: as much in action as in intention

tamquam alter idem (or **tanquam alter idem**) [as if a second self]: a completely trustworthy person

tandem: at length

tanquam optimum maximum: at its best and greatest

tantum: so much; as much

te judice [you being the judge]: in your judgment

te nosce: know thyself

tempore (temp. or **t.**): in the time of

tempus: time; a season

tempus anima rei: time is the essence of the thing

tempus continuum: time running on without interruption

tempus deliberandi: time for deliberation

tempus instat: this is the time; this is the moment

tempus me deficit: I have no time

tempus omnia revelat: time reveals all things

tempus semeste: six months

tenet: he/she holds

terminus (pl. **termini**): a limit either of space or of time; a boundary

terminus a quo [the point from which]: the beginning point

terminus ad quem [the point to which]: the ending point

terra: land

terra culta: cultivated land

terra non secta: untilled earth

terra nova: newly cleared land

tertium nihil est: there is no third choice

testamentum: a last will

testamentum omne morte consummatum: wills are brought to maturity entirely by death

testatio mentis: a testament

testator (f. **testatrix**): a person who makes a will

teste: by the evidence or witness of

testes ponderantur, non numerantur: witnesses are weighed, not counted

testis (pl. **testes**): a witness

testis gravis: an important witness

testis unus, testis nullus: one witness is no witness

titulus [title]: a label or inscription

tortum: crooked; twisted; wrong

totidem verbis: in so many words

toties quoties: as often as it shall happen

toto genere: in every respect

totum: the whole

traditio rei: delivery of a thing

transeat in exemplum: let it become an example or a precedent

transfugium [going across]: desertion

transit terra cum onere: land passes with its burdens (also, **terra transit cum onere**)

transitus: transit; transition

transitus vetitus: no trespassing

transmarinus [from beyond the sea]: foreign

tributum: tax; taxation

tu quoque [you as well]: a statement accusing the accuser of the same charge

tunc: then

turpis: base; foul

tuta: safe; secure

tutamen (pl. **tutamina**): protection; a protective pact

tutor (f. **tutrix**): a guardian

tutus accessus non fuit: there was no safe access

typographum: typewritten

U

uberrima fides [superabounding faith]: implicit trust

ubi jus, ibi remedium: where there is law, there is remedy

ubi jus incertum, ibi jus nullum: where the law is uncertain, there is no law

ubi mel, ibi apes: where there is honey, there are bees

ubi supra (u.s.) [where above]: in the place mentioned above

ultimatum: a final proposal

ultimo loco: in the last place

ultimum or **ultimus** (**ult.**): to the last; the ultimate or extreme

ultimum supplicium [ultimate punishment]: the death penalty

ultimus haeres [the last heir]: the final heir (i.e., the crown)

ultra fines mandati: beyond the limits of the mandate

ultra licitum: beyond the legal limit

ultra mare: beyond the sea

ultra petita: beyond that which was sought

ultra posse nemo obligatur: no one is obligated to do more than he/she is able

ultra valorem: beyond the value

ultra vires [beyond one's power]: beyond legal authority

una cum: together with

una voce [with one voice]: unanimously

unde nihil habet: whereof he/she has nothing (e.g., a widow without dower)

unde petit judicium: whereof he/she demands a judgment

undique: from all sides; in every respect

unico contextu: by one and the same act

uno animo [with one spirit]: unanimously

uno consensu: unanimously

uno ore [one mouth]: unanimously

uno tempore: at the same time

uno verbo: in a word

usque ad: as far as; up to

usque ad filum aquae: as far as the thread of the stream

usque ad sententiam: until the pronouncing of judgment

usus: use

usus bellici: use in warfare

usus et fructus (or **usus fructus**): the use or enjoyment of the property of another

usus loquendi: usage in speaking; customary language

ut antiquum: as in ancient times

ut audivi: as I have heard

ut credo: as I believe

ut fit: as is commonly the case

ut infra (**ut i.** or **ut inf.**): as below (as stated or cited below)

ut supra (**ut sup.** or **u.s.**): as above (as stated or cited above)

uti non abuti: it is to use, not to abuse

uti possidetis [as you possess]: with the possessions held at the present time

utilitas: usefulness; utility

utitur jure suo: he/she exercises his/her right

uxor (**ux.**): a wife

V

vacatio: freedom; immunity

vadium mortuum [a dead pledge]: a mortgage

vadium vivum: a security by which money borrowed is repaid out of profits gained from the fruits of the land against which it is borrowed (also, **vivum vadium**)

vel faciendo vel delinquendo: either by act or by omission

vel non: whether or not

venalis: [for sale]: commercial

venalis populus venalis curia patrum [the people and the senators are equally venal]: everyone has his/her price

venditio: selling

venia necessitati datur: (fig.) necessity knows no law

venire facias [to make to come]: a writ from a judge ordering the sheriff to summon a jury

venire facias de novo [to make to come anew]: a second writ from a judge ordering the sheriff to summon another jury for a new trial

venit et defendit: he/she comes and defends

venit et dicit: he/she comes and says

venter inspiciendo (or **de venter inspiciendo**): examining the womb (historically, a writ commanding a sheriff to examine a woman, in the presence of twelve male jurors and twelve women, to determine if she truly is with child and, if so, when the child is likely to be born)

verba: words; language

verba generalia generaliter sunt intelligenda: general words are to be understood generally

verba jactantia: boastful words (i.e., words spoken in jest and, hence, not legally binding upon the person or persons speaking them)

verba solennia: solemn words (i.e., words essential to validity)

verba volant, scripta manent: spoken words fly away, written ones remain

verbatim et literatim [word for word and letter for letter]: an exact copy

verbi causa: for instance

verbo: in name only

verborum obligatio: a verbal obligation

verbum sapienti (**verb. sap.**): a word to the wise

verbum sat sapienti (**verb. sat.**): a word to the wise is sufficient

veredictum: a verdict

veritas: truth

veritas convicii: the truth of the accusation

veritas convicii an excusat?: does the truth of a libel excuse its publication?

veritas nihil veretur nisi abscondi: truth fears nothing save concealment

veritas nunquam perit: truth never dies

veritas omnia vincit: truth conquers all things

veritas praevalebit: truth will prevail

veritatem dies aperit: time reveals the truth

veritatis simplex oratio est: the language of truth is simple

versus (**v.** or **vs.**): toward; against

verus: true; genuine

veto [I forbid]: the refusal of a chief executive to execute an order

vi aut metu: by force or fear

vi et armis: with force and arms

via actionis: by means of an action

via alta: a highway

via amicabili: in a friendly way

via juris: by means of law

via publica: a public way

via regia [the king's highway]: a public highway

via trita via tuta: the trodden path is the safe path

viagium: a voyage

vicarius non habet vicarium: a delegate cannot have a delegate

vice versa (**V.V.**) [with the meaning or order reversed]: conversely

vicecomes: a sheriff

vicinus: neighbor; neighboring

vicus: district

vide (**v.**): see

vide infra (**v.i.**): see below

vide supra (**v.s.**): see above

videlicet (**viz.**) [that is to say]: namely; to wit

vidi, scivi, et audivi: I saw, I knew, and I heard

vigore cujus: by the force of which

viis et modis: by ways and means

vilis: cheap; inferior; worthless

vinculum: a bond or tie; a relation or connection

vinculum matrimonii: the bond of marriage

vindex injuriae: an avenger of wrong

vir: a man

vir et uxor: husband and wife

vir sapit qui pauca loquitur: wise is the person who talks little

virtus: virtue; strength

virtute cujus: by virtue of which

virtute officii: by virtue of office

vis: power; force

vis et metus: force and fear

vis major [superior force]: an inevitable accident (e.g., an act of God)

vis vel metus: force or fear

vitae summa (or **summa vitae**): life span

vitium: a fault or crime

viva voce [by a living voice]: orally (i.e., by oral examination); by word of mouth

vivax: long-lived

vix or **vixdum**: hardly; scarcely; with difficulty

vixit . . . annos (v.a.): he lived . . . years

volenti non fit injuria: a person cannot claim injury for something he/she willingly did

voluntas: will; volition; intention

voluntas habetur pro facto: the will is taken for the deed

voluntas legis: the spirit of the law

voluntas pro facto: the will for the deed

voluntas pro facto reputatur: the will is to be taken for the act (a reference to treasonable offenses)

voluntas testatoris: the will of the testator

voluntatis non necessitatis: a matter of choice, not of necessity

votum captandae mortis alienae: an earnest desire for the death of another

vox audita perit, litera scripta manet: the voice that is heard perishes, the letter that is written remains

vox populi (pl. **voces populi**): the voice of the people

vulgi opinio: public opinion

vulgo concepti (or **vulgo quaesiti**): illegitimate children of unknown paternage

vulgus amicitias utilitate probat: the common crowd seeks friendships for their usefulness

vulnus: injury; wound

RELIGIOUS LATIN

A

a cruce salus: salvation is from the Cross

a Deo lux nostra: our light comes from God

a dextris: on the right

a longe: from afar

a progenie in progenies: from generation to generation

a saeculo [from the ages]: from the beginning of time

a sinistris: on the left

ab aeterno: from the beginning of time

ab infima ara: from the bottom of the altar

ab ira tua: from your wrath

ab omni malo: from all evil

ab omni peccato: from all sin

abacus: a small table or shelf for holding cruets

abbas: an abbot

abbas primas: abbot primate (i.e., head abbot

abbatia: abbey

abbatissa: an abbess

ablutio: ritual washing (i.e., the mixing of water and wine during the Mass)

absconditus: hidden

absens or absum: absent

absit: God forbid

absit omen: may there be no evil omen in it

absolutus: absolved

abyssus abyssum invocat: deep calls unto deep

accentus: part of a church service chanted or sung by the priest and his assistant at the altar, distinguished from **concentus**, which is sung by the congregation or choir

acceptabilis: acceptable

accidens: accident (i.e., a quality or attribute, as opposed to **substantia**)

accipiens: a recipient

acclinus: prostrate

acerra: an incense boat

acetum: vinegar

acolythus: an acolyte

acta sanctorum: holy deeds of the martyred saints

actus: deed

actus Dei: an act of God

actus purus [pure act]: a reference to God as a complete and perfect Being

acupictura: embroidery

ad aperturam libri [at the opening of the book]: wherever the book opens (a reference to a certain type of prognostication)

ad astra [to the stars]: to an exalted place

ad Benedictionem Sanctissimi Sacramenti: at Benediction of the most Blessed Sacrament

ad clerum: to the clergy

ad completorium: at Compline

ad credendum: to believe

ad extra: outwardly; external

ad extremum: finally

ad gentes: to the nations

ad hunc modum: in this way

ad inferos descendere: to descend into the lower world

ad invicem: one with another

ad laudem et gloriam nominis sui: to the praise and glory of his name

ad laudes: at Lauds

ad limina apostolorum or **ad limina** [to the threshold of the Apostles]: to the highest authority; also, a bishop's official visit to the pope

ad majorem Dei gloriam (A.M.D.G.): to the greater glory of God (motto of the Society of Jesus, the Jesuits)

ad multos annos: for many years

ad nonam: at None

ad ostium ecclesiae [at the church door]: at the marriage

ad patres [to the fathers]: dead; passed away

ad perpetuitatem: forever

ad primam: at Prime

ad referendum [for reference]: for further consideration by or for the approval of a superior

ad sextam: at Sext

ad summam: on the whole; in general

ad summum: to the highest point

ad tempus: at the time; on time

ad tertiam: at Terce

ad ultimum: utterly

ad verbum: literally

ad vesperas: at Vespers

ad vitam aeternam: for life eternal; for all time

aditus: access

adjutorium: help

adjutorium nostrum in nomine Domini: our help is in the name of the Lord

adjuvante Deo labor proficit: with God's help, work prospers

admirabilis: admirable

admonitus: warned; admonished

adnotatio: annotation; comment

Adoremus: Let us adore

adventus: coming

adversus (adv.): adverse; against

adversus hujusmodi non est lex: against such there is no law (Galatians 5:23)

advocatus diaboli: the devil's advocate (opposite of **promotor fidei** in an ecclesiastical argument in favor of the beatification of a person)

adytum: sanctuary

aedicula: chapel; tabernacle

aedificatus: built

aere perennius [more lasting than bronze]: everlasting

aeternitas: eternity; eternal life

aeternus: eternal

affectus: affection; disposition

affixus: affixed; fastened

afflictus: afflicted

agnus: a lamb

Agnus Dei: Lamb of God (the concluding section of the Latin Mass)

alabastrum: alabaster

alleluia or **alleluja**: Hallelujah

Alma Redemptoris Mater: Dear Mother of the Redeemer

almarium: the sacristy

almus: kind; gracious

altare: an altar

alte: highly; deeply

alteri sic tibi: do to another as to thyself

altum silentium: silence from on high

altus: high; deep

ama: a cruet

amabilis: lovable

amarus: bitter

amemus Deum: let us love God

amen [so be it]: amen

amen dico vobis: truly I say to you . . .

amicus: friend

amor: love

amor nummi: love of money

amor vincit omnia: love conquers all things

amphora: a jug

amplexus: an embrace

amplus: abundant; ample

ampulla: a cruet

amygdala (or **amygdalum**): almond

anathema: an ecclesiastical condemnation resulting in banishment from the Church

ancilla: a handmaid

ancora: an anchor

angelicus: angelic

angelo nuntiante: by the message of an angel

angelus: angel

Angelus Domini: the Angel of the Lord

angustus: narrow

aniles fabellae: old wives' tales

anima: soul; breath of life

anima bruta [the brute soul]: the vital principle of lower animals

Anima Christi: Spirit of Christ

anima divina: the divine soul

anima humana: the human soul

anima mundi [the spirit of the universe]: the creative and energizing force that permeates all nature

anima sensibilis: conscious life (i.e., human and animal life)

anima vegetabilis (or **vegetalis**): vegetable life (i.e., plant life)

animatus: animated; inspired

animus (pl. **animae**): soul; mind

anno Christi: in the year of Christ

anno Domini (A.D.): in the year of our Lord

anno Hebraico (A.H.): in the Hebrew year (see also **anno mundi**)

anno Hejirae/Hegirae (A.H.): in the year of the Hegira (from the first year of the Muslim era, beginning 622 C.E.)

anno humanae salutis (A.H.S.): in the year of man's redemption

anno mundi (A.M.): in the year of the world since its creation (see also **anno Hebraico**)

anno post Christum natum (A.P.C.N.): in the year after the birth of Christ

anno salutis (A.S.): in the year of redemption

annulus or **anulus**: a ring

Annuntiatio: the Annunciation

annus: year

annuus: annual

ante Christum (A.C.): before Christ

ante Christum natus (A.Ch.N.): before Christ's birth

ante sacellum: in front of the chapel

ante Thronum: before the Throne

antimensium: a consecrated cloth used in place of an altar

antiphona: antiphon

antiquatus: archaic; antiquated

antiquitatis memoria: ancient memory

antiquum documentum: the Old Testament

antiquus: ancient; old

antistes sacrorum: bishop

apage Satanus!: away with you, Satan!

apertus: open

apologia pro vita sua: a defense or justification of the conduct of one's life

apostolicus: apostolic

apostolus: apostle

apparitio: an appearance; apparition

aptus: suitable

apud: with; near

aqua: water

aquila: eagle

ara: an altar

arbitrium: will; judgment

arbor: tree

arca: ark; chest

arcana caelestia [heavenly secrets]: celestial mysteries

arcanum arcanorum [secret of secrets]: a reference to the hidden keys that unlock the secrets of nature underlying alchemy, astrology, and magic

arcanus: secret; esoteric

Archangelus [archangel]: one of the nine orders of angels

arcus: bow

ardens: burning

ardor [flame]: heat; ardor

arduus: steep; lofty

arenaria: catacomb

Argentum et aurum non est mihi: Silver and gold have I none (Acts 3:6)

arx: fortress; stronghold; citadel

ascensio: ascension

asinus: ass; donkey

aspectus: sight; appearance; countenance

asperges [thou shalt sprinkle]: the sprinkling with holy water at the beginning of the High Mass

aspersio: sprinkling

Assensus [assent]: an essential item in Medieval Christian faith (together with **Fiducia** and **Notitia**)

at spes non fracta: but hope is not broken

Athanasius contra mundum [Athanasius against the world]: referring to the stand made by St. Athanasius against heresy in the early fourth century C.E.

atque: and also

atra cura [black care]: (fig.) in mourning

atratus [clothed in black]: in mourning

attentus: attentive

auctoritas: authority

Auctoritate Domini Nostri Jesu Christi, Sanctorum Apostolorum Petri et Pauli, ac Nostra: By the power of our Lord Jesus Christ, the holy Apostles Peter and Paul, and by our own authority

audacia or **audentia**: courage

audientia: hearing; attention

auditio: report

auditus: hearing; audible

augur: a soothsayer

aureola: halo

aureus: golden

aurichalcum: brass

auris or **auricula**: ear

aurora: dawn

aurum: gold

auspex [bird-watcher]: a diviner

auspicium [divination by watching birds]: an omen

auxilium: help; aid

Ave Maria: Hail Mary (a salutation to the Virgin Mary)

Ave Regina Caelorum: Hail, Queen of Heaven (a salutation to the Virgin Mary)

axis mundi: center of the world

azymus: unleavened

B

bacillum or **baculus**: a staff or crozier

baculus pastoralis: a bishop's crozier

baldachinum: a canopy

baptisma or **baptismus**: baptism

Baptista: John the Baptist

baptistarium: baptistry

baptizator: the minister of baptism

barathrum: an abyss

Beata Maria (B.M.): Blessed Mary

Beata Virgo (B.V.): the Blessed Virgin

Beata Virgo Maria (B.V.M.): the Blessed Virgin Mary

beatae memoriae (B.M.): of blessed memory

Beati mundo corde: Blessed are the pure in heart (Matthew 5:8)

Beati misericordes: Blessed are the merciful (Matthew 5:7)

Beati mites: Blessed are the meek (Matthew 5:4)

Beati pauperes spiritu: Blessed are the poor in spirit (Matthew 5:3)

Beati pacifici: Blessed are the peacemakers (Matthew 5:9)

Beati qui esuriunt et sitiunt iustitiam: Blessed are those who hunger and thirst for righteousness (or justice) (Matthew 5:6)

Beati qui in via Domini ambulant: Blessed are those who walk in the way of the Lord

Beati qui lugent: Blessed are those who mourn (Matthew 5:5)

beatissimus: most blessed

beatitudo: beatitude; happiness

Beatius est magis dare quam accipere: It is more blessed to give than to receive (Acts 20:35)

beatus [blessed]: a heavenly saint; also, a candidate for beatification in the Catholic Church

bene: well

bene orasse est bene studuisse: to have prayed well is to have striven well

bene vale (b.v.): farewell

Benedicamus Domino: Let us bless the Lord

benedicite!: bless you!

benedictio: benediction; blessing

Benedictus: blessed (a section of the Latin Mass)

Benedictus Dominus Deus Israel: Blessed be the Lord God of Israel

Benedictus qui venit in nomine Domini: Blessed is he who comes in the name of the Lord (Luke 13:35)

beneficium [a kindness or favor]: a benefice

beneplacitum: approval

benigno numine: by the favor of heaven

benignus: benign; kind

Biblia: Bible

biblicus: biblical

blasphemia: blasphemy

blasphemus: a blasphemer

bombacium: cotton

bombyx: cotton wadding; silk

bona fide [in good faith]: sincerely; genuinely

bonis quod bene fit haud perit: whatever is done for good men is never done in vain

bonitas: goodness

bonum: good

Bonum certamen certavi, cursum consummavi, fidem servavi: I have fought the good fight, I have finished the course, I have kept the faith (2 Timothy 4:7)

bonum diffusivium sui: diffusing his goodness (a reference to the inherent goodness of the divine creation)

bonum ecclesiae: the good of the church

breviarium [summary or abridgement]: a medieval devotional book containing the Psalms and other sacred writings

brevis: brief; short

bruma: the winter solstice

bulla [a seal]: a papal document bearing the official seal of his office

bullarium: collection of papal bulls

C

cadus: a cask

caecus: blind

caelebs or **caelibis**: unmarried

caelestis: heavenly; divine

caeli enarrant gloriam Dei: the heavens tell of the glory of God

caelicola: a resident of heaven

caelitus: from heaven

caelitus mihi vires: my strength is from heaven

caelum: the heavens

calix: chalice

calvaria: skull

candela: a candle; lamp

candidatus: clothed in white

canistrum: a basket

canon: ecclesiastical rule

canonisatio (or **canonizatio**): canonization

cantate Domino: sing unto the Lord

canticum [canticle]: a hymn

Canticum Canticorum: the Song of Songs (Song of Solomon)

Canticum Simeonis: the Canticle of Simeon

cantillatio: chanted portions of a religious service

cantio or **cantus**: a song; a chant

cantor: a singer

cantoris: to be sung by the cantorial side of the antiphonal

cantus firmus [fixed song]: a Gregorian melody

cantus planus [plain song]: a Gregorian chant

capella: a chapel; a choir

cappa: cape; cloak

captivitas: captivity

captivus: captive

caput: head; chapter

caputium: hood

cardinalis: a cardinal

caritas (or **charitas**): love or charity

carmen: a song

Carmen Christi: Song of Christ (a reference to the Pauline hymn to the incarnation of Christ in Philippians 2:5–11)

carnalis: carnal

caro: flesh

carpentarius: a carpenter

carus: precious; dear

cassus: empty; vain

castus: chaste

casula: chasuble

casus fortuitus [a fortunate fall]: a chance happening

catechesis: oral instruction

catechumenatus: the process of formal entrance into the Catholic Church

catechumenus (f. **catechumena**): an adult seeking formal entrance into the Catholic Church

catena: chain

catholicus: catholic; universal

causa causans [the cause that causes all things]: the Great First Cause

causa mali: an evil cause

causalitas: causality

cede Deo: submit to God

celebritas: feast; celebration; observance

celer: swift

celsitudo: eminence; loftiness

celsus: high

Cena Domini or **Coena Domini**: the Lord's Supper

cenaculum: upper room

censor librorum: an official censor of books

censura: censure

centrum: center

centum (C.): one hundred

cereus: a candle

cernuus: prostrate

certamen: contest; a fight

certitudo salutis: assurance of salvation

certo: certainly

certum est quia impossibile est: it is true because it is impossible (Tertullian)

certus: certain

charismata: spiritual gifts (also **charismaticus**)

charitas (or **caritas**): love or charity

Cherubim: one of the nine orders of heavenly angels (two cherubim were said to have guarded the Ark of the Covenant)

chorus: a choir

chrisma: consecrated oil

Christe, Fili Dei vivi: O Christ, Son of the Living God

Christi crux est mea lux: the cross of Christ is my light

christianitatus curia [Christian court]: an ecclesiastical court

christianus: christian; a Christian

Christianus sum: I am a Christian

christifidelis: a faithful Christian

Christo et Ecclesiae: for Christ and the Church

Christus: Christ

Christus Dominus: Christ the Lord

Christus praedicatur quod resurrexit a mortuis: It is preached that Christ rose from the dead (1 Corinthians 15:12)

ciborium: a vessel for holding the Host

cinis: ashes

circiter (c. or circ.): around; about

circulus: a circle

circum sacra: concerning sacred things

cithara [zither]: a harp

Civitas Dei: the City of God (in opposition to the Earthly City of St. Augustine)

Civitas Terrena: the Earthly City (in opposition to the City of God of St. Augustine)

clam: secretly

clamor: clamor; shouting

claustrum: an enclosure (i.e., a cloister)

clavis: key

clavus: a nail

clemens: clement; merciful

clementer: mercifully

clementia: clemency; goodness

clerici non ponentur in officiis: the clergy should not be placed in temporal offices

clericus: a cleric; also, a secular priest

codex: a book

codex rescriptus: a palimpsest

coelestis: heavenly

Coelestis aulae janua: Gate of Heaven

coelibatus: celibacy

coelitus: from heaven

coelum: the heavens

coena (or cena): supper

Coena Novissima: the Last Supper

coenobium: a monastery

cogitatio: thought

cognitus: known

cognoscitivus: cognizant; aware

coincidentia oppositorum: said of a god that is both creative and destructive

collatus: brought together; collected

collectanea: a miscellany; an anthology

collegium (pl. **collegia**) [a college]: a body or society of persons with common interests or pursuits

Collegium Sacrum: college of cardinals

collis: hill

colluvies vitiorum (coll. vit.) [a collection of filthy vices]: a den of iniquity

columba: a dove

columna: a pillar

comes: companion; associate

comitatus: a following

Commemoratio Omnium Fidelium Defunctorum: Feast of All Souls

comminus: close up; close at hand

commiseratio: pity

commixtio: mingling

commodum: at the right time

communicatio essentiae [communication of essence]: a doctrine which teaches that Christ the Son receives his divine essence from God the Father

communicatio idiomatum [communication of similarities]: the transference of divine qualities to humans

communio: communion

communio sanctorum: communion of the saints

communis: common

communitas: community or fellowship

commutatio: change

compar: similar; like

compassio: compassion

compendium: a summary

Completorium: the office of Compline

complexio oppositorium: mutually opposed positions

concentus [concord or harmony]: part of the church service sung or chanted by the congregation or choir, distinguished from **accentus**, which is sung by the priest and his assistant at the altar

concessus: given; granted

concilium: council

concio ad clerum: discourse to the clergy

concionator: a preacher

conclave: a room that can be locked

concordia: peace; harmony

concursus: concourse; gathering

condemnatio: condemnation

conditio: condition

conferentia: conference

confessarius: a confessor

confessio [confession]: the sacrament of Reconciliation; the tomb of a martyred saint

confestim: immediately

confidelis: a fellow believer

confidentia: confidence

confirmatus: confirmed

Confitemini ergo alterutrum peccata vestra: Confess your sins to one another (James 5:16)

confiteor [I confess]: a prayer of public confession

Confiteor Deo omnipotenti: I confess to God the Almighty

confiteor tibi in cithara: I will praise you upon the harp

confixus: fixed

connubium: marriage

conscientia mala: a bad conscience

conscientia recta: a good conscience

consensus: agreement

consilium [deliberation]: a council or assembly; advice

consolatio: consolation; encouragement

consors: consort

consortio or **consortium**: companionship; partnership

conspectus: view; survey

conspiciendus: notable; worthy to be beheld

constat: it is certain

constitutivus: constituent

constitutus: settled; agreed upon

consubstantialis [of the same nature (as)]: consubstantial

consuetudo: custom

consuetus: accustomed

Consummatum est: It is finished (one of the Seven Last Words of Christ; John 19:30)

consummatus: finished; completed; perfected

contemplatio: contemplation

contemptus: contemptible

contigit: it happens

continuo: continually

contra (**con.** or **cont.**): against; on the opposite side

contra mundum: against the world

contradictio: contradiction

contrarietas: opposition

contrarium: opposite

contristatus: compassionate

contritus: contrite

contumelia: outrage; ignominy; reproach

convenientia: harmony; agreement

conventus: an assembly

convexus: vaulted

convivium: banquet

copia: abundance; plenty

copiosus: copious; plentiful

copulatus: joined; united

cor: heart

Cor Jesu Sacratissimum, miserere nobis: Most Sacred Heart of Jesus, have mercy on us

cor unum, via una: one heart, one way

coram: before; in the presence of

corculum: little heart

cornu: horn

cornu salutis: a horn of salvation

corona: crown; rosary

corona lucis [crown of light]: a circular chandelier hung from the central interior roof of a church or cathedral

corporalis or **corporeus**: bodily; physical; corporeal

corpus [a body or corpse]: a body or collection of writings

Corpus Christi [body of Christ]: a festival in honor of the Holy Eucharist

Corpus Juris Canonici: the body of canon law

corpus theologicum: the body of theological writings

corrumpunt mores bonos colloquia mala: bad company corrupts good character (1 Corinthians 15:33)

cotidianus (or **cotidie**): every day; daily

creatio ex nihil [creation from nothing]: the doctrine that God created the world from absolute nothingness

creator: creator

creatura: creature

crede Deo: trust God

credendum (pl. **credenda**) [a thing to be believed]: an article of faith

credens: one who believes

Credo [I believe]: a section of the Latin Mass; a creed

Credo, Domine: Lord, I believe

credo ecclesiam: I believe in the church

Credo in unum Deum: I believe in one God

credo quia absurdum (est): I believe it because it is absurd

credo quia impossibile (est): I believe it because it is impossible

credo ut intelligam: I believe so that I might understand (i.e., belief precedes knowledge)

cruce, dum spiro, fido: while I have breath, I trust in the Cross

cruciatio: torment

cruciatus: torture

Crucifigatur: Let him be crucified

crucifixus: a crucifix

crucis supplicium: crucifixion

cruentus or **cruentatus**: bloody; bloodstained

crux: cross

crux commissa: the tau (T) cross

crux decussata: the chi (X) cross of St. Andrew or St. Patrick

crux mihi ancora: the Cross is my anchor

crux stellata: a type of cross in which its arms extend into stars

cucullus non facit monachum: the cowl does not make the monk

culpa: fault

cultor: worshipper

cultus: worship; reverence

cultus dei: worship of the gods

cultus deorum [care of the gods]: reverence or divine service

cum nimbo [with a cloud]: the halo surrounding the head of saints in sacred art

cum sacerdote: with the priest

cunabula: a cradle

cuncta fausta: all things are favorable

cunctus: all collectively; the whole

cupidus: desirous of

cura animarum: the care of souls

curatus: a curate

cursor: a messenger

Cursus: the Divine Office; the Breviary

custodia: custody; protection

custos martyrum: keeper of relics

custos morum: a custodian of morals

D

Da gloriam Deo: Give glory to God

Da mihi pacem: Give me peace

daemoniacus: possessed by a demon

daemonium: an evil spirit; a demon

dante Deo: by the gift of God

date et dabitur vobis: give and it shall be given to you (Luke 6:38)

de cetero: as for the rest

de fide: of the faith (i.e., required as an article of faith)

de industria: by labor

de longinquum: from afar

de Maria Virgine: of the Virgin Mary

de profundis clamavi ad te, Domine: out of the depths I have cried to you, O Lord (Psalms 130:1)

de tibi credita: entrusted to thee

de verbo in verbum (or **de verbo**) [word for word]: literally

dea: a goddess

debitum naturae [the debt of nature]: death

Decalogus: the Ten Commandments

decani: to be sung by the decanal side of the antiphonal

decorus: decorous; befitting

decretalis: decretal

decuma (or **decima**) [a tenth part]: a tithe

Dedit illis potestatem spirituum immundorum: He gave them power over unclean spirits (Matthew 10:1)

deduc me: lead me

defessus: weary

defunctus: dead; deceased

Dei gratia: by the grace of God

Dei gratias: thanks be to God

Dei irati: the wrath of God

Dei judicium: judgment of God (also, trial by ordeal)

Dei propitii: the favor of God

Dei Verbum: the Word of God

deitas: deity; divinity

delectamentum: amusement; delight

delictum: sin

delinquens: a shortcoming; a failing

delubrum: a shrine; temple

demissus: humble; lowly; bent; hanging

denique: at length; at last

denique caelum: heaven at last! (Crusaders' battle cry)

Deo adjuvante non timendum: with God's help, nothing need be feared

Deo date: give unto God

Deo favente [with God's favor]: by the grace of God

Deo gratias: thanks be to God

Deo juvante: with God's help

Deo monente: with God's warning (i.e., a warning from God)

Deo, Optimo, Maximo (D.O.M.): to God, the Best, the Greatest (motto of the Benedictine Order)

Deo volente (d.v. or **D.V.)**: God willing

deoscatum: kissed devoutly

depositus: divested

deprecatio: an entreaty

derelictus: forsaken

Descendat nunc de cruce, et credimus ei: Let him come down from the cross, and we will believe him (Matthew 27:42)

desertus: forsaken

desideratum: something desired

desiderium: desire

desolatus: forsaken

desponsatus: espoused

detrimentum: loss

Deum esse credimus: we believe in the existence of God

Deus: God

Deus absconditus: the hidden God (the Lutheran doctrine that, despite the advent of Christ, God's nature is not fully revealed to humanity)

Deus autem spei repleat vos omni gaudio et pace in credendo: May the God of hope fill you with joy and peace in believing (Romans 15:13)

Deus avertat!: God forbid!

Deus det!: God grant!

Deus est regit qui omnia: there is a God who rules all things

Deus est summum bonum: God is the greatest good

deus est suum esse: God is his own being

Deus Fortis: Mighty God

deus ignotus: an unknown or ignorant god

Deus incognitus: the unknown, unknowable God

Deus meus: My God; O my God

Deus misereatur: God be merciful

deus mobilis: a changing or changeable god

Deus nobiscum, quis contra?: God with us, who can be against us?

Deus pro nobis: God for us (i.e., those aspects and manifestations of God open to the finite human mind; also, God's direct relation to humans through Christ)

Deus providebit: God will provide

Deus salutaris noster: God our Savior

Deus vobiscum: God be with you

Deus vult: God wills it! (the rallying cry of the First Crusade)

devictus: beaten; subjugated

devius: astray

devotio: devotion

devotus: devout; devotional

dextimus: on the right hand or side

diabolicus: diabolical

diabolus: a devil

diaconus: a deacon

diadema: a diadem

dialogus: a philosophical discussion

dicitur [it is called]: it is said to be

Dies Azymorum [the Days of Unleavened Bread]: the feast of Passover

Dies Dominicus: the Lord's Day (i.e., Sunday)

dies festus: holy day

Dies Irae [day of wrath]: Day of Judgment (a section of the Requiem mass)

differentia: distinction

difficulter: with difficulty

diffusus: diffused

digitus: finger

dignitas: dignity

Dignitatis Humanae: Of Human Dignity (papal encyclical on human rights, 1965)

dignus: worthy

Dignus est operarius cibo suo: The worker is worthy of his meal (Matthew 10:10)

dignus vindice nodus: a knot worthy of a liberator (i.e., a difficulty needing divine intervention)

dilectus: beloved

diligens: diligent; industrious

Diliges proximum tuum tanquam te ipsum: You shall love your neighbor as yourself (Mark 12:31)

diluculum: daybreak

diluvium: flood

dirige nos Domine: direct us, O Lord

dirus: fearful; horrible

dirus auditu: dreadful to hear

dirus visu: dreadful to see

discessus: departure

disciplina: discipline; order

discipulus: disciple

ditat Deus: God enriches

diurnus: daily; per day

dives: rich; wealthy

divina particula aurae [divine particle of light]: the divine spirit in the human person

divinitas [divinity]: the power of prophecy or divination

Divinitatis Baccalaureus (D.B.): Bachelor of Divinity

Divinitatis Doctor (D.D.): Doctor of Divinity (an honorary degree)

divinitatis sensus: an awareness of the divine presence in the world

divinitus: divinely; by divine power; miraculously

divinitus accidit: it happened miraculously

Divinum auxilium maneat semper nobiscum: May the Divine assistance remain with us always

Divinum officium: the Divine Office (an official service of prayer); also, **Officium Divinum**

divinus: divine; superhuman

divisio: separation

divitiae: riches

divus: a saint; a divine

dixi: I have spoken

Dixit Dominus: the Lord has spoken it

Doctores Ecclesiae: Doctors of the Church

doctrina: teaching; doctrine; instruction

doctus: learned

documentum: law; testament

dogmaticus: dogmatical

dolens: grief-stricken

dolor: pain; sorrow; suffering

dolorosus: sorrowful

dominatus: mastery; dominating power

Domine, ad adjuvandum me festina: O Lord, make haste to help me

Domine dilexi decorem domus tuae: I have loved the beauty of your house, O Lord.

Domine illuminatio mea: O Lord, my light

Domine, non sum dignus: O Lord, I am not worthy

Domine, salva nos, perimus: Lord, save us, we are perishing (Matthew 8:25)

dominicium [lordship]: a building that has been consecrated to God

Domino, Optimo, Maximo (D.O.M.): the Lord, the Best, the Greatest (an alternative rendering of the motto of the Benedictine Order)

Domino viso: they have seen the Lord

dominus (f. domina): lord; master

Dominus Deus Sabaoth, pleni sunt caeli et terra gloria tua: Lord God of hosts, the heavens and the earth are full of your glory

Dominus illuminatio mea: the Lord is my light

Dominus providebit: the Lord will provide

Dominus vobiscum: the Lord be with you

domus: house

Dona Nobis Pacem: Grant us peace

donec (don.): while; as long as

donum: a gift

donum superadditum: additional endowment (i.e., a reference to those divine gifts humans lost at the Fall, such as knowledge, eternal happiness, and love)

dormientium: of them that sleep (i.e., of the dead)

dormitio: sleep; death

dubitatio: doubt

dubius: doubtful

ductus: leadership

dulcior melle: sweeter than honey

dulcis: tender; sweet

dum: while

dupliciter: doubly

durus multis videtur hic sermo: this seems a hard saying to many

dux or **ductor:** leader

E

e or **ex:** out of; from

ebenus: ebony

eboreus or **eburneus:** made of ivory

ebrietas: drunkenness

ebur: ivory

ecce: behold

Ecce Agnus Dei: Behold the Lamb of God

Ecce Homo: Behold the Man (a representation of Christ crowned with thorns)

Ecce quomodo amabat eum: Behold how much he loved him (John 11:36)

ecclesia: a church

ecclesia ecclesiae decimas solvere non debet: a church ought not to pay tithes to a church

Ecclesia meliorari non deteriorari potest: the Church can make its position better, but not worse

Ecclesia non moritur: the Church does not die

ecclesia reformata, ecclesia semper reformada: (fig.) the reformed church is the church ever reforming itself (or: ever in need of reform)

ecstasis or **extasis**: ecstasy

Editio Vulgata [common edition]: the Latin Vulgate Bible

efficax: efficacious

effusio: outpouring

ego: I

Ego baptizo in aqua: I baptize with water (John 1:26)

elatio: exaltation

elatus: raised up; elevated

electio: choice; election

electus: chosen; elected

eleemosyna: alms

elementum: an element; a first principle

elogium: a saying; maxim

Emitte lucem tuam et veritatem tuam: Send forth your light and your truth

encyclica epistola: a papal encyclical

enim: for

enimvero: to be sure; certainly

ens (pl. **entia**): being or existence; an entity

Ens Entium [Being of Beings]: the Supreme Being

enuntiatim or **enuntiatio**: enunciation; a proposition

episcopalis: episcopal

episcopus: a bishop

epistola or **epistula**: a letter; an epistle

epulae or **epulum**: a feast

erratum (pl. **errata**): an error; mistake

eruditio: instruction; learning

esse: being; existence (as opposed to **posse**)

essentia: essence

Estote autem invicem benigni, misericordes, donantes invicem: But be kind to one another, merciful, forgiving one another (Ephesians 4:32)

esuriens: a hungering person

Et beatus est qui non fuerit scandalizatus in me: And blessed is the one who is not offended in me (Matthew 11:6)

Et cum oratis, non eritis sicut hypocritae: And when you pray, be not as the hypocrites (Matthew 6:5)

Et cum spiritu tuo: and with thy spirit (liturgical response to **Dominus vobiscum**, the Lord be with you)

Et ecce nihil dignum morte actum est ei: And behold nothing worthy of death has been done by him (Luke 23:15)

et ejusmodi: and the like

Et erunt omnes docibiles Dei: And they all will be taught of God (John 6:45)

Et fidelium animae per misericordiam Dei requiescant in pace: And may the souls of the faithful, through the mercy of God, rest in peace

Et lux in tenebris lucet: And the light shines in the darkness (John 1:5)

Et mundus eum non cognovit: And the world knew him not (John 1:10)

et omnibus sanctis tuis: and with all your saints

Et verbum caro factum est: And the Word was made flesh (John 1:14)

ethnicus: heathen

etiam atque etiam: again and again

Eucharistia: the Holy Eucharist

eucharisticus: eucharistic

euge!: well done!

eunuchus: a eunuch

evangelium: the Gospel

eversor: destroyer

ex animo [from the heart]: sincerely

ex cathedra [from the chair]: officially; with authority

ex dono Dei: by the gift of God

ex illo: since then

ex improviso: unexpectedly

ex ipso ore procedit benedictio et maledictio: out of the same mouth comes blessing and cursing (James 3:10)

ex more [according to custom]: habitually

ex nihilo, nihil fit: from nothing, nothing is made

ex officio (e.o.): by virtue of one's office

ex opere operantis: out of the work (i.e., a reference to the efficacy of the sacrament coming from the goodness of the one dispensing it)

ex opere operato: out of the operation of the work (i.e., a reference to the efficacy of the sacrament despite the moral condition of the one dispensing it)

ex parte: from the viewpoint of

ex professo: openly; avowedly

ex toto: wholly

ex visitatione Dei: by the visitation of God

exaltus: exalted

examen: test; struggle; agony

Exaudi nos, Domine: Graciously hear us, O Lord

excellentia: eminence; distinction

excelsum: height; high position

excelsus: lofty; sublime

excursus: a digression

exemplar: pattern; model

exercitatio: practice

exercitia spiritudia: spiritual exercises

Exi a me, quia homo peccator sum, Domine: Depart from me, Lord, for I am a sinful man (Luke 5:8)

eximius: exalted

exitus: death

exoratio: petition

exorcismus: exorcism

exsecratio: a curse

exsilium or **exilium**: exile; banishment

exsultatio: joy; exultation

extollentia: haughtiness

extra ecclesiam nulla salus: there is no salvation outside the church

extremus: extreme; last

F

fabricator: maker

facies Dei revelata: the revealed face of God

factum: deed; fact

factum est: it is done; it came to pass (that)

factura: handiwork

faenerator: a money-lender

fallacia: a fallacy

falsa religio: false religion

falsus: false

falx or **falcis**: sickle; scythe; pruning hook

fames: famine; hunger

familia: family

famosus: renowned; infamous

famulus (f. **famula**): servant

fanaticus: frenzied; fanatical

fanum [a temple and its grounds]: a holy place

fas: divine command; fate

fascia: a band; ribbon

favilla: glowing embers; ashes (of the dead)

februum: religious purification

felicitas: happiness

felix: happy; fortunate

felix culpa!: O fault most fortunate! (Augustine's allusion to the Fall of humanity that necessitated the coming of the Redeemer)

femina (f.): woman

ferax: fertile; fruitful

feria: weekday

Feria Quarta Cinerum: Ash Wednesday

Feria Quinta in Coena Domini: Maundy Thursday

Feria Sexta in Parasceve: Good Friday

feriatio: a feast

ferox: fierce; courageous

fertilis: fruitful

ferus: wild; a wild beast

ferventer: fervently

festinantes: with haste

festivitas: festivity

festuca: mote

festum: a feast; a feast day

Festum Festorum [the greatest of the feasts]: Easter

Festum Magorum [feast of the Magi]: Epiphany

Festum Stellae: Epiphany

festus or **festivus**: festive

fiat (ft.) [let it be so!]: amen

fiat Dei voluntas: God's will be done

fiat lux: let there be light (Genesis 1:3)

fiat voluntas tua: Thy will be done (Matthew 6:10)

fidei coticula crux: the Cross is the touchstone of faith

fideles: the faithful

fidelis: faithful

fideliter: faithfully

fides: faith

fides et ratio: faith and reason

fides quaerens intellectum: faith seeking understanding (i.e., belief before understanding)

Fiducia [trust]: an essential item in Medieval Christian faith (together with **Assensus** and **Notitia**)

figmentum: fiction

figulus: a potter

Fili David: Son of David

filia: daughter

filioque [and from the Son]: the clause later added to the Nicene Creed by the Roman Church that precipitated further schism between Roman and Byzantine Christianity

filius: son

Filius autem hominis non habet ubi capet reclinet: For the Son of Humanity has nowhere to lay his head (Matthew 8:20)

Filius hominis traditur in manus peccatorum: The Son of Humanity is being betrayed into the hands of sinners (Matthew 26:45)

fimbria: hem; fringe; border

fimbriatus: fringed

finis: end; finish

finitimus: bordering on

finitum non capax infiniti: the finite cannot contain the infinite (a doctrine reaffirming the humanity of Christ)

firmamentum: firmament

firmitas: firmness; stability

firmus: firm

fixura: perforation; piercing

fixus: affixed; fastened

flagellum or **flagrum**: a whip or scourge

flagitiosus: shameful; disgraceful

flamen: spirit; breath

flatus vocis: a mere word; not real (St. Anselm)

flectamus genua: let us kneel

fletus: weeping

florens: budding; blossoming

flores curat Deus: God takes care of the flowers

floreus or **floridus**: flowery

flumen or **fluvius**: river

foecundus: fruitful; fecund

fons: fountain; source

fons malorum: the source of evils

fonticulus: a spring

foras (or **foris**): out of doors; outwardly; in public

formido: fear; dread

fornix: arch; an arcade

fortis: brave; strong

fortitudo: bravery; courage

fragilis: weak

frater: brother

fraternitas: brotherhood

fraternus: brotherly; fraternal

fratres: brothers and sisters

fraus: deception

fremebundus: murmuring

frigescens: nondevout

frons [foliage]: a chaplet

frons: forehead

fructu non foliis arborem aestima: judge a tree by its fruit, not by its leaves

fructus (fruct.): fruit

frumentum: corn; grain; meal

frustra: in vain

fulgidus: shining; resplendent

fundamen or **fundamentum**: foundation

fundus animae: the basis or basic essence of the soul

funus: funeral

furiosus: a madman

furtum: theft

futurum or **futurus**: future

G

galerum (or **galericulum**): skull-cap

galerus: a cardinal's hat

gallicinium: a cock's crow

gallus: a cock

gamut (a contraction of **gamma ut**): the complete scale (i.e., a reference to the music scale developed by Guido d'Arezzo which is based on a medieval song whose seven phrases ascend in successive major scale tones in solfeggio fashion [ut re me fa sol la si]; hence: *Ut* queant laxis, *Re*-sonare fibris, *Mi*-ra gestorum, *Fa*-muli tuorum, *Sol*-ve polluti, *La*-bii reatum, *S*-anctae *I*-ohannes)

Gaudere cum gaudentibus, flere cum flentibus: Rejoice with those that rejoice, weep with those that weep (Romans 12:15)

gaudium (or **gaudimonium**): joy; delight

Gaudium et Spes: Joy and Hope

Gehenna: Hell

geminus (pl. **gemini**): a twin

gemitus: groaning

gemma: jewel

generatim: in general

generatio: generation

Genetrix or **Genitrix** [mother]: God the Mother (i.e., the Virgin Mother)

Genitor [father]: God the Father

Genitus [the begotten]: God the Son

gens: people (i.e., the Gentiles)

gentilis: gentile

genu flexo: kneeling

genus: race

germana: sister

gladius: sword

globulus: a bead

Gloria in altissimis Deo, et super terram pax in hominibus bonae voluntatis: Glory to God in the highest, and on earth peace to men of good will

Gloria in Excelsis Deo: Glory be to God Most High (the "greater doxology")

Gloria Patri: Glory be to the Father (the "lesser doxology")

Gloria tibi, Domine: Glory be to you, Lord

gloriatio: boasting

gloriosus: glorious

gratia: grace

gratia Dei: by the grace of God

gratia praeveniens: prevenient grace (i.e., a doctrine of St. Augustine holding that God not only provides grace but also the desire within the individual believer to receive it)

gratiae: thanks

Gratias agamus Domino Deo nostro: Let us give thanks to the Lord our God

Gratias agimus tibi: We give thee thanks

gratis: freely

gratus Deo: pleasing to God

H

Habemus Papam! [we have a father!]: the cheer of the people upon the election of a new Catholic pope

habitaculum: living quarters

habitatio: dwelling

habitus: disposition; habit; garb

haedus or **hoedus**: goat

haereditas: inheritance

halitus: breath

haruspex: an augur who examined entrails of sacrificed animals or other natural phenomena, such as lightning, to foretell the future

hastile: the staff of a cross

hebdomada (hebdom.): the week

hebdomadarius: a choir official serving for a week

heroicus: heroic

hibernagium: the season for sowing winter grain

hic: this

Hic est enim sanguis meus novi testamenti: This is the new covenant in my blood (Matthew 26:28)

hiems: winter

Hierosolyma: Jerusalem

hinc: here

historia: history

historicus: historical

hoc est: that is

Hoc est corpus meum: This is my body (Matthew 26:26)

Hoc facite in meam commemorationem: Do this in remembrance of me (Luke 22:19)

Hodie mecum eris in paradiso: Today, you shall be with me in Paradise (one of the Seven Last Words of Christ; Luke 23:43)

hodierna or **hodierna die**: this day; on this day

holocaustum: a burnt offering

homagium: homage

homilia: a homily

homo (pl. **homines**): human being; man

homo homini aut deus aut lupus: to man, man is either a god or a wolf (Erasmus)

homo religiosus: religious man (Eliade)

Honora patrem et matrem: Honor your father and your mother (Matthew 15:4)

honorabilis: honorable

honorificus: honorary

hora: hour

horae canonicae [canonical hours]: hours for prayer

horologium: a clock

Horrendum est incidere in manus Dei viventis: It is a fearful thing to fall into the hands of a living God (Hebrews 10:31)

Hosanna in excelsis: Hosanna in the highest

hospes [stranger]: a guest

hostia [victim]: an animal given in sacrifice

hostilis: hostile

hostis: a stranger; an enemy

Humanae Vitae: Of Human Life (papal encyclical on birth control, 1968)

humanitas: humanity

humanus: human

humilis: humble

humilitas: humility

humiliter: humbly

hymnus: a hymn

hypocrisis: hypocrisy

hypocrita: a hypocrite

hyssopus or **hyssopum**: hyssop (in the Bible, a plant whose twigs were used for sprinkling water in certain Jewish rituals)

I

idolatra: an idolator

idolatria or **idololatria**: idolatry

idolium: the temple of an idol

idolothytum: food offered to idols

idolum: idol

ieiunium or **ieiunus** (also **jejunium**): days of abstinence; fasting

Iesus Nazarenus, Rex Iudaeorum (I.N.R.I.): Jesus of Nazareth, King of the Jews (the title placard appended to the Cross by Pontius Pilate at Christ's Crucifixion; cf., John 19:20)

igitur: therefore

ignavus: slothful; idle

ignis: fire

ignitus: purified; refined

ignotus (ign.): unknown

Ille vos docebit omnia: He will teach you all things (John 14:26)

illibatus: unsullied

Illum oportet crescere, me autem minui: He must increase, but I must decrease (John 3:30)

illustris: glorious

imaginatio: imagination

imago: image

imago Dei: the image of God (a reference to the divine nature of the human person)

imitatio: imitation

imitatio Dei: imitation of God (a reference to religious rituals or other symbolic acts that replicate some divine action or sacred event, such as the Jewish Passover, the Christian Eucharist, the Hajj)

Immaculata Conceptio: Immaculate Conception

immaculatus: immaculate; spotless

immarcescibilis: imperishable

immaterialis: immaterial

immemor: unmindful

immeritus: unmerited

immersio: immersion

immoderantia: excess

immolatio: offering

immortalis: immortal

immortalitas: immortality

immutatio: change

imperator (f. **imperatrix**): imperial ruler

impermissus: forbidden

impietas: impiety; unbelief

impius: wicked; godless

impletus: fulfilled

impoenitens: impenitent

impollutus: undefiled

impotens: powerless

impotentia: poverty

impransus: fasting

imprimatur: the official approval of the Church

imprimis: first of all; especially

impudens or **impudicus**: shameless; unchaste

impuritas: moral impurity

in absentia (i.a.): in absence

in Adventu: in Advent

in aeternum: forever

in altum: on high

in Bethlehem Juda: in Bethlehem of Judea

in caelo quies: in heaven is rest

in caelo salus: in heaven is salvation

in Christi nomine: in Christ's name

in commendam [in trust for a time]: a benefice held by a person in absence of an incumbent

in conspectu divinae majestatis tuae: in the sight of your divine majesty

in corpore [in body]: in substance

in cruce spero: I hope in the Cross

in Dei nomine: in the name of God

in Deo speravi: in God have I trusted

in detrimentum animi: to the detriment of the soul

in dextram: on the right side

in dies: from day to day; daily

in ecclesiis benedicam Te, Domine: I will bless you in the churches, O Lord

in essentialibus: in the essentials

in excelsis: in the highest

in facie ecclesiae: before the church

in fine: finally

in hoc signo spes mea: in this sign is my hope (a reference to the Cross of Christ)

in hoc signo vinces: by this sign you will conquer (Emperor Constantine's vision before the decisive Battle of the Milvian Bridge, 312 C.E., which, according to Eusebius, inspired the Chi-Rho [XP] monogram, the labarum)

in hora mortis nostrae: in the hour of our death

in hymnis et canticis: in hymns and songs

in illa die: on that day

in illo tempore [in those days]: in the Golden Age (i.e., in the time when gods and goddesses walked the earth)

in latitudine: at liberty

In manus tuas commendo spiritum meum: Into Thy hands I commend my spirit (one of the Seven Last Words of Christ; Luke 23:46)

in medio: in the midst

in medio mei: within me

in memoriam [in memory]: in memory of

in meo corde: within my heart

in modico: in little things

in necessariis unitas, in dubiis libertas, in omnibus caritas: in things essential unity, in things doubtful liberty, in all things love

in nobis: within us

in nomine: in the name of

in nomine Domini: in the name of the Lord

in nomine Patris et Filii et Spiritus Sancti: in the name of the Father, the Son, and the Holy Spirit

in omne tempus [for all time]: forever

in omnibus caritas: in all things love

In Paradisum [into paradise]: a funeral hymn

in partibus infidelium (i.p.i.) or **in partibus (i.p.)** [in the lands of the unbelievers]: a titular bishop whose title is that of an extinct Roman Catholic see

in peccatis natus es totus [you were altogether born in sin]: you are a sinner from birth (John 9:34)

in perpetuum: forever

in persona Christi: in the person of Christ

in pontificalibus [in pontificals]: in episcopal robes

in populo: among the people

in posterum: in the future

in principio (in pr.): in the beginning

in proximo: near at hand

in remissionem peccatorum: to the remission of sins

in rerum natura: in the nature of things

in saecula [into the ages of ages]: forever

in saecula saeculorum [for ages of ages]: forever and ever

in sacris: in sacred matters

in se: in itself

in sempiternum: forever

in solo Deo salus: in God alone is salvation

in somnio pacis: in the sleep of peace

in spiritu humilitatis: in the spirit of humility

in te, Domine, speravi: in thee, O Lord, have I put my trust

in unitate Spiritus Sancti: in the unity of the Holy Spirit

in vanum: in vain

in vias et sepes: into the highways and byways

inane corpus: without a soul

inanis: empty; void

inargentatus: silver-plated

inauratus: gold-plated; gilt

incarnatus: incarnate

incassum: in vain

incensarium: a censer

incensum: incense; frankincense

incertus: uncertain

inclementia: unmerciful

inclina cor meum: incline my heart

inclusa: recluse

inclusus: enclosed

incolumis: safe; unharmed

incolumitas: safety

inconcessus: forbidden

incorporeus: incorporeal

inculpabilis: innocent

incunabula: swaddling clothes; infancy

indetonsus: untonsured

Index Expurgatorius: a list of the books from which offending passages must be purged before they may be read by Catholics

Index Librorum Prohibitorum: a list of prohibited books drawn up at the Roman Catholic Council of Trent, first published in 1557, and regularly updated

indignus: unworthy

inditus: given; endowed

individuus: undivided

indivisio: oneness

indubitanter: undoubtedly

Induite vos armaturam Dei: Put on yourselves the armor of God (Ephesians 6:11)

indulgentia: indulgence; forgiveness

indultum: a dispensation

industria: diligence

indutus: clothed

ineffabilis: ineffable

infantes expositi et inventi: foundlings

infelix: unhappy

infermentatus: unleavened

inferus: below; coming from the lower world

infidelis: faithless; disloyal

infidelitas: unbelief; infidelity

infinitus: infinite

Infirmatur quis in vobis?: Is any among you sick? (James 5:14)

infirmus: weak; infirm

infloratus: haughty; puffed up

influxus: inpouring; a flowing in; influence

infra caelum: beneath the heavens

infunde: pour forth

infusio: pouring

ingenitus: innate

inimicus: enemy

iniquitas: iniquity

iniquus: wicked

injustus: unjust

inlectus: unread

inlotus: unwashed; unclean

innocens or **innocentia**: innocent

innuba or **innupta**: husbandless; unmarried

innumerabilis or **innumerus**: innumerable

inobedientia: disobedience

inopia: poverty; want

inops: helpless; needy

insperatus: unexpected

instar: in place of

institutum: institute; a religious order

instrumentum: instrument; tool

insuper: moreover

integritas: virginity

intelligens: intelligent

intelligibilis: intelligible

inter nos [between ourselves]: mutually

intercedens or **intercessor**: a mediator

Intercedite pro nobis: Intercede for us

intercessio: intercession

interdictum: a prohibition

interim: in the meantime

interitus: destruction; ruin

interlunium: the period during the new moon

internuntius: a messenger; a mediator

internus: internal

interpretatus: translated; interpreted

intertextus: interwoven

intextus: woven

intimus: inmost; innermost

intrabilis: accessible

introibo ad altare Dei: I will go to the altar of God

introitus: introit

intuitivus: intuitive

intumulatus: unburied

intus: inside; within

inultus: unpunished

inunctio: anointing

inurbanus: rude; unpolished

invictus: invincible

invidia: hatred; envy; ill will

invisibilis: invisible

Invitatorium: the Invitatory (i.e., the call to prayer)

invitus: unwilling

invocans: one who calls upon

invocatio: an invocation

Ioannes or **Joannes**: St. John (the Apostle John)

Ioannes Baptista or **Joannes Baptista**: St. John the Baptist

ipse dixit [he himself has spoken it]: a dictum

ipse dixit Dominus: the Lord himself has spoken it

Ipsum Esse: Being Itself (i.e., God)

ira: anger; wrath

ira deorum: the wrath of god; divine retribution

irrescindibilis: irrevocable

it prex caeli: prayer goes heavenward

ita et viri debent diligere uxores ut corpora sua: so men ought to love their wives as their own bodies (Ephesians 5:28)

ite, missa est [go, there is a dismissal]: the Mass is over

item: in like manner

iter: a journey

itinerarium: itinerary

iucunditas or **jucunditas**: joy

iusiurandum or **jusjurandum**: an oath; a vow

iussa: by order; by command

iuventus (f. **iuventa**): a youth

J

Jacobus: St. James

jaculum: dart; javelin

janua: a door

jejuniosus or **jejunus**: fasting

jejunium or **jejunus** (also **ieiunium**): days of abstinence; fasting

Jerosolyma: Jerusalem

Jesu bone pastor: Jesus, Good Shepherd

Jesu Deus fortis: Jesus, mighty God

Jesu Deus noster: Jesus, our God

Jesu Deus pacis: Jesus, God of peace

Jesu Fili Dei vivi: Jesus, Son of the Living God

Jesu nostri miserere: Jesus, have mercy on us

Jesu Pater pauperum: Jesus, Father of the poor

Jesu refugium nostrum: Jesus, our refuge

Jesu Rex Gloriae: Jesus, King of Glory

Jesus Christus Filius Tuus Dominus noster: Jesus Christ Your Son and our Lord

Joannes or **Ioannes**: St. John (**n.b.** the Apostle John)

Joannes est nomen ejus: his name is John (Luke 1:63)

Jubilate Deo: rejoice in God

jubilatio: jubilation; rejoicing

jubilum: a shout of joy

jucunditas or **iucunditas**: joy; pleasure

jucundus or **iucundus**: pleasant; pleasing; agreeable

Judaeus: Jew

Judaicus: Jewish

judex: judge

judicium: judgment

judicium Dei: the judgment of God

jugum: yoke

jure divino: by divine right or divine law

jus canonicum: canon law

jus divinum: divine law

jus sacrum: sacred law

jusjurandum or **iusiurandum**: an oath; a vow

jussa: by order; by command

justificatio: justification

justitia: justice

Justorum autem animae in manu Dei sunt: But the souls of the righteous are in the hands of God (Wisdom 3:1)

justus: just

juvante Deo: God helping

juventus (f. **juventa**): a youth

juxta or **iuxta** (jux. or **iux.**): near; close by

K

Kyrie eleison (K.e. or **K.E.)**: Lord, have mercy (the opening section of the Latin Mass)

L

labellum: a small vessel for washing

labor: labor; work

labrum: a basin

lac: milk

lacrimae Christi (sing. **lacrima Christi**): the tears of Christ

lacrimae rerum [the tears of things]: the human condition

lacrimosus: tearful; sorrowful

lacuna: pool; a gap (e.g., in a text)

laetatio: rejoicing

laetificus: joyous

laetitia: joy; happiness

laetus: joyful

laicus: layperson

lamentatio: weeping; lamentation

lampada or **lampas**: torch; lamp

lana: wool

lancea: lance; spear

laneus: woolen; soft as wool

lapis: stone

lapsus: lapse; error

lassus: weary

latria: divine worship

latus: side

laudabilis: worthy of praise

laudatio: commendation; praise

laudatus: praiseworthy

Laudes Divinae: Divine Praises

Laudetur Jesus Christus in saecula: Let Jesus Christ be forever praised

laurea: wreath

Laus Deo: Praise be to God

Laus Deo Semper (L.D.S.): Praise be to God always

Laus tibi Christe: Praise be to you, O Christ

Laus tibi Domine, Rex aeternae gloriae: Praise be to You, O Lord, King of everlasting glory

Lavabo inter innocentes manus meas: I will wash my hands among the innocent (Psalm 26:6)

lavacrum: the water of baptism

Lectio [a reading]: a lesson or epistle, given during the Divine Office

Lectionarium: Book of Lessons for the Divine Office

lector: a reader

legatus a latere: a papal legate

Lemuria: a Roman festival held in May to expel ghosts

lenis: smooth; gentle

leniter: softly; kindly

leo: a lion

lepra: leprosy

leprosus: leprous

levis: light (in weight)

lex: a law or precept

lex aeterna: eternal law (i.e., the laws that underlie the natural world)

libamen or **libamentum** (also **labatio**): a libation; an offering to the gods

libellus: a letter or petition; a little book

libenter: freely; willingly

liber (pl. **libri**; **L.** or **lib.**): a book

liber: free

Libera nos, Domine, ab omnibus malis: Deliver us, Lord, from all evils

Libera nos, Jesu: Deliver us, Jesus

liberatus: set free; freed

libertas: liberty; freedom

liberum arbitrium [free will]: free choice

libido: lust; desire

libra: a pair of scales

librarius: a copyist

ligatus: bound; connected

lignarius: a carpenter

lignum: wood; the Cross

lilium: lily

limbus [limbo]: the border regions of hell

limbus infantium [infants' paradise]: limbo for unbaptized children

limbus patrum [paradise of the Fathers]: the place for the souls of the righteous before the first advent of Christ

limbus puerorum: children's paradise

limen: threshold

lingua: speech; language

litteratura: learning

litteratus (or **literatus**): learned

liturgia: liturgy

locum tenens (pl. **locum tenentes**): a substitute or deputy, esp. for a physician or a cleric

locus: place

logos: word

longe lateque: far and wide

Lucas: St. Luke

lucerna: lamp

lucidus: lucid; clear; bright

lucifer [light-bringing]: the morning star; the angel Lucifer

lucis ante terminum: before the end of day(light)

lucis et pacis: light and peace

luctus: grief; mourning

lucus: a sacred grove

ludere cum sacris: to trifle with sacred things

ludibrium: mockery; derision

lues: plague; pestilence

lumen: light

lumen fidei: light of faith

Lumen Gentium: Light of the Nations

lumen gratiae: light of grace

lumen naturale rationis: natural light of reason (i.e., knowledge of divine things without the direct assistance of God)

luna: the moon

lunaris: lunar

lupus: a wolf

lustralus: holy; blessed; purifying

lustratio: sacrificial purification

lustrum: a purifying sacrifice

lutum: clay

lux: light

lux in tenebris: light in darkness

lux mundi: the light of the world

lux perpetua luceat eis: let perpetual light shine on them

lux sum mundi: I am the light of the world

lux venit ab alto: light comes from above

lyra: a lyre

M

maceratio: mortification

mactatio: a sacrifice (a reference to the sacrificial death of Christ)

macula: stain

maeror: sadness; grief

magicus: magical

magis magisque: more and more

magister: master; teacher

magister dixit: the master has spoken it (an invocation of the authority of Aristotle in Medieval scholasticism)

Magisterium: Roman Catholic tradition, its authority, teachings, and holy offices

Magna Mater: the Great Mother (i.e., a deity related to the ancient cult of Mithras)

magna voce: aloud

magnalia: wonderful things

Magnificat: hymn of praise offered during Vespers

Magnificat Anima Mea Dominum: My soul magnifies the Lord (the Hymn of the Virgin at the Annunciation; Luke 1:46)

magnificus: magnificent

magnus (mag.): great

magus (pl. magi): a wizard or magician

majestas: majesty

Majestas Dei: the Majesty of God

major: larger; greater

Major autem horum est charitas: But the greatest of these is love (1 Corinthians 13:13)

majores: forefathers; elders

majusculae [uncials]: large capital letters characteristic of early Latin manuscripts

male: badly

male gratus: unthankful

maledicus: cursed; accursed

maledictio or **maledictum**: curse

malevolentia: ill will; malice

malum: apple

malum (pl. mala): an evil

malus: bad; wicked

mandatum: a command

mane: morning; in the morning

mane prima sabbati: early the first day (of the week)

manes: spirits of the dead

manibus extensis: with hands extended

manibus junctis: with hand joined

manna [manna]: spiritual food

manus: hand

manuscriptum (MS; pl. manuscripta, MSS): a manuscript

Maranatha [Even so Lord come]: the Lord cometh

mare: sea

Mare Nostrum [our sea]: the Mediterranean Sea

Mare Rubrum: the Red Sea

margarita: pearl

marmoreus: made of marble; marble-like

martyrium: martyrdom

Mater Christi: Mother of Christ

Mater Dei: Mother of God

Mater dolorosa: the sorrowing Mother (a reference to Mary's sorrows at the Cross)

Mater et Magistra: Mother and Teacher (papal encyclical on social progress, 1961)

materia: matter; material

Matutinum [night watch]: Matins

matutinus: of the morning

maxime: greatly

maximus: highest; greatest

me paenitet [I regret it]: I'm sorry

mea culpa: by my own fault (also **per meam culpam**)

mea maxima culpa: by my most grievous fault

mecum: with me

medice, cura te ipsum: physician, heal yourself (Luke 4:23)

medicinalis operatio: healing power

medicus: a physician

meditatio: meditation

medius fidius: so help me God

mellitus: sweet as honey

memor: mindful

memorare: to remember

memorari testamenti sui sancti: mindful of his Holy Testament

memoria: memory

memoriale: remembrance

mendacium: a lie

mendax: false; lying; mendacious

mendicus: a beggar

mensa: a table; an altar

mensis: month

mentiens: a deceiver

mercenarius: a hired servant

meretrix: a harlot

meritum: merit; reward

meta: goal; destination; turning point

metaphysica: metaphysics

meus: my; mine

Meus cibus est ut faciam voluntatem ejus, qui misit me: My food is to do the will of him who sent me (John 4:34)

mica: morsel; crumb

Mihi vivere Christus est, et mori lucrum: For me to live is Christ, and to die is gain (Philippians 1:21)

miles: a soldier

minime vero: by no means

minimus: least

minister: servant

ministerium: ministry

minusculae [small letters]: lower-case Roman letters in later Latin manuscripts

mirabile dictu: wonderful to say

mirabilia: wonders; miracles

mirabiliarius: a wonderworker; a miracle worker

mirabilis: wonderful; marvelous

miraculum: miracle

miscebis sacra profanis: mixing sacred things with profane

miseratio: mercy

miserator Dominus: the merciful Lord

Misereatur tui omnipotens Deus: May God Almighty have mercy on you

miserere mei: have mercy on me

miserere nobis: have mercy on us

misericordia: mercy; compassion

misericors: merciful

Missa (pl. **Missae**): the Mass

Missa ad canones: a Mass in canonic style

Missa ad fugal: a Mass in fugal style

Missa bassa: Low Mass

Missa brevis: a brief Mass

Missa cantata: Mass sung, but without deacon and sub-deacon

Missa catechumenorum: Mass of the catechumens

Missa fidelium: Mass of the faithful

Missa Latina: Latin Mass

Missa pro populo: [Mass for the people]: Mass of obligation (also **propopulo**)

Missa solemnis: High Mass

missio: the act of sending

missus: sent

mitis: meek

mitra: a ceremonial headdress worn by popes, bishops, abbots, and other religious leaders

modicus: moderate; a little

modus: manner

moechus (f. **moecha**): an adulterer

mola: a millstone

momentum: movement; motion

mons: mount; a mountain

monumentum: tomb; sepulchre

mors: death

mors janua vitae: death is the gate of life

mors omnia solvit: death dissolves all things

mors omnibus communis: death is common to all persons

morte devicta: death being overcome

mortificatus: being put to death

mortuus: dead

morum praecepta: moral teaching

mos: custom

mosaicus: Mosaic (i.e., pertaining to Moses)

mox: soon

Moyses: Moses

mulier: a woman

multa nocte: late at night

multi sunt vocati, pauci vero electi: many are called but few are chosen (Matthew 22:14)

multo: much; more

mundanus: mundane

mundus: the world

munera: offerings

mutatio: change

myrrha: myrrh

mysteria: cultic mysteries; secret rites

mysterium: mystery

mysterium fascinosum [a fascinating mystery]: the feeling of awe-inspiring fascination in the presence of the Almighty

mysterium fide: the mystery of faith

mysterium stupendum [an astounding mystery]: to be dumbfounded or thunderstruck by the awareness of the presence of the Almighty

mysterium tremendum [a tremendous mystery]: the feeling of awful dread in the presence of the Almighty

mysticus: mystic

N

nardus or **nardum**: nard oil

natatoria Siloe: the pool of Siloam

nativitas: nativity; birth

natum de Maria Virgine: born of the Virgin Mary

natura naturans: nature naturing (a reference to God as the creative principle of created things, i.e., the infinite creating the finite)

natura naturata: nature natured (a reference to created things which find their principle being in God, i.e., the finite dependent on the infinite)

naturae bonitas: innate goodness

natus: born

navis [a boat]: nave of a church

ne fronti crede: trust not to appearances

ne me perdas: let me not be lost

Ne Temere [not rashly]: a decree by the Roman Catholic Church invalidating all marriages not consecrated before a priest and the proper witnesses

ne timeas: do not fear

nefandus: abominable

nefarius: wicked

nefas: an abomination

nefastus: inauspicious; forbidden

nemo: no one

nequaquam: no!

nequitia: iniquity

nescio: I know not

nexus: tie; connection

nihil: nothing

nihil ex nihilo: nothing comes from nothing

nihil obstat: the official approval of the contents of a treatise or book

nihil obstat quominus imprimatur: nothing hinders the work from being published (i.e., the phrase that indicates acceptability to the Censor of the Roman Catholic Church, printed on the title page of a published work)

nihil sub sole novum or **nil novi sub sole**: there is nothing new under the sun

nihilominus: nevertheless

nil: nothing

nil nisi Cruce: nothing except by the Cross

nil sine Deo: nothing without God

nimbus: cloud; halo

nimium ne crede colori: (fig.) trust not too much in appearances

nisi Dominus frustra: except the Lord [build it, those who build it build] in vain (after Psalm 127)

Nisi esset hic a Deo, non poterat facere quicquam: If this man were not of God, he could do nothing (John 9:33)

nobilis: noble

nodus: knot; difficulty

noli me tangere: touch me not (John 20:17)

noli timere (sing.): fear not

nolite aliquid a Deo quaerere nisi Deum: ask of God nothing but God himself (St. Augustine)

nolite dare sanctum canibus: do not give that which is sacred to dogs (Matthew 7:6)

Nolite deficere bene facientes: Do not cease to do good (2 Thessalonians 3:13)

nolite judicare: judge not

Nolite judicare secundum faciem, sed justum judicium judicate: Do not judge after the appearance, but judge a righteous judgment (John 7:24)

Nolite judicare ut non judicemini: Judge not that you be not judged (Matthew 7:1)

Nolite mirari, fratres, si odit vos mundus: Do not marvel, brethren, if the world hates you (1 John 3:13)

Nolite thesaurizare vobis thesauros in terra: Do not lay up for yourselves treasures on the earth (Matthew 6:19)

nolite timere: (pl.) fear not; do not be afraid

nolo episcopari [I do not wish to be made a bishop]: official refusal of a royal offer of a bishopric

nomen (nom.; pl. **nomina)**: name

nomen est omen: the name is an omen

non Angli sed angeli: not Angles but angels (Pope Gregory the Great, upon seeing English youths for sale in the slave market at Rome)

non ens [the nonexistent]: a nonentity

Non ergo amplius invicem judicemus: Therefore let us no longer judge one another (Romans 14:13)

non nobis, Domine: not to us, O Lord (Psalm 115:1)

non obstante (non. ob.): notwithstanding

Non reliquam vos orphanos: I will not leave you orphans (John 14:18)

nosce te ipsum or **nosce teipsum**: know thyself

noster: our

nostrum omnes: all of us

Notitia [understanding]: an essential item in Medieval Christian faith (together with **Assensus** and **Fiducia**)

notus: known

nova religio: a new religion

novena (pl. **novenae**): a nine-day period of religious observance or devotion

novitius: novice

novus: new

nox (pl. **noctis**): night

nulla ex parte: in no way

nullus: none

numen: a spirit or deity; divine will

numen divinum: the will of heaven

numen loci [spirit places]: sacred places

numen praesens: spirit presence (i.e., the feeling of some spiritual presence)

nunc: now

Nunc Dimittis servum tuum, Domine: Now let your servant depart, O Lord (Simeon's prayer of rejoicing at the sight of the Christ child; Luke 2:29, offered during Compline)

nuncupatus: called; pronounced

nuntio or **nuncio** [messenger]: a nuncio (i.e., a papal ambassador)

nuptiae [nuptials]: marriage

O

O Mater mea, memento me esse tuum: O my Mother, remember I am yours

O Salutaris Hostia: O Saving Victim (first words of the hymn used at the beginning of the Benediction of the Blessed Sacrament)

obedientia: obedience

obiter: on the way; in passing

obitus: death; destruction

oblatio: offering

obsequium: homage

obsequium religiosum: religious submission

observantia: observance

obviam: on the way; hence

occultus: secret; hidden

octava: the eighth day following a church festival

odium: hatred; bitter dislike

odium theologicum [the hatred of rival theologians]: the bitterness of theological controversy

officium: duty; office

olea sancta: holy oils (sing. **oleum sanctorum**)

oleum catechumenorum: oil used at baptism

oleum infirmorum: oil for anointing the sick

Olivetum: Mount Olive; Olivet

omissio: omission

omne initium difficile: every beginning is difficult

omne trinum perfectum: every perfect thing is threefold

omnia ad Dei gloriam: all things for the glory of God

omnia bona bonis: to the good all things are good

omnia desuper or **omnia de super**: all things are from above

omnia munda mundis: to the pure all things are pure

omnia per ipsum facta sunt: all things were made through him (John 1:3)

omnia vanitas: all is vanity

omnia vincit amor: love conquers all things

omnino: by all means

omnipotens: all-powerful

Omnipotens Sempiterne Deus: O Almighty Everlasting God

Omnipotentia Dei: Almighty God

omnis: all; every

omnis honor et gloria: all honor and glory

Omnis sermo malus ex ore vestro non procedat: Let no evil speech proceed out of your mouth (Ephesians 4:29)

omnituens: all-seeing

onustus: laden

operatio: action

Oportet Deo obedire magis quam hominibus: It is necessary for us to obey God rather than men (Acts 5:29)

Oportet vos nasci denuo: You must be born again (John 3:7)

opposuit natura [nature has opposed]: it is contrary to nature

ops: power

optimus: the best

Opus Dei [work of God]: the Divine Office

opus operatum (pl. **opera operata**): a work wrought (a reference to the inherent efficacy of the Blessed Sacrament)

ora et labora: pray and work

ora pro nobis: pray for us

ora pro nobis peccatoribus: pray for us sinners

oraculum: prophecy; oracle

orantes autem, nolite multum logui: but when you pray, do not say much (Matthew 6:7)

orare bonum est: it is good to pray

orate fratres: pray, brothers

orate pro anima: pray for the soul of . . . .

orate pro invicem: pray for one another (James 5:16)

orate pro nobis: pray for us

oratio: prayer

orationes ante Missam: prayers before Mass

oratorium: oratory; chapel

Orbis Factor: Maker of the World

orbis terrae (or **orbis**): the world

ordinarius: an ordinary (i.e., a bishop)

ordines majores [major orders]: the higher offices of the Catholic Church

ordines minores [minor orders]: the lower offices of the Catholic Church

ordo: order; rite

ordo albus [white order]: the Augustinian Order

ordo griseus [grey order]: the Cistercian Order

Ordo Missae: the Order of the Mass

ordo niger [black order]: the Benedictine Order

ordo sancta [holy orders]: the Sacrament of Catholic priesthood

Oremus: Let us pray

oriens: the east

origo mali: the origin of evil

ornatus: decorated; adorned

ortus: rising (of the sun)

os (pl. **ora**): mouth

Osanna in excelis: Hosanna in the highest

osculo Filium hominis tradis?: you betray the Son of Humanity with a kiss? (Luke 22:48)

osculum: a kiss

osculum pacis: kiss of peace

ostium [door]: entrance; gate

ostrinus: purple

otiosus: useless; idle

ovis: sheep

P

Pacem in Terris: Peace on Earth (papal encyclical on world peace, 1963)

pacem meam do vobis: my peace I give you (John 14:27)

pacifer: peace-bringing

pacificus: peaceful

pacificum: a peace offering

Paenitemini igitur et convertimini: Repent, therefore, and be converted (Acts 3:19)

pallium: a ceremonial mantle worn over the shoulders by a priest

panem sanctum: the holy bread

panem sanctum vitae aeternae et calicem salutis perpetuae: the holy bread of eternal life and the cup of everlasting salvation

panis: bread

Panis Angelicus: [Angelic Bread]: manna; also, a Eucharistic hymn

Panis Coelicus: Bread from Heaven

pannus: cloth; swaddling clothes

papalis legatus: a papal legate (i.e., an envoy)

parabola: parable

Paraclitus: Paraclete; Comforter (i.e., the Holy Spirit)

Paradisus: Paradise; also, a church vestibule

Parasceve: Good Friday

Parce nobis, Domine: Spare us, O Lord

parens: parent

parochia: parish

parochialis: parochial

parochus: a parish priest

particeps: partaker

partitio: a division

parva componere magnis: to compare small things with great

parvus: small

Pascha: Easter

Pascha Annotinum: an anniversary of a baptism

Pascha Clausum: Low Sunday

Pascha Competentium: Palm Sunday

Pascha Floridum: Palm Sunday

Pascha Rosarum: Pentecost Sunday

paschalis: paschal (pertaining to Easter)

passio: passion

pastor: shepherd

Pastor Pastorum [pastor of pastors]: a papal appellation

Pater, in manus tuas commendo spiritum meum: Father, into Your hands I commend my spirit (one of the Seven Last Words of Christ; Luke 23:46)

patera: bowl

Paternoster or **Pater Noster** [Our Father]: the Lord's Prayer

paternus: fatherly

patina: small dish

patrinus: patron; sponsor

patrocinium: patronage

patronus: advocate

pauci: few

paucis: in a few words

Paulus: St. Paul

pauperes ac debiles: the poor and the feeble

Pax Dei: Peace of God (i.e., the Church's protection of non-combatants during war)

Pax Domini sit semper vobiscum: may the Peace of the Lord be with you always

Pax Ecclesiae: Peace of the Church (i.e., the Church's protection of non-combatants during war)

pax potior bello: peace is more powerful than war

pax vobiscum: peace be with you

peccator: sinner

peccatores te rogamus audi nos: we sinners beseech you to hear us

peccatum: sin

peccavi (pl. **peccavimus**) [I have sinned]: a confession of guilt

pectus: breast; heart

peculiaris: unique

pedilavium: ritual foot-washing (cf., John 13:2–17)

Pentecostalis: Pentecostal

penuria: want

per annulum et baculum: by ring and staff (symbols of office)

per Christum Dominum nostrum: through Christ our Lord

per Dominum nostrum: through our Lord

per Dominum nostrum Jesus Christum: through Jesus Christ our Lord

per evangelica dicta deleantur nostra delicta: by the words of the Gospel, may our sins be blotted out

per gloriam tuam: through your glory

per hujus aquae et vini mysterium: by the mystery of this water and wine

per ipsum, et cum ipso, et in ipso: through him, and with him, and in him

per meam culpam: by my own fault (also **mea culpa**)

per mysterium sanctae incarnationis tuae: through the mystery of your holy incarnation

per omnia saecula saeculorum [through all the ages of the ages]: through all eternity

per resurrectionem tuam: through your resurrection

per se esse: to exist by its own being

per singulos dies benedicimus te, Domine: day by day we bless you, Lord

per somnum [asleep]: in a dream

per totum: throughout

per viam dolorosam: by the way of sorrows

percontans: inquiring

peregrinatio: journey

peregrinatio sacra: a pilgrimage

perennis: eternal

perfectus: perfect

perfidia: treachery

perforatus: pierced

periculum: danger; peril; risk

peritus: experienced; skilled

persecutio: persecution

persona: a person

pervigil: vigilant

pervigilium: a vigil

petens: petitioner

Petite, et dabitur vobis; quaerite, et invenietis; pulsate, et aperietur vobis: Ask, and it shall be given to you; seek, and you shall find; knock, and it shall be opened to you (Matthew 7:7)

petra: rock

Petrus: St. Peter

pharisaeus: pharisees

pharmaceutria: a sorceress

piacularis: atoning

piaculum: sin; a sin offering

pietas: piety; devotion

pietatis causa: for the sake of piety

pileolus: a skull-cap

piscis: fish

pius: godly; devoted

placeat tibi: may it be pleasing to you

placebo: the first antiphonal in the vespers for the dead

plenarius: full; complete

plenius: more fully

Plenum gratiae et veritatis: full of grace and truth (John 1:14)

plenus: full

ploratus: weeping; lamentation

pluralitas: plurality

plusquam: more than

poena: punishment

poena damni: pain of the damned (a reference to the anguish the damned experience in hell as a result of their separation from God)

poena sensus: pain of judgment (a reference to the means by which humans will be tortured in hell, e.g., Dante's *Inferno*)

poenitens: penitent

poenitentia: repentance; penance

pompa funebris: a funeral procession

pone altare: behind the altar

pontifex: a priest or high priest

Pontifex Maximus [the high priest of the Roman cultus]: a papal appellation

pontificale: pontifical (a book of rites)

pontificalia [pontificals]: the vestments and insignia of a bishop

pontificatus: pontificate

pontificium: the papacy; papal power

populus: people

populus gaudeat: let the people rejoice

porcus: swine

porta: gate

portio: portion

portus: harbor

posse [to be able]: potential; possibility (as opposed to **esse**)

post Christum natum (P.Ch.N.): after Christ's birth

posterior: the latter

posterus: subsequent

postulans: a petitioner

potentia: power; strength

potestas: power; authority

prae oculis habeatur: let it be held before the eyes

praecelsus: sublime

praecique: principally

praeconium: praise

praecordia: inmost heart

praedicatio: sermon; preaching

praedicator: preacher

praedictus: aforementioned; predicted

praeditus: endowed with

praelatus: a superior

praesentia: presence

praesepe or **praesepium**: manger; trough

praesidium: protection

praetantissimus: most excellent

praeter or **preter**: beyond

praeteritis, praesentibus, et futuris: past, present, and future

praxis: practice

precatio: prayer; entreaty

precibus infirmis: with ineffective prayers

presbyter: a priest

pretiosus: precious

prex: a prayer

prima cum luce: at daybreak

prima inter pares: first among her equals

primario: primarily

primitiae: the first fruits

primo: first of all; in the first place

primogenitus: firstborn

primus: first; foremost

primus inter pares: first among his equals

princeps: prince

principium: beginning

pristinus: pristine; former; original

privatem: privately

privativus: deprived

pro Deo et Ecclesia: for God and the Church

pro Ecclesia et Pontifice: for Church and Pope

pro libito: at pleasure

pro populo [for the people]: a Mass of obligation

pro redemptione animarum suarum: for the redemption of their souls

probrus: shameful

procurator: proxy

prodigium: a prodigy

profanus: not sacred; profane

profluens: flowing

profundus: deep; profound

progenies: race; generation

Progenies viperarum, quis demonstravit vobis fugere a futura ira?: You brood of vipers, who warned you to flee from the wrath to come? (Matthew 3:7)

promotor fidei: promoter of the faith (opposite of **advocatus diaboli** in an ecclesiastical argument in favor of the beatification of a person)

prophetia: prophecy

propinquus: near

propitiatio: propitiation

propitius: merciful; forgiving

proprius: proper; personal; one's own

prospera: prosperity

protectio: protection

protoparens: first parent

providentia: providence

prudens: prudence

psalmista: a psalmist

psalmus or **psalmum**: a psalm

psalterium: psaltery

pulchritudo: beauty

puncto temporis: in an instant

purgatio: purification

purgatus: purged

purpura: purple cloth

purpureus: purple

Q

Quadragesima [fortieth]: Lent (i.e., the forty-day period of fast preceding Easter, beginning on Ash Wednesday)

quaere verum: seek after truth

quaesumus: we beseech

quasi vestigias nostras insistere: as if walking in my footsteps

Quasimodo Geniti: Low Sunday (i.e., the first Sunday after Easter)

Qui stat, caveat ne cadat: Let the one who stands be careful lest that one fall (1 Corinthians 10:12)

Qui videt me, videt eum qui misit me: He who sees me sees the one who sent me (John 12:45)

Quicunque Vult Servari: Whoever Will be Saved (the beginning of the Creed of Athanasius)

Quid est veritas?: What is truth? (Pontius Pilate; John 18:38)

Quid mihi prodest, si mortui non resurgunt?: What does it profit me if the dead do not rise? (1 Corinthians 15:32)

quidditas: essence (i.e., "whatness")

quidem: in fact

quies: rest; peace

Quinquagesima: the Sunday before Ash Wednesday

Quinque Viae: the Five Ways (i.e., the five arguments of Aquinas for the existence of God)

Quis nos separabit a caritate Christi?: Who will separate us from the love of Christ? (Romans 8:35)

Quo Vadis, Domine?: Whither goest Thou, Lord?

quo animo?: with what spirit or intention?

quoad sacra: as regards sacred things

quod avertat Deus! [which may God avert!]: God forbid!

quod Deus bene vertat!: may God grant success!

quod dixi dixi: what I have said I have said

quod non habet principium non habet finem: that which has no beginning has no end

quod non legitur non creditur: what is not read is not believed

quod scripsi scripsi: what I have written I have written (Pontius Pilate; John 19:22)

R

radix: a root; foundation

radix enim omnium malorum est cupiditas: for the love of money is the root of all evil (1 Timothy 6:10)

ratio: reason; account

ratiocinium: reasoning

recitatio: recitation

reconciliatus: reconciled

reconditus: hidden; concealed

recordatus: mindful

redemptio: redemption

redemptor: redeemer

redime me et miserere mei: redeem me and have mercy on me

refrigerium: refreshment

refugium: refuge

regalis or **regius**: royal

regeneratio: regeneration

Regina angelorum: Queen of angels

Regina Coeli: Queen of Heaven

Regina pacis: Queen of peace

regnum: kingdom

Regnum Dei: Kingdom of God

regula: rule

religio illicita: an unlawful or illegal religion

religio laici: a layperson's religion

religio licita: a lawful or legal religion

religio loci: the sanctity of a place

religio naturalis: natural religion

religiosus: religious

reliquiae [the remains]: relics

remissio: remission

requiem: a mass for the dead

Requiem aeternam dona eis, Domine, et lux perpetua luceat eis: Give them eternal rest, O Lord, and let perpetual light shine on them

requies: rest

requiescat in pace (R.I.P., pl. **requiescant)**: may he/she rest in peace

requiescit in pace (R.I.P.): he/she rests in peace

rerum natura [things of nature]: the natural world; the universe

res divina [divine things]: sacrificial service to the gods

res gestae: deeds

res religiosa: religious matters; also, cemeteries

res sacrae: sacred or consecrated things

res sanctae: holy or inviolable things

Res Tota Simul [the whole thing at the same time]: a Medieval Christian definition of eternity (also **Totum Simul**)

resipiscentia: repentance

restat: it remains

resurgens: risen one

resurrectio: resurrection

retributio: reward

Retro Satana!: Get behind, Satan!

reus: guilty

revelatio: revelation

reverenter: reverently

Rex Judaeorum: King of the Jews

Rex Pacificus: King of Peace

Rex regum: King of kings

rhetorica: rhetoric

rite: in proper form

rituale: a ritual manual for priests

ritus: ceremony

rogatio: a petition

rogus: funeral pyre

Roma locuta, causa finita: Rome has spoken, the case is closed

Romae: at Rome

rosarium: rosary

rota: wheel

ruina: ruin

ruri: in the country

S

Sabaoth [armies]: the Heavenly Host

Sabbatum: Sabbath

sacellum: sanctuary; shrine; chapel

sacer or **sacra**: sacred; holy; consecrated

sacerdos: a priest

sacra mysteria: the sacred mysteries

Sacrae Ordines: Holy Orders

Sacrae Theologiae Baccalaureus (S.T.B.): Bachelor of Sacred Theology

sacramentum: sacrament

sacrarium: sacred place

sacrificium: sacrifice

sacrilegium: sacrilege

sacrilegus: a sacrilegious person

Sacrosanctae et Individuae Trinitati: To the Most Holy and Undivided Trinity

sacrosanctus: sacrosanct (i.e., most holy)

sacrum oleum: consecrated oil

Sacrum Romanum Imperium (S.R.I.): the Holy Roman Empire

Sacrum Septenarium: the sevenfold gifts of the Holy Spirit: knowledge, wisdom, counsel, understanding, piety, fortitude, and reverence of the Lord

saeclum or **saeculum**: the world

saecularis: secular

sal terrae: the salt of the earth

salus animarum: the salvation of souls

salus mundi: the salvation or welfare of the world

salus per Christum Redemptorem: salvation through Christ the Redeemer

salutare: salvation; savior (**n.b.**, an ecclesiastical Latin form)

salutaris: saving

salutis exitum: a safe or salvific death

salva conscientia: without compromising one's conscience

salva fide: without compromising one's faith; without breaking one's word

salvator: savior

salve [may you be safe]: God's speed (a salutation)

Salve Regina: Hail Queen

salvo pudore: without offense to modesty

salvus: saved

Sancta Dei Genitrix: Holy Mother of God

Sancta Scriptura: the Holy Scriptures

Sancta Sedes [the Holy See]: Rome

Sancta Trinitas: O Holy Trinity

Sancta Virgo virginum: Holy Virgin of virgins

sanctissimi (SS.): of the most holy

Sanctissimi Nominis Jesu: of the most holy name of Jesus

Sanctissimum Sacramentum: the most Holy Sacrament

sanctitas: sanctity; holiness

sanctum sacrificium: a holy sacrifice

sanctum sanctorum: holy of holies; also, a private room; a place of retreat

sanctus: holy; consecrated

sanguis: blood

sapere recta: to be truly wise

sapiens: wise

sapientia: wisdom

Satanas: Satan

satis: enough

saucius: wounded; injured

Saulus: Saul (i.e., St. Paul)

saxum: rock; stone

schisma: division

schola: school

scientia: knowledge; learning

scio: I know

Scio enim cui credidi: I know in whom I have believed (2 Timothy 1:12)

scotista: a Scotist (i.e., a follower of the philosopher Duns Scotus)

scriba: scribe

Scriptura Sancta: the Holy Scriptures (or simply **Scriptura**)

scriptus: written

Secreta: the Secret prayer of the Mass

Secretum Missae: the Canon of the Mass

secta: a school of thought

secundum (sec.): according to

sedato corde: with calm heart

sedes: chair

Sedes Apostolica: the Apostolic See

sedes confessionalis: the confessional

semel abbas, semper abbas: once an abbot, always an abbot

semel pro semper: once for all

semper: always

sempiterna gloria [everlasting glory]: immortality

sempiternus: everlasting; eternal

senex: elder

sensus: feeling; sense; understanding

Septem Psalmi Poenitentiales: the Seven Penitential Psalms

Septemviri epulones: a college of priests in charge of sacrificial feasts (previously **Tresviri epulones**)

sepulchrum: grave; tomb

sepultura: burial

sepultus (S.): buried

Seraphim: one of the nine orders of heavenly angels, usually placed as first before the others

sermo: sermon; speech

Serva me, defende me, ut rem et possessionem tuam: Preserve me, defend me, as your property and possession

servitus: servitude

servus: servant

Servus Servorum Dei [Servant of the Servants of God]: a papal appellation

Si Deus pro nobis, quis contra nos?: If God is for us, who is against us? (Romans 8:31)

Si fallor, sum: If I am deceived, then I exist (St. Augustine's refutation of skepticism through one's self-awareness of deception)

Si quis dixerit quoniam diligo Deum, et fratrem suum oderit, mendax est: If anyone says "I love God" and hates his brother, he is a liar (1 John 4:20)

Sic enim dilexit Deus mundum, ut Filium suum unigenitum daret: For God so loved the world that he gave his only-begotten Son (John 3:16)

Sic totum omnibus quod totum singulis: So that the whole was given to all and the whole to each

sidus: star

signaculum: mark; seal; the mark of circumcision

signum: sign; miracle

silentium: silence

similitudo Dei: the likeness of God

Simon Petrus: Simon Peter (i.e., St. Peter)

simonia: simony

simoniacus: a simoniac (a reference to the sin of Simon Magus, who tried to buy sacred power)

simplicitas: simplicity

simul et semel: at one and the same time

simulacrum: image; likeness

sincerus: sincere

sine cruce, sine luce: without the Cross, without light

sine maculis [without stain]: spotless

singularis: singular

Sion: Zion

sit pro ratione voluntas: let goodwill stand for reason

Sitio: I thirst (one of the Seven Last Words of Christ; John 19:29)

situs: situated; situation, position

societas: society

socius: a companion; an ally

sodalitas: confraternity

Sol Invictus: the Invincible Sun (the Sun God of ancient Mithraism whose festival was celebrated each year on December 25th)

sola fide: faith alone (a doctrine of the Protestant Reformers)

sola gratia: grace alone (a doctrine of the Protestant Reformers)

sola salus servire Deo: our only salvation is in serving God

sola scriptura: scripture alone (a doctrine of the Protestant Reformers)

solatium: solace

solemnis: solemn

solemnitas: solemnity

soli Deo gloria: to God alone be glory

solus: alone; only

somnus: sleep

sophia: wisdom

sordidus: filthy; unclean

soror: a sister

sortes Biblicae: casting a fortune with the Book (a reference to divination by the selection of random passages from the Bible)

soter: a savior

speculum aeterni Patris: mirror of the eternal Father (a reference to the Crucifixion as an image of the eternal love of God)

specus or **spelunca**: cave; den

Spera in Deo: Hope in God

spes: hope

spes mea Christus: my hope is in Christ

spes mea in Deo: my hope is in God

spes tutissima coelis: the safest hope is in heaven

spina: thorn

spiramen [breathing]: inspiration

spiritalis or **spiritualis**: spiritual

spiritus: spirit

Spiritus autem blasphemia non remittetur: But blasphemy against the Spirit will not be forgiven (Matthew 12:31)

Spiritus Sanctus: the Holy Spirit

Spiritus Sanctus in corde: the Holy Spirit in the heart

spolia sua [from one's own spoils]: out of one's excess

sponte: voluntarily

Stabat Mater: the Mother was standing (a Latin hymn inspired by the suffering of the Virgin Mother at the Crucifixion)

stabularius: an innkeeper

stabulum: an inn; stable

stacte: oil of myrrh

stella: star

Stella Matutinia: Morning Star

stella monstrat viam: the star shows the way

Stephanus: St. Stephen

stola [robe]: a liturgical vestment worn by priests during Mass

studium: enthusiasm; zeal

stultus: foolish; a fool

stupens: astonished

suavis: sweet; good

suavitas: sweetness; goodness

sub cruce salus: salvation under the Cross

sub hoc signo vinces: under this sign you will conquer (variation of **in hoc signo vinces**)

subdiaconus: a subdeacon

subito: suddenly

sublevatus: lifted up

substantia: substance

subtilitas: subtlety

subtracta a praesentibus: withdrawn from consciousness

succinctus: girded

sudarium: a cloth or napkin

suffragium: prayer; intercession

sui: of his, her, or its own; of himself, herself, or itself

sui generis [of its own kind]: unique; one of a kind; something in a class by itself

summa or **summae**: a compendium of philosophical thoughts or theological conclusions, the most famous being the *Summa Theologica* of St. Thomas Aquinas

summum bonum: the highest or chief good (i.e., God)

summus: highest

summus mons: the top of the hill

super capita nostra: over our heads

superbia: pride

superbus: proud

supernus: heavenly

supplex: suppliant

supplicatio: prayer; supplication

supplicium: entreaty; also, torture or punishment

supra caelos: beyond the heavens

supra intelligentiam: beyond understanding

supra memoriam meam: beyond my recognition

sursum: upward

sursum corda; habemus ad Dominum: Lift up your hearts; We have lifted them up to the Lord

Symbolum Apostolorum: the Apostles' Creed

Symbolum Nicenum: the Nicene Creed

synagoga: synagogue

synodus: a council

T

tabernaculum [tent]: the container placed on the High Altar that holds the Sacrament

tacens: silent

tactus: touch

taedet: it wearies

tandem: at length

Tanto tempore vobiscum sum?: Have I been with you so long? (John 14:9)

Tantum Ergo: so great, therefore (a Eucharistic hymn)

tantus: such; so great

tardus: slow

Tartarus: the Underworld; Hell

Te Deum, Laudamus: We praise Thee, O God (an ancient Christian hymn)

Te igitur: You, therefore (part of the Eucharistic liturgy of the Latin Mass)

te nosce: know thyself

te rogamus, audi nos: we beseech you, hear us

tecum: with you

temperantia or **temperatio**: temperance; moderation

templa quam dilecta!: how lovely are thy temples!

templum: temple; consecrated ground

temporalia festa: temporal feasts

tempus: time; season

Tempus meum prope est: My time is at hand (Matthew 26:18)

tenax: tenacious

tenebrae: darkness

tenebrae aeternae: eternal darkness

tentatio: test; temptation

tepens: lukewarm; tepid

ter [thrice]: three times

ter arduae: three-times heavy

terminus: end; limit

terra: earth

terra es, terram ibis: you are dust, and to dust you will return (Genesis 3:19)

terra est gloria Dei pleni: the earth is full of the glory of God

terra firma [solid earth]: dry land; firm footing

terra incognita (pl. **terrae incognitae**) [an unknown land]: an unknown region or subject

terra marique: by land and sea

terrae filius (pl. **terrae filii**) [son of the earth]: a person of lowly birth

terrenus: earthly

Tersanctus [thrice holy]: the Trisagion (a liturgical hymn)

tertius: third

testimonium: testimony; witness

testimonium internum (or **testimonium Spiritus Sanctus internum**): internal testimony (a reference to the internal witness of the Holy Spirit that inspires faith within those who seek the truth of the Gospel)

textus receptus (**text. rec.**): the received text (i.e., the scriptural tradition that has been handed down from generation to generation)

theologia crucis: theology of the cross (the emphasis of Protestant reformers on the sacrificial death of Christ on the Cross, as opposed to **theologia gloriae**)

theologia gloriae: theology of glory (Martin Luther's pejorative label for Church doctrines that did not lay proper stress on the sacrificial death of Christ on the Cross; as opposed to **theologia crucis**)

theologus: theologian

theophania: a manifestation of divinity in human form

theristrum: a veil

thesaurus: treasure

threnus: lamentation

thronus: throne

thuribulum [an incense burner]: a censer

timeo hominem unius libri: I fear the man of one book (St. Thomas Aquinas)

timidus: fearful

tinniens or **tinnitus**: tinkling; ringing; clanging

tonsura: tonsure

tormentum: torment

tota die: all the day

Totum Simul: the whole at the same time (a Medieval Christian definition of eternity; also **Res Tota Simul**)

totus: whole

traditor: betrayer

tranquillus: calm; tranquil

trans media varia: through various means

transfiguratio: transfiguration (i.e., change of appearance)

tremendus: dreadful

tremens: trembling

Tresviri epulones: a college of priests who had charge of sacrificial feasts (later **Septemviri epulones**)

Treuga Dei (or **Treva Dei**): Truce of God (during the Middle Ages, the suspension of hostilities and private warfare during certain religious holidays, on pain of excommunication)

tribus: tribe

triduum: a three-day period

trinitas [three-in-one]: trinity (the doctrine of the unity of the Christian Trinity, i.e., of the Father, the Son, and the Holy Spirit)

trinus: triune

triplex munus [triple service]: referring to Christ as fulfilling the triple roles of prophet, priest, and king

Trisagion: thrice holy (a liturgical hymn)

tristis: sad; sorrowful

triumphalis: triumphal

triumphator: in triumph

triumphus: a triumphal procession

Tu, Domine, gloria mea: Thou, O Lord, are my glory

Tu es filius meus dilectus, in te complacui: You are my beloved son, in you I am well pleased (Mark 1:11)

Tu est Christus, filius Dei vivi: You are the Christ, the son of the living God (Matthew 16:16)

Tu solus sanctus: Thou alone art holy

tuba: a trumpet

tumultus: rising

tumulus: a grave

turba: crowd; assembly

turbatus: troubled

tus or **thus**: incense

tutus: safe; secure

U

uberrima fides: superabounding faith

Ubi est qui natus est rex Iudaeorum?: Where is he who is born king of the Jews? (Matthew 2:2)

ultra fidem: beyond belief; incredible

ultra mensuram: beyond measure

umbilicus [the navel]: the center or middle point

umbra: shadow; shade

una cum: together with

una sabbatorum [a sabbath]: the first day of the week

una sancta: one holy (a reference to the divine nature of the Christian Church)

unanimus: of one mind or spirit

unctio: anointing

unicus: sole; single

unigena or **unigenitus** [of the same race]: only-begotten

unio mystica: mystical union (a reference to the mystical union of the human consciousness with the divine consciousness)

unitas: unity

Unitas Fratrum [Unity of Brethren]: official name of the Moravian Church

universus: whole; entire

Unum scio, quia caecus cum essem, modo video: One thing I know, that though I was blind, now I see (John 9:25)

urbi et orbi: to the city [Rome] and the world

urbs: city

usus: use

ut digni efficiamur promissionibus Christi: that we may be worthy of the promises of Christ

utcumque placuerit Deo: as it shall please God

uterus: womb

Utinam frigidus esses aut calidus: Would that you were cold or hot (Revelation 3:15)

V

vade in pacem: go in peace

Vade post me, satana: Get thee behind me, you satan! (Matthew 16:23; also, **Vade retro me, satana**; Mark 8:33)

vae soli: woe to the solitary person (Ecclesiastes 4:10)

valde: exceedingly, greatly, very much

valde mane: very early in the morning

vanitas vanitatum, omnia vanitas: vanity of vanities, all is vanity (Ecclesiastes 1:2)

vanus: vain

varia lectio (pl. **variae lectiones**): a variant reading

variorum notae: notes of various commentators

vates: a prophet

vaticinium: a prophecy or revelation

velociter: quickly

venerabilis: venerable

veneratio: veneration

Veni, Sancte Spiritus: Come, Holy Spirit

Veni Sanctificator Omnipotens Aeterne Deus: Come Almighty and Eternal God, the Sanctifier

venia: grace; favor; pardon

Venit enim Filius hominis salvare, quod perierat: For the Son of Humanity has come to save that which had been lost (Matthew 18:11)

Venite, exultemus Domino [O Come, let us exalt the Lord]: a musical setting of Psalm 95

venter: womb

ventus: wind

ver sacrum: an offering of the first fruits given during spring

vera religio: true religion

veraciter: truthfully

verax: truthful

Verbi Dei Minister (V.D.M.): Minister of the Word of God

verbi gratia (v.g.): for example

verbum: word

verbum sapienti (verb. sap.): a word to the wise

verbum sat sapienti (verb. sat. sap. or verb. sat.): a word to the wise is sufficient

vere: truly; rightly

veritas: truth

veritas a Deo est: truth is from God

veritas nunquam perit: truth never dies

veritas omnia vincit: truth conquers all things

veritas praevalebit: truth will prevail

vernaculus: vernacular

vero: in truth

versiculus: verse

verus: true; genuine

vesica piscis [a fish bladder]: the aura surrounding the heads of sacred figures in Medieval and Renaissance Christian art (cf., **cum nimbo**)

Vesperae: Vespers (Evensong)

vesperi: in the evening

vester: your; yours

vestigium: footstep

vestigium Dei: vestige of God (a doctrine teaching that, despite the Fall, creation still reflects traces of its divine origins)

vestimentum: vestment

vestitio: investiture

vestitus: clothed

vetus: old

Vetus Testamentum (V.T.): the Old Testament

vetustissimus: very old; very ancient

vexillum: banner

via: way

via affirmativa [the affirmative way]: the way to knowledge of or union with God that is gained through affirmation of the positive aspects of the world (also known as **via positiva**)

via crucis, via lucis: the way of the Cross is the way of light

Via Dolorosa: the way of sorrows (i.e., the route Jesus walked on his way to his crucifixion)

via eminentiae [the way of eminence]: the positive way to knowledge of or union with God that is gained by affirming those perfections in the world that point to the eminence of God

via illuminativa [the way of enlightenment]: the way to God through illumination, whether mystical, inspirational, or relevatory

via Matris: the Seven Sorrows of Mary, the Mother of God, en route to the Crucifixion of Christ

via negativa or **via negationes** [the negative way]: the way to knowledge of or union with God that is gained through negation of the world

via positiva [the positive way]: the way to knowledge of or union with God that is gained through affirmation of the positive aspects of the world (also known as **via affirmativa**)

via purgativa [the way of purgation]: the way to knowledge of or union with God that is gained through purification by ascetic practices

via unitiva [the way of union]: the way to knowledge of or union with God that is gained by perfection of the self

viator: wayfarer

vicarius: vicar; a representative

vicarius non habet vicarium: a vicar cannot have a vicar

victima: victim (i.e., an animal offered in sacrifice)

victor rex: conquering king

victoria: victory

vide et crede: see and believe

Videte ne contemnatis unum ex his pusillis: See that you do not despise one of these little ones (Matthew 18:10)

videtur: it seems; it appears

vidit et erubit lumpha pudica Deum: the modest water saw God and blushed (a reference to Christ's first miracle, the turning of water into wine; John 2:1–11)

vidua: widow

viduus: bereaved; deprived

vigil: watchful

vigilate et orate: watch and pray

vigilia: a nightwatch

Vigiliae: the Night Office; Matins

vigilium: the eve of a church festival

vincit omnia veritas: truth conquers all things

vinculum: chain; fetter; bond

vinculum matrimonii: the bond of marriage

vinum (vin.): wine

vir: man

virginitas: virginity

Virgo [a maiden girl or virgin]: the Virgin

Virgo Sapientissima: the Virgin Wisest of All

Virgo Sponsa Dei: the Virgin Bride of God

virgo vestalis: a vestal virgin

virtute officii: by virtue of office

vis: power; strength

vis medicatrix: healing power

visibilis: visible

visum et approbatum: seen and approved

visus: sight

vita: life

vita beata: the blessed life; happiness

vitalis: vital; life-giving

vitis: vine

vitium: sin; vice

vitulus: a calf

viva vox: living voice (a reference to the "still small voice" of God heard by the prophet Elijah; 1 Kings 19:12)

vividus: full of life

vivificans: life-giving

vivificus: vivifying; quickening

vivus: fresh; alive

vocatio: vocation; calling

volente Deo: God willing

voluntas: will; free will

vorago: an abyss

vos (estis) lux mundi: you are the light of the world (Matthew 5:14)

vos (estis) sal terrae: you are the salt of the earth (Matthew 5:13)

votum: offering; vow

vox (pl. voces): voice

vox clamantis in deserto: the voice of one crying in the desert (John 1:23)

vox populi, vox Dei: the voice of the people is the voice of God

vulgaris: common

vulneratus: wounded

vultus: face; countenance

vultus est index animi: the face is the index of the soul

Z

zelotes: zealot

zelotypus: jealous

zodiacus: the zodiac

zona: girdle; sash

ABBREVIATIONS

A

a. [ana]: of each

a.a.s. or **A.A.S.** [anno aetatis suae]: in the year of his/her age

A.C. [ante Christum]: before Christ

a.c. [ante cibum or ante cibos]: before meals

A.Ch.N. [ante Christum natum]: before Christ's birth

A.D. [anno Domini]: in the year of our Lord

a.d. [ante diem]: before the day

a.d. [auris dextra]: right ear

A.H. [anno Hebraico]: in the Hebrew year (see also **A.M.** [anno mundi])

A.H. [anno Hegirae]: in the year of the Hegira (i.e., the beginning of Islam)

a.h.l. [ad hunc locum]: at this place

A.H.S. [anno humanae salutis]: in the year of humanity's redemption

a.h.v. [ad hanc vocem]: at this word

a.j. or **ant. jentac.** [ante jentaculum]: before breakfast

A.M. [anno mundi]: in the year of the world since its creation

a.m. or **A.M.** [ante meridiem]: before noon

A.M.D.G. [ad majorem Dei gloriam]: to the greater glory of God (motto of the Jesuits)

a.p. or **ant. prand.** [ante prandium]: before dinner

A.P.C.N. [anno post Christum natum]: in the year after the birth of Christ

A.R. [anno regni]: in the year of the reign

A.S. [aetatis suae]: of his/her age or lifetime

A.S. [anno salutis]: in the year of redemption

a.s. [auris sinistra]: left ear

a.u.c. [ab urbe condita]: from the founding of the city

a.v. [ad valorem]: according to the value

a.v. [annos vixit]: he/she lived (so many years)

aa or **aa.** [ana]: of each

ab init. [ab initio]: from the beginning

abd. or **abdo.** or **abdom.** [abdomen]: the abdomen; belly

abs. febr. [absente febre]: in the absence of fever

abs. re. [absente reo]: the defendant being absent

acerb. [acerbus]: sour

acet. [acetum]: vinegar

acid. [acidum]: acid

acm. [acme]: the height of the fever

ad [ad]: up to; so as to make

ad 2 vic. [ad duas vices]: in two doses

ad 2nd vic. [ad secundam vices]: for the second time

ad 3 vic. [ad tres vices]: for three times

ad def. an. [ad defectionem animi]: to the point of fainting

ad deliq. [ad deliquilium]: to fainting

ad effect. [ad effectum]: until effectual

ad eund. [ad eundem (gradum)]: to the same (degree or standing)

ad fin. [ad finem]: finally

ad grat. acid. [ad gratam aciditatem]: to an agreeable sourness or acidity

ad grat. gust. [ad gratum gustum]: to an agreeable taste

ad inf. or **ad infin.** [ad infinitum]: to infinity (i.e., forever)

ad init. [ad initium]: at the beginning

ad int. or **ad inter.** [ad interim]: in the meantime; meanwhile; temporarily

ad lib. [ad libitum]: at will (i.e., to improvise)

ad loc. [ad locum]: to or at the place

ad part. dol. [ad partes dolentes]: to the painful parts

ad pond. omn. [ad pondus omnium]: to the weight of the whole

ad sat. [ad saturandum]: to saturation

ad sec. vic. [ad secundum vicem]: to the second time

ad ter. vic. [ad tertiam vicem]: to the third time

ad us. [ad usum]: according to customary use

ad us. ext. [ad usum externum]: for external use

ad val. [ad valorem]: according to value

ad. or **add.** [adde]: let there be added (i.e., add)

ad. feb. or **adst. febr.** [adstante febre]: in the presence of fever

add. part. dol. [adde partem dolente]: add to the painful part

addend. [addendus]: to be added

adf. [adfinis]: neighboring; having an affinity with (sometimes abbreviated **aff.** [affinis])

adhib. or **adhibend.** [adhibendus]: to be used; to be administered

admov. [admove or admoveatur]: apply; let there be applied

ads. or **adsm.** [ad sectam]: at the suit of

adst. febr. [adstante febre]: in the presence of fever

adv. [adversus]: against

ae. or **aetat.** [aetatis]: of the age

aeg. [aeger]: a medical excuse; a patient

aeq. [aequalis]: equal

aet. [aetas]: at the age of

aet. or **aetat.** [aetatis; anno aetatis suae]: of the age; in his/her lifetime

ag. or **Ag.** [argentum]: silver

aggred. febr. [aggrediente febre]: on the approach of fever

agit. [agita]: shake

agit. ante sum. [agita ante sumedum]: shake before taking

agit. vas. [agitato vase]: the vial being shaken

alb. [albus]: white

aliq. [aliquot]: some; a few

aliquant. [aliquantillum]: a very little

aliquot. [aliquoties]: some; sometimes

alt. . . . alt. . . . [alter. . . alter. . .]: the one . . . and the other . . .

alt. die. or **altern. dieb.** [alternis diebus]: every other day

alt. hor. or **altern. hor.** [alternis horis]: every other hour

alt. noct. [alternis noctes]: every other night

altern. [alternus]: alternate

alv. adst. [alvo adstricta]: the bowels being confined or constricted

alv. deject. [alvi dejectiones]: discharge from the bowels

amp. [amplus]: large; ample

ampul. [ampulla]: a small bottle

antitox. [antitoxinum]: antitoxin

aperi. [aperiens]: a gentle purge

apert. [apertus]: clear; open

applan. [applanatus]: flattened

applic. or **applicet.** [applicetur]: let there be applied

aq. [aqua]: water

aq. aerat. [aqua aerata]: carbonated water

aq. astr. [aqua astricta]: frozen water (i.e., ice)

aq. bull. [aqua bulliens]: boiling water

aq. comm. [aqua communis]: common water (i.e., tap water)

aq. dest. [aqua destillata]: distilled water

aq. ferv. [aqua fervens]: hot water

aq. fluv. [aqua fluvialis]: river water

aq. font. [aqua fontalis, aqua fontana, or aqua fontis]: spring water

aq. fort. [aqua fortis]: nitric acid

aq. mar. [aqua marina]: seawater

aq. naph. [aqua naphae]: orange-flower water

aq. niv. [aqua nivalis]: snow water

aq. pluv. [aqua pluvialis]: rainwater

aq. pur. [aqua pura]: pure water

aq. reg. [aqua regia]: royal water (a mixture of nitric and hydrochloric acids that dissolves platinum and gold)

aq. sal. [aqua saliens]: a jet of water

aq. tep. [aqua tepida]: lukewarm water

aq. vit. [aqua vitae]: a distilled spirit (e.g., whiskey)

arom. [aromaticus]: aromatic

ascr. [ascriptum]: ascribe to

au. or Au. [aurum]: gold

aug. [augeatur]: let it be increased

aur. [auri or auribus]: to or for the ear

aurin. [aurinarium]: an ear cone

auristill. [auristillae]: ear drops

B

b. or bac. [bacillum]: bacillus

b. [bis]: twice

B.A. [balneum arenae]: a sand bath

b.d. [bis die]: twice a day

b.i.d. or bis in d. [bis in die]: twice a day

B.M. [balneum maris or balneum mariae]: a saltwater bath

B.M. [Beata Maria]: Blessed Mary

B.M. [beatae memoriae]: of blessed memory

b.m. or B.M. [bene misce]: mix well

b.p. [bonum publicum]: the common good

B.T. [balneum tepidum]: a warm bath

b.t.d. [bis terve die]: two or three times a day

b.t.i.d. [bis terve in die]: two or three times a day

B.V. [balneum vaporis]: a vapor or steam bath

B.V. [Beata Virgo]: the Blessed Virgin

b.v. [bene vale]: farewell

B.V.M. [Beata Virgo Maria]: the Blessed Virgin Mary

Ba. [barium]: barium

baln. anima. [balneum animale]: part of a freshly killed animal applied to a patient's body or limb

baln. aren. [balneum arenae]: a sand bath

baln. mar. [balneum maris or mariae]: a saltwater bath

baln. med. [balneum medicatum]: a medicated bath

baln. sicc. [balneum siccum]: a bath of dry ashes

baln. tep. [balneum tepidum]: a warm bath

baln. vap. [balneum vaporis]: a vapor or steam bath

bals. [balsamum]: balsam

bib. [bibe or bibat]: drink; let him drink

bid. [biduum]: two days

bihor. [bihorium]: during two hours

bis ind. [bis indies]: twice a day

bol. [bolus]: a large pill

bon. art. [bonae artes]: good qualities or character

bon. pub. [bonum publicum]: the common good

brach. [brachio]: to the arm

brom. [bromidum]: bromide

buginar. [buginarium]: a nasal bougie

bull. [bulliat or bulliens]: let it boil; boiling

but. [butyrum]: butter

C

c̄ [cum]: with

c̄ dup. [cum duplo]: with twice as much

c̄ pen. [cum penicillo]: with a camel-hair brush

c̄ pt. aeq. [cum parte aequale]: with an equal quantity

c̄ tant. [cum tanto]: with as much

c. or **C.** [centum]: one hundred

c. or **ca.** [circa]: about

c. or **cib.** [cibus]: meal; food

c. or **circ.** [circiter or circum]: around; about

c. [congius]: gallon

c. [costa]: rib

c.a.v. [curia advisari vult]: the court wishes to be advised or to consider

c.m. [cras mane]: tomorrow morning

c.m.s. [cras mane sumendus]: to be taken tomorrow morning

c.n. [cras nocte]: tomorrow night

c.n.s. [cras nocte sumendus]: to be taken tomorrow night

c.p. or **cor pul.** [cor pulmonale]: right ventricular failure

C.R. [custos rotulorum]: principal justice of the peace in an English county

c.v. [cras vespere]: tomorrow evening

c.v. [curriculum vitae]: a résumé

caerul. [caeruleus]: blue

calef. [calefactus or calefiat]: warmed; let it be warmed

cap. [cape or capiat]: take

cap. [capiti]: to the head

cap. or **caps.** [capsula]: capsule

capiend. [capiendus]: to be taken

caps. amylac. [capsula amylacea]: a cachet

caps. gelat. [capsula gelatina]: a gelatin capsule

caps. vitrea [capsula vitrea]: a glass capsule

carb. [carbonas]: carbonate

carbas. [carbasus]: gauze

cat. or **catapl.** or **cataplasm.** [cataplasma]: a poultice

cath. [catharticus]: a cathartic

cent. [centum]: hundred

cerat. [ceratum]: cerate (i.e., wax)

cereol. [cereolus]: an urethral bougie

cet. par. [ceteris paribus]: other things being equal

cf. [confer]: compare

Ch.D. [Chirurgiae Doctor]: Doctor of Surgery

chart. [charta]: prescription paper; powder

chart. cerat. [charta ceratum]: waxed paper

chartul. [chartula]: small paper

cib. [cibus]: meal; food

cit. [citissime]: as quickly as possible

cito disp. [cito dispensatur]: let it be quickly dispensed

cl. [chlorum]: chlorine

co. or **comp.** [compositus]: compounded

coch. [cochleare]: a spoonful

coch. amp. or **coch. ampl.** [cochleare amplum]: a tablespoonful

coch. infant. [cochleare infantis]: a teaspoonful

coch. mag. [cochleare magnum]: a tablespoonful

coch. mag. ij [cochlearia magna duo]: two tablespoonfuls

coch. max. [cochleare maximum]: a tablespoonful

coch. med. [cochleare medium]: a dessertspoonful

coch. min. [cochleare minimum]: a teaspoonful

coch. mod. [cochleare modicum]: a dessertspoonful

coch. parv. [cochleare parvum]: a teaspoonful

coch. parv. iij [cochlearia parva tria]: three teaspoonfuls

coch. plen. [cochleare plenum]: a tablespoonful

coct. [coctio]: boiling

col. [cola]: strain

colat. [colatur; colatus]: let it be strained; strained

colatur. [colaturae]: a strained liquid; the substance strained

colen. [colentur]: let them be strained

colet. [coleatur]: let it be strained

coll. or **collyr** [collyrium]: an eyewash

collod. [collodium]: a collodion

collun. [collunarium]: a nose wash

collut. [collutorium]: a mouthwash

color. [coloretur]: let it be colored

comp. [compositus]: compound(ed)

con. or **conj.** [conjunx or conjux]: a spouse (either husband or wife)

con. [contra]: against

conf. [confectio]: a confection

cong. [congius]: a gallon

cons. [conserva]: a conserve; also, keep

cons. [consonans]: tinkling

consperg. [consperge]: sprinkle; dust

cont. [contra]: against

cont. bon. mor. [contra bonos mores]: contrary to good morals

cont. rem. [continuantur remedia]: let the remedy be continued

conter. [contere]: rub together

contin. [continuetur]: let it be continued

contu. [contusus]: bruised or crushed

coq. [coque]: cook; boil

coq. ad med. consump. [coque ad medietatis consumptionem]: boil to the consumption of half (or render by one half)

coq. in S.Q.A. [coque in sufficiente quantitate aquae]: boil in a sufficient quantity of water

coq. S.A. [coque secundum artem]: boil according to method or practice

coqu. [coquantur]: let them be boiled

corp. [corpori]: to the body

cort. [cortex]: a peel (e.g., bark)

cr. [cras]: tomorrow

crast. [crastinus]: for tomorrow; on the morrow

crep. [crepitus]: discharge of wind or gas from the bowels

cui. or **cuj.** [cuius or cujus]: of which

cujusl. [cujuslibet]: of any

cum aq. [cum aqua]: with water

cur. adv. vult [curia advisari vult]: the court wishes to be advised or to consider

curat. [curatio]: a dressing

cyath. [cyathus]: a glassful

cyath. amp. [cyathus amplus]: a tumblerful

cyath. mag. [cyathus magnus]: a tumblerful

cyath. vin. [cyathus vinosis]: a wineglassful

cyath. vinar. [cyathus vinarius]: a wineglassful

D

d. or **D.** [da]: give

d. or **D.** [dosis; pl. doses]: a dose

d. or **dex.** [dexter or dextra]: right

d. [decretum]: a decree or an ordinance

d. [dentur]: let them be given

d. [detur]: let it be given

d. et s. or **det. et sig.** [detur et signatur]: let it be given and labeled

d. in p. aeq. [dividatur in partes aequales]: let it be divided into equal parts

d.a.s.f. or **don. alv. sol. fuer.** [donec alvus soluta fuerit]: until the bowels are opened

D.B. [Divinitatis Baccalaureus]: Bachelor of Divinity

D.Ch. [Doctor Chirurgiae]: Doctor of Surgery

D.D. [Divinitatis Doctor]: Doctor of Divinity (an honorary degree)

d.d. [dono dedit]: given as a gift (e.g., a donation)

D.O.M. [Deo (or Domino), Optimo, Maximo]: to God (or the Lord), the Best, the Greatest [motto of the Benedictine order]

D.P. or **Dom. Proc.** [Domus Procerum]: the House of Lords

d.p. or **D.P.** [directione propria]: with proper directions

d.s.p. [decessit sine prole]: died without issue

D.T. [delirium tremens]: an acute delirium caused by alcohol poisoning

d.t.d. or **D.T.D.** [detur talis dosis]: give of such a dose

d.t.d. iv [dentur tales doses iv]: let four such doses be given

d.v. or **D.V.** [Deo Volente]: God willing

dand. [dandus]: to be given

dd. [detur ad]: let it be given to

de d. in di. or **d.d. in d.** [de die in diem]: from day to day

dearg. pil. [deargentur pilulae]: let the pills be silvered

deaur. pil. [deaurentur pilulae]: let the pills be gilded

deb. spiss. [debita spissitudine]: of a proper consistency

dec. [decanta]: pour off

decoct. [decoctio or decoctum]: a decoction

decub. [decubitus]: lying down

decub. hor. [decubitus hora]: at bedtime

deglut. [deglutiatur]: let it be swallowed

dej. alv. [dejectionis alvi]: stools

del. [delineavit]: he/she drew it

dent. [dentur]: let them be given

dent. tal. dos. [dentur tales doses]: let such doses be given

dentif. [dentifricium]: dentifrice

dep. [depuratus]: to be purified

depilat. [depilatorium]: a depilatory

destil. [destillatus]: distilled

det. [detur]: let it be given

det. ad [detur ad]: let it be given to

det. in dupl. [detur in duplo]: let twice as much be given

dext. [dexter]: right

dext. lat. [dextra lateralis]: right side

dieb. alt. [diebus alternis]: every other day

dieb. tert. [diebus tertiis]: every third day

dig. [digeratur]: let it be digested

dil. [dilue]: dilute or dissolve

dil. or **dilut.** [dilutus]: diluted

diluc. [diluculo]: at daybreak

dim. [dimidius]: one half

dimid. [dimidium]: half; the half

direc. prop. [directione propria]: with proper directions

disp. [dispensa]: dispense

div. [divide or dividatur]: divide; let it be divided

div. in par. aeq. [dividatur in partes aequales]: let it be divided into equal parts

dol. urg. [dolore urgente]: when the pain is severe

dolent. part. [dolenti parti or dolentibus partibus]: to the painful part(s)

don. [donec]: until

don. alv. sol. fuer. [donec alvus solutas fuerit]: until the bowels are moved

dos. [dosis]: dose

dos. aug. ad gtt. iv [dosis augeatur ad guttas iv]: let the dose be increased to four drops

dr. or **drach.** [drachma]: a drachm (dram)

dup. [duplum]: twice as much

dur. dol. or **dur. dolor.** or **durant. dol.** [durante dolore]: the pain continuing

E

e lact. [e lacte]: with milk

e paul. aq. [e paullo aquae]: with a little water

e paux. aq. [e pauxillo aquae]: with a little water

e quol. veh. [e quolibet vehiculo]: with any vehicle

e quov. liq. [e quovis liquido]: with any liquid

e vin. [e vino]: with wine

e.g. [exempli gratia]: for example

e.m.p. [ex modo praescripto]: after the manner prescribed

e.o. [ex officio]: by virtue of office

ead. [eadem]: the same

ed. [edulcora; edulcoratus]: sweeten; sweetened

efferv. [effervesentia]: effervescence

ejusd. [ejusdem]: of the same

elect. [electuarium]: an electuary

elix. [elixir]: an elixir

emend. [emendatis]: emended

emp. [emplastrum]: a plaster

emul. or **emuls.** [emulsio or emulsum]: an emulsion

en. or **enem.** [enema]: a clyster

epistom. [epistomium]: a stopper

et al. [et alibi]: and elsewhere

et al. [et alii or et aliae]: and others

et conj. [et conjunx]: and spouse (either husband or wife)

et seq. [et sequens]: and the following

et seq. [et sequentes or et sequentia]: and what follows

et ux. [et uxor]: and wife

etc. [et cetera]: and so forth

evan. [evanescere]: to disappear

ex adf. or **ex aff.** [ex adfinis or ex affinis]: from affinity

ex aq. [ex aqua]: in water; with water

ex art. [ex arte]: according to the rules or methods of the practice

ex gr. [ex gruppa]: from the group of

ex mod. prae. [ex modo praescripto]: after the manner prescribed; as directed

ex. gr. [exempli gratia]: for example

exc. [excudit]: he/she fashioned it

exhib. [exhibeatur]: let it be exhibited

ext. [extende or extensus]: spread

ext. or **extr.** [extractum]: an extract

F

f. or **F.** [fac]: make

f. [femina]: female

f. [femininum]: feminine

f. or **ft.** [fiat or fiant]: let it/them be made

F.D. [Fidei Defensor]: Defender of the Faith (an appellation of the English Monarch)

f.h. [fiat haustus]: let a draught be made

f.l.a. or **F.L.A.** [fiat lege artis]: let it be made according to practice or the usual method

f.m. [fiat mistura]: let a mixture be made

f. pil. [fac pillulam]: make a pill

f.r. [folio recto]: on the front of the page (i.e., the right-hand page)

f.s.a.r. or **F.S.A.R.** [fiat secundum artis regulas]: let it be made according to the rules of practice

f.v. [folio verso]: on the back of the page (i.e., the left-hand page)

far. [farina]: flour

fasc. [fasciculus]: a bundle or packet

Fe. or **ferr.** [ferrum]: iron

feb. dur. [febre durante]: the fever continuing

fec. [fecit]: he/she made or did it

fem. intern. [femoribus internus]: the inner side of the thighs

ferv. [fervens]: hot; boiling

ff. [fecerunt]: they made or did it

fi. fa. [fieri facias]: cause it to be done

fi. fe. [fieri feci]: I have caused it to be done

fel. mem. [felicis memoriae]: of happy memory

fel. rec. [felicis recordationis]: of happy recollection

fict. [fictilis]: made of potter's clay

Fid. Def. [Fidei Defensor]: Defender of the Faith (an appellation of the English Monarch)

filt. [filtra]: a filter

fl. or **fld.** [fluidus]: liquid, fluid

fl. or **flor.** [floruit]: flourished

flav. [flavus]: yellow

fldext. or **fldxt.** [fluidextractum]: fluid extract

flor. [flores]: flowers

fol. [folium]: a leaf

form. [formula]: a prescription

fort. [fortis]: strong

fot. [fotula]: fomentation

fract. dos. [fracta dosi]: in divided doses

frem. or **frem. voc.** [fremitus vocalis]: vocal fremitus

freq. [frequenter]: frequently

fruct. [fructus]: fruit

frust. [frustillatim]: in little pieces

ft. [fiat]: let it be made; make

ft. cataplasm. [fiat cataplasma]: let a poultice be made

ft. cerat. [fiat ceratum]: let a cerate be made

ft. chart. [fiant chartae]: let powders be made

ft. collyr. [fiat collyrium]: let an eyewash be made

ft. confec. [fiat confectio]: let a confection be made

ft. elect. [fiat electuarium]: let an electuary be made

ft. emp. [fiat emplastrum]: let a plaster be made

ft. emuls. [fiat emulsum]: let an emulsion be made

ft. garg. [fiat gargarisma]: let a gargle be made

ft. h. or **ft. haust.** [fiat haustus]: let a draught be made

ft. infus. [fiat infusum]: let an infusion be made

ft. inject. [fiat injectio]: let an injection be made

ft. linim. [fiat linimentum]: let a liniment be made

ft. m. or **ft. mist.** [fiat mistura]: let a mixture be made

ft. mas. [fiat massa]: let a mass be made

ft. p. or **ft. pulv.** [fiat pulvis]: let a powder be made

ft. pil. [fiant pilulae]: let pills be made

ft. pot. [fiat potio]: let a potion be made

ft. pulv. subtil. [fiat pulvis subtilis]: let a fine powder be made

ft. solut. [fiat solutio]: let a solution be made

ft. suppos. [fiant suppositoria]: let suppositories be made

ft. troch. [fiant trochisci]: let lozenges be made

ft. ung. [fiat unguentum]: let an ointment be made

ft. vs. [fiat venaesectio]: let the patient be bled

G

g. or **gt.** [gutta]: a drop

g.g.g. [gummi guttae gambiae]: gamboge (a cathartic derived from an Asiatic gum resin)

garg. [gargarisma]: a gargle

gel. [gelatum]: jelly

gel. quav. [gelatina quavis]: in any kind of jelly

gland. [glandula]: a gland

glob. [globulus]: a little ball; a small drop

glyc. or **glycer.** or **glyct.** [glyceritum]: glycerite

gossyp. [gossypium]: cotton

gr. or **grav.** [gravida]: pregnant

gr. or **grn.** [granum or grana]: grain or grains

grad. [gradatim]: step by step; gradually

grat. [gratus]: pleasant; agreeable

grm. [gramma]: a gram

gtt. [guttae]: drops

gutt. [gutturi]: to or for the throat

gutt. quis. [guttis quisbusdam]: with a few drops

guttat. [guttatim]: drop by drop; by drops

H

H. [hora]: hour; hydrogen

h. [haustus]: a draught

h.a. [hoc anno]: in this year

h.d. or **H.D.** [hora decubitus]: at bedtime

H.I. [hic iacet or hic jacet]: here lies

H.I.S. [hic iacet sepultus]: here lies buried

h.l. [hoc loco]: in this place

h.m. [hoc mense]: in this month

H.M.P. [hoc monumentum posuit]: he/she erected this monument

h.n. [hac nocte]: tonight; this night

h.q. [hoc quaere]: look for this

H.S. [hic sepultus]: here [lies] buried

h.s. or **H.S.** [hora somni]: at the hour of sleep; at bedtime

h.s. [hoc sensu]: in this sense

h.t. [hoc tempore]: at this time

h.t. [hoc titulo]: under this title

hab. corp. [habeas corpus]: a writ of habeas corpus

habt. [habeat]: let him/her have

hac noct. [hac nocte]: tonight; this night

haer. [haeres]: an heir

haust. [haustus]: a draught

hebdom. [hebdomada]: a week; a seven-day period

her. [heres]: an heir

hir. or **hirud.** [hirudo]: a leech

hoc vesp. [hoc vespere]: this evening

hor. altern. [horis alternis]: every other hour

hor. decub. [hora decubitus]: at bedtime

hor. interim. [horis intermediis]: at intermediate hours

hor. quad. or **hor. quadrant.** [horae quadrante]: a quarter of an hour

hor. som. [hora somni]: at bedtime

hor. un. spat. [horae unius spatio]: after one hour; at the end of an hour

hyd. [hydor]: water

hydr. or **hydrarg.** [hydrargyrum]: mercury

I

i or **j** [unus]: one

i.a. [in absentia]: in absence

i.c. [inter cibum or inter cibos]: between meals

i.e. [id est]: that is

I.N.R.I. [Iesus Nazarenus Rex Iudaeorum]: the title placard appended to the Cross of Christ by Pontius Pilate at the Crucifixion (John 19:20)

i.p.i. [in partibus infidelium]: a titular bishop whose title is that of an extinct Roman Catholic see

i.q. [idem quod]: the same as

ib. or **ibid.** [ibidem]: in the same place (in a book)

id. [idem]: the same

id. ac [idem ac]: the same as

ign. [ignotus]: unknown

IHS [Jesu]: Jesus (from the first three letters of Jesus in Greek)

ii or **ij** [duo]: two

iii or **iij** [tres]: three

iiij or **iv** [quattuor]: four

illic. [illico]: immediately

illinend. [illinendus]: to be smeared

impon. [imponatur]: let there be put on

impr. [imprimis]: first

in aq. [in aqua]: in water

in aq. bull. [in aqua bulliente]: in boiling water

in aur. dext. [in aurem dextram]: into the right ear

in aur. sinist. [in aurem sinistram]: into the left ear

in d. or **ind.** [in dies or indies]: from day to day; daily

in lim. [in limine]: in the beginning

in litt. [in litteris]: in correspondence

in loc. ferv. [in loco fervente]: in a hot place

in loc. frig. [in loco frigido]: in a cool or cold place

in ocul. dext. [in oculum dextrum]: into the right eye

in ocul. sinist. [in oculum sinistrum]: into the left eye

in pr. [in principio]: in the beginning

in pulm. [in pulmento or in pulmentum]: in a gruel

in scat. [in scatula]: in a box

in sing. aur. [in singulas aures]: into each ear

in trans. [in transitu]: in transit; on the way

in ut. [in utero]: in the womb

in vas. claus. [in vaso clauso]: in a closed vessel

in vit. [in vitro]: in glass

in viv. [in vivo]: in a living body

inc. [incide]: cut

inf. [infra]: below

inf. [infunde]: pour in

inf. or infus. [infusum]: an infusion

infra dig. [infra dignitatem]: beneath one's dignity

infric. [infricetur]: let it be rubbed in

infund. [infundatur]: let there be infused

inhal. [inhaletur]: let it be inhaled

init. [initio]: in or at the beginning (referring to a passage in a book or treatise)

inj. or inject. [injectio or injectum]: an injection

inj. enem. [injiciatur enema]: let an enema be injected

inj. hyp. [injectio hypodermica]: hypodermic injection

inspir. [inspiretur]: let it be breathed (into)

instill. [instilletur or instillentur]: let it/them be dropped in

insuff. [insufflatio]: an insufflation

int. [internus]: internal

int. [intime]: intimately

int. cib. [inter cibos]: between meals

int. noct. or inter noct. [inter noctem]: during the night

interm. [intermedius]: intermediate

inv. [invenit]: he or she designed it

involv. [involve]: roll

iod. [iodinium or iodum]: iodine

J

J.D. [Juris or Jurum Doctor]: Doctor of Law (a professional degree)

J.U.D. [Juris Utriusque Doctor]: Doctor of both Canon and Civil laws

jent. or jentac. [jentaculum]: breakfast

jug. [jugulo]: to or for the throat

jul. [julapium or julepus]: a mixture; a julep

jux. [juxta]: near; next to

K

K. [kalium]: potassium

K.e. or K.E. [Kyrie eleison]: Lord, have mercy (the opening section of the Latin Mass)

L

l. or lib. [libra]: book

l.a. [lege artis]: by the rules of the art

l.c. [loco citato]: in the place cited

l.d. [loco dolenti]: to the painful spot

L.D.S. [libra, solidus, denarius]: pound, shilling, penny

L.H.D. [Litterarum Humaniorum Doctor]: Doctor of Humanities

L.S. [locus sigilli]: the place of the seal

l.s.c. [loco supra citato]: in the place cited before

lact. [lacte; lacteus]: in milk; milky

laev. [laevus]: left

lat. or latitud. [latitudine]: in width

lat. [latus]: wide

lat. dol. [lateri dolenti]: to the painful side (i.e., the side affected)

lavat. [lavatio]: bathing; washing; also, a washing apparatus

lb. [libra]: a pound

Li. [lithium]: lithium

lim. [limon]: lemon

lin. [linimentum]: a liniment

lin. [linteum]: lint

linct. [linctus]: a soothing cough syrup

liq. [liquor]: liquor; a solution

Lit. Hum. [Litterae Humaniores]: the Humanities (e.g., ancient Classics)

Litt.D. [Litterarum Doctor]: Doctor of Letters

LL.D. [Legum Doctor]: Doctor of Laws

loc. cit. [loco citato]: in the place cited

loc. dol. [loco dolenti]: to the painful spot

loc. laud. [loco laudato]: in the place cited with approval

long. or **longitud.** [longitudine]: in length

loq. [loquitur]: he/she speaks

lot. [lotio]: a lotion

lumb. [lumborum]: the loins

M

m. or **M.** [meridies]: noon

m. or **M.** [misce]: mix

m. or **min.** [minimum]: a minim; a drop; a very small amount

m. [mane]: morning

m. [masculinum]: masculine

m. [masculus]: male

m. [mentum]: chin

m. or **mut.** [mutitas]: dull

m.b. [misce bene]: mix well

M.D. [Medicinae Doctor]: Doctor of Medicine

m.d. [modo dicto or more dicto]: as directed

m. dict. [more dicto or modo dicto]: as directed

m. et n. [mane et nocte]: morning and night

m. et sig. [misce et signa]: mix and label

m. ft. [mistura fiat]: make a mixture

m. ft. m. [misce fiat mistura]: mix to make a mixture

m.m. [mutatis mutandis]: with the necessary changes being made

m.o. [modus operandi]: modus operandi

m. pr. or **m. prim.** [mane primo]: very early in the morning

m.s. [more solito]: in the usual manner

m.s.a. [misce secundum artem]: mix according to practice

m. seq. [mane sequenti]: the following morning

M.V. [Medicus Veterinarius]: a veterinarian

mac. [macera]: macerate (i.e., soak)

mag. [magnus]: large

man. [manipulus]: a handful

mas. or **mass.** [massa]: a mass

mas. pil. [massa pilularum]: pill mass

mat. [matutine]: in the late morning (i.e., before noon)

matut. [matutinus]: in or of the morning

max. [maximus]: the maximum; the greatest

med. [medius]: medium

mediet. [medietas]: half

meli. [melior]: better

mens. or **mensur.** [mensura]: a measure; by measure

mic. pan. [mica panis]: a crumb of bread

min. [minimum]: a minim; a drop; a very small amount

minut. [minutum]: a minute

misc. [misceatur]: let it be well mixed

mist. [mistura]: a mixture

mit. or **mitt.** [mitte]: send

mit. tal. or **mitt. tal.** [mitte tales]: send such

mitig. [mitigatio]: alleviation

mitt. sang. [mitte sanguinem]: bleed

mob. [mobile vulgus]: the fickle masses (i.e., the mob)

mod. [modicus]: medium-sized

mod. praesc. or **mod. praes.** [modo praescripto]: as prescribed or directed

moll. [mollis]: soft

mor. dict. or **more dict.** [more dicto]: as directed

mor. sol. or **more sol.** [more solito]: in the usual manner

mort. [mortalis]: mortal

MS [manuscriptus]: manuscript

MSS [manuscripta]: manuscripts

muc. or **mucil.** [mucilago]: mucilage

N

n. [natus]: born

n. [neutrum]: neuter

n. [nocte]: at night

n.b. or **N.B.** [nota bene]: note well

n. et m. [nocte et mane]: night and morning

n.l. [non licet]: it is not permitted

n.l. [non liquet]: it is not clear; it is not proven

n.m. [nocte maneque]: night and morning

n.n. or **nom. nov.** [nomen novum]: new name

n.p. or **N.P.** [nomen proprium]: proper name

n.p.o. [nihil per os]: nothing by mouth

n.p.s. [nomen proprium signetur]: let the common name be written on the label

n.r. [non repetatur]: let it not be repeated (i.e., no refill)

n.t.s.n. or **ne tr. s. num.** [ne tradas sine nummo]: do not deliver unless paid (i.e., c.o.d.)

Na. [natrium]: sodium

neb. [nebula]: a spray or mist; a spray solution

ni. [nisi]: unless

nig. [niger]: black

nih. [nihil]: nothing

no. or **No.** [numero]: in number

nob. [nobis]: to us

noct. [nocte]: at night

noct. manq. [nocte maneque]: at night and in the morning

nol. contend. [nolle contendere]: a plea of "no contest" to criminal charges by the defendant without admitting guilt

nol. pros. [nolle prosequi]: an entry into court records indicating a stay or discontinuance of proceedings, either wholly or in part

nom. [nomen]: name

nom. dub. [nomen dubium]: doubtful name

nom. nud. [nomen nudum]: undesignated

non lic. [non licet]: it is not permitted

non liq. [non liquet]: it is not clear; it is not proven

non obs. [non obstante]: notwithstanding

non pros. [non prosequitur]: a legal judgment where the plaintiff does not appear

non rep. [non repetatur]: let it not be repeated (i.e., no refill)

non seq. [non sequitur]: it does not follow

nov. [novum]: something new

nov. nom. [novum nomen]: new name

nov. spec. [novum species]: a new species

nup. [nuper]: lately

O

o. or **O.** [octarius]: a pint

o. [oculus]: eye

o. alt. h. [omni alterna hora]: every other hour

o.b. or **O.B.** [omni bihora]: every two hours

o.c. [opere citato]: in the work cited

o.d. [oculus dexter]: right eye

o.d. or **O.D.** [omni die]: every day; daily

o.h. or **O.H.** [omni hora]: every hour

o.l. [oculus laevus]: left eye

o.l.s.i. [oleum lini sine igni]: cold drawn linseed oil

o.m. or **O.M.** [omni mane]: every morning

o.m.v.n. [omni mane vel nocte]: every morning or night

o.n. or **O.N.** [omni nocte]: every night

o.o. [oleum olivae]: olive oil

o.o.o. [oleum olivae optimum]: the best olive oil

o.q.h. or **o.4.h.** [omni quarta hora]: every four hours

o.q.h. or **omn. quad. hor.** [omni quadranta hora]: every fifteen minutes

o.s. [oculus sinister]: left eye

o. sext. h. [omni sexta hora]: every six hours

o.s.h. or **o. sing. h.** [omni singula hora]: every single hour

o.t.h. or **o. ter. h.** or **o.3.h.** [omni tertia hora]: every three hours

o.u. or **oc. unit.** [oculi unitas]: both eyes together

o.u. or **oc. ut.** [oculus uterque; oculo ultroque]: in each eye; in both eyes

O₂ or **Oc₂** [oculi unitas]: both eyes together

ob. [obiit]: he/she died

ob. [obiter]: incidentally

ob. dict. [obiter dictum]: an unofficial expression of opinion

ob. s.p. [obiit sine prole]: he/she died without issue

oblat. [oblatum]: a cachet

ocul. [oculis or oculo]: to or for the eyes

ol. [oleum]: oil

ol. ol. [oleum olivae]: olive oil

omn. [omnis]: all; every

omn. bid. [omni biduo]: every two days

omn. bih. [omni bihora]: every two hours

omn. die [omni die]: every day; daily

omn. hor. [omni hora]: every hour

omn. man. [omni mane]: every morning

omn. man. vel noct. [omni mane vel nocte]: every morning or night

omn. noc. [omni nocte]: every night

omn. quart. hor. or **omn. 4 hor.** [omni quarta hora]: every four hours

omn. sec. hor. or **omn. 2 hor.** [omni secunda hora]: every two hours

omn. tert. hor. or **omn. 3 hor.** [omni tertia hora]: every three hours

op. [opus]: a musical compostion

op. cit. [opere citato]: in the work cited

ope pen. [ope penicilli]: by means of a camel-hair brush

opt. [optimus]: the optimum; the best

ov. [ovum]: egg

ovi alb. [ovi albumen]: the egg white

ovi vit. [ovi vitellum]: the egg yolk

ovil. jus. [ovillum jusculum]: mutton broth

ox. or **oxy.** or **oxym.** [oxymel]: a mixture of honey, vinegar, and water

oz. [uncia]: an ounce

P

. . . [placebo]: satisfy the patient (i.e., give a placebo)

P. [perstetur]: let it be continued

P. [pondere]: by weight

p. [partim]: in part

p.a. [parti affectae or partibus affectis]: to the affected part(s)

p.a. [per annum]: by the year

p.a.a. [parti affectae applicandus]: to be applied to the affected part

P.ae. or **p.ae.** [partes aequales]: in equal parts

p.c. or **per cent.** [per centum]: by the hundred

p.c. or **pon. civ.** [pondus civile]: avoirdupois weight

p.c. [post cibum or post cibos]: after meals

P.Ch.N. [post Christum natum]: after Christ's birth

P.D. or **Phar. D.** [Pharmaciae Doctor]: Doctor of Pharmacy

p.g. [persona grata]: an acceptable or welcome person

p. in u. m. [perga in usu medicinarum]: continue to use the medicine

p.m. or **P.M.** [post mortem]: after death

p.m. or **P.M.** [post meridiem]: after noon

p.n.g. [persona non grata]: an unacceptable or unwelcome person

p.o. [per os]: by mouth

p.o.e. [peracta operatione emetici]: when the action of the emetic has ended

p.p. [per procurationem]: by proxy; by the action of

p.p. or **punct. prox.** [punctum proximum]: near point

p.p.a. or **P.P.A.** [phiala prius agitata]: after first shaking the bottle

p.r. or **per rect.** [per rectum]: by rectum

p.r. or **punct. rem.** [punctum remotum]: far point

p.r.a. or **pro rat. aet.** [pro ratione aetatis]: according to the age of the patient

p.r.n. or **P.R.N.** [pro re nata]: occasionally; whenever necessary; as needed

p.s.d.l. [post singulas dejectiones liquidas]: after each loose bowel movement

p.s.s.l. [post singulas sedes liquidas]: after each loose stool

p.t. [pro tempore]: temporarily

pact. [pactum]: a contract or agreement

par. aff. or **part. aff.** [pars affecta or partem affectam]: the part affected

part. dolent. [partem dolentem]: the part in pain

part. vic. [partitis vicibus]: in divided doses

pas or **pastil.** [pastillum or pastillus]: a small lozenge; a breath lozenge

pass. [passim]: throughout

past. [pasta]: paste

paul. [paullum]: a little

pb. or **Pb.** [plumbum]: lead

pct. [per centum]: by the hundred

pect. [pectus or pectori]: breast; chest; to the chest or breast

pedet. [pedetentim]: step by step; by degrees

pedil. [pediluvium]: a bath for the feet

pen. cam. or **penic. cam.** or **penicul. cam.** [penicillum camelinum or peniculum camelinum]: camel-hair brush

pend. [pendens]: weighing

per cent. or **p.c.** [per centum]: by the hundred

per mens. [per mensem]: by the month; monthly

per mil. [per mille]: by the thousand

per omn. [per omnes]: by all

per stirp. [per stirpes]: by families; by representation

per tot. cur. [per totam curiam]: by the entire court

per. op. emet. [peracta operatione emetici]: when the action of the emetic has ended

per. pro. [per procurationem]: by proxy

perfric. [perfrictus]: let it be rubbed

perg. in us. med. [perga in usu medicinarum]: continue to use the medicine

pess. [pessus]: a pessary (i.e., a vaginal suppository)

Ph.D. [Philosophiae Doctor]: Doctor of Philosophy

phos. [phosphas]: phosphate

pigm. [pigmentum]: a paint

pil. [pilula; pl. pilulae]: a pill

pinx. [pinxit]: he/she painted it

pl. [pluralis]: plural

poc. or **pocul.** [poculum or poculus]: a cup or cupful

pocill. [pocillum]: a small cup

poll. [pollex]: an inch

poll. sex [pollices sex]: six inches

pomer. or **pomerid.** [pomeridianus]: of the afternoon

pond. [pondere]: by weight

pond. civ. [pondus civile]: avoirdupois weight

pone aur. [pone aurem]: put behind the ear

postul. [postulent]: may require

pot. [potus]: a drink

P.P. [pastor pastorum]: a papal appellation

PPS [post postscriptum]: an additional postscript

ppt. [praecipitatus]: precipitated

praep. [praeparatus]: prepared

prand. [prandium]: dinner

prim. [primus]: first

prim. luc. [prima luce]: early in the morning

prim. m. [primo mane]: early in the morning

pro capill. [pro capillis]: for the hair

pro dos. [pro dose]: for a dose

pro jug. [pro jugulo]: for the throat

pro ocul. [pro oculis]: for the eyes

pro ocul. dext. [pro oculo dextro]: for the right eye

pro ocul. laev. [pro oculo laevo]: for the left eye

pro pot. com. [pro potu communi]: for a common drink

pro rat. aet. [pro ratione aetatis]: according to age

pro rect. [pro recto]: rectal

pro sing. ocul. [pro singulis oculis]: for each eye

pro tem. [pro tempore]: temporarily

pro ureth. [pro urethra]: urethral

pro us. ext. [pro usu externo]: for external use

pro vag. [pro vagina]: vaginal

prolong. [prolongatus]: prolonged

prox. [proximum]: near

prox. or **prox. m.** [proximo mense]: in the next or following month

PS [postscriptum]: postscript

pt. [perstetur]: let it be continued

pt. aeq. [partes aequales]: in equal parts

pug. [pugillus]: a pinch; small handful

pulm. [pulmentum]: gruel

pulv. [pulvis]: a powder

pulv. consper. [pulvis conspersus]: a dusting powder

pulv. subt. [pulvis subtillisimus]: the very finest powder

pur. [purificatus]: purified

pxt. [pinxit]: he/she painted it

pyx. [pyxis]: a pill box

Q

q. alt. h. [quaque alterna hora]: every other hour

q. sext. h. [quaque sexta hora]: every six hours

q.d. [quaque die]: every day

q.d. [quasi dictum; quasi dicat]: as if said; as if one should say

q.d. or **Q.D.** [quater die]: four times a day

q.e. [quod est]: which is

Q.E.D. [quod erat demonstrandum]: which was to be demonstrated or proven

Q.E.F. [quod erat faciendum]: which was to be done

q.h. or **Q.H.** [quaque hora]: every hour

q.i.d. [quater in die]: four times a day

q.l. or **Q.L.** or **q.lib.** [quantum libet]: as much as you please; liberally

q.m. or **Q.M.** [quaque mane]: every morning

q.n. [quaque nocte]: every night

q.o.s. or **quot. op. sit** [quoties opus sit]: as often as required

q.p. or **Q.P.** or **q. pl.** [quantum placet]: as much as you please; liberally

q.q.h. or **qq. 4 h.** [quaque quarta hora]: every fourth hour

q.s. or **quant. sat.** [quantum satis]: as much as satisfies

q.s. or **quant. suff.** [quantum sufficit or quantum satis]: as much as suffices

q.s.h. or **q. sing. h.** [quaque singula hora]: every single hour

q.t.h. or **q. ter. h.** or **qq. 3 h.** [quaque tertia hora]: every third hour

q.v. or **Q.V.** [quantum vis]: as much as you will

q.v. [quod vide]: (sing.) which see

qq. or **Qq.** [quaque]: each, every

qq. or **Qq.** [quoque]: also

qq. hor. or **Qq. hor.** [quaque hora]: every hour

qq.v. [quae vide]: (pl.) which see

qt. [quantitas]: quantity

qt. dupx. or **qt. dx.** [quantitas duplex]: twice the quantity

qu. [quaere]: a question or query

quad. [quadrantis]: a quarter

quadrihor. [quadrihorio]: every four hours

quadrupl. [quadruplicato]: four times as much

quamp. [quamprimum]: immediately

quart. hor. [quartis horis]: every four hours

quat. [quattuor]: four

quib. [quibus]: to which; with which

quiesc. [quiescat]: may it rest

quin. vel sex. in d. [quinquies vel sexies in die]: five or six times a day

quinq. [quinque]: five

quint. [quintus]: fifth

quot. or **quotid.** [quotidie]: daily

quot. op. sit [quoties opus sit]: as often as required

R

R. [regina]: queen

R. [rex]: king

r. or **rem.** [remotum]: far

r. in p. or **red. in pulv.** [reductus in pulverem]: reduced to a powder

R.I.P. [requiescat in pace; requiescit in pace]: may he/she rest in peace; he/she rests in peace

rad. [radix]: root

ras. [rasurae]: shavings

rat. [ratio]: proportion

rec. [recens]: fresh

rect. [rectificatus]: rectified

red. [reductus]: reduced

red. in pulv. [redigatur in pulverem]: let it be reduced to a powder

reg. hep. [regio hepatis]: region of the liver

reg. umb. [regio umbilici]: umbilical region

reli. or **reliq.** [reliquum or reliquus]: the remainder; the remaining

ren. [renovetur]: renew

rep. or **repet.** or **rept.** [repetatur]: let it be repeated

res. [resina]: resin

retin. [retinendus]: retained

rub. [ruber]: red

℞ [recipe]: take

S

s [sine]: without

S. [sulfur]: sulphur/sulfur

s. or **S.** [sepultus]: buried

S. or **Sal.** [Salutem dicit!]: Greetings!

S. or **Sig.** [signa]: that which is to be written on the label of a prescription

s. or **sig.** [signetur]: let it be written; label

s.a. or **S.A.** [secundum artem]: according to practice

s.a. [sine anno]: without date

s.a.l. [secundum artis legis]: according to the rules of the art

s.d. or **sem. die** [semel die]: once a day

s.d. [sine die]: indefinitely

s.f. or **sp. frum.** [spiritus frumenti]: whiskey

s.f.c. or **sub fin. coct.** [sub finem coctionis]: toward the end of boiling

s.i. [sine igni]: cold

s.i.d. or **S.I.D.** [semel in die]: once a day

s.l. [secundum legem]: according to law

s.l. or **sen. lat.** [sensu lato]: in a broad sense

s.l. or **seq. luce** [sequenti luce]: the following day

s.l. [sine loco]: without place

s.l.a. [sine loco et anno]: without place and year

s.l.a.n. [sine loco, anno vel nomine]: without place, year, or name

s.l.p. [sine legitima prole]: without legitimate issue

s.m.p. [sine mascula prole]: without male issue

s.n. or **S.N.** [secundum naturam]: according to nature; naturally

s.n. [sine nomine]: anonymous

s.n.p. [signetur nomine proprio]: label with proper name

s.n.v. or **si n. val.** [si non valeat]: if it does not respond

s.o.s. [si opus sit]: if necessary

s.p. [sine prole]: without issue

s.p.s. [sine prole supersite]: without surviving issue

s.r. [secundum regulam]: according to rule

S.R.I. [Sacrum Romanum Imperium]: the Holy Roman Empire

s.s. or **sen. str.** [sensu stricto]: in a strict sense

s.s.s. or **S.S.S.** [stratum super stratum]: layer upon layer

s.s.v. [sub signo venemi]: under a poison label

S.T.B. [Sacrae Theologiae Baccalaureus]: Bachelor of Sacred Theology

s.v. (pl., **s.vv.**) [sub verbo or sub voce]: [look] under the word

s.v. [spiritus vini]: an alcoholic spirit

s.v.g. [spiritus vini gallici]: brandy

s.v.p. or **si vir. perm.** [si vires permittant]: if strength permits

s.v.r. [spiritus vini rectificatus]: alcohol

s.v.t. [spiritus vini tenuis]: proof spirit; half alcohol and half water

sacch. [saccharum; saccharatus]: sugar; sugar-coated

sacch. alb. [saccharum alba]: white sugar

saep. [saepe]: often

saepiss. [saepissime]: very often

Sal. or **S.** [Salutem dicit!]: Greetings!

sang. [sanguis]: blood

sang. miss. [sanguinis missura]: blood-letting

sat. [saturatus]: saturated

sc. or **sculpt.** [sculpsit]: he/she sculptured it

sc. [scilicet]: that is to say; namely; to wit

scan. mag. [scandalum magnatum]: defamation or slander of notable or high-ranking persons

scap. [scapula]: shoulder blade

scat. [scatula]: box

sci. fa. [scire facias]: a writ to enforce, annul, or vacate a judgment, patent, charter, or other matter of record

scr. [scrupulus or scrupulum]: a scruple

scrob. cord. [scrobiculus cordis]: the pit of the stomach

sec. [secundum]: according to

sec. [secundus]: second

sec. art. [secundem artem]: according to practice; scientifically; artificially

sec. hor. [secundis horis]: every two hours

sec. leg. [secundum legem]: according to law

sec. nat. [secundum naturam]: according to nature; naturally

sec. reg. [secundum regulam]: according to rule

sed. [sedes]: stool

sem. [semen]: seed; semen

sem. die [semel die]: once a day

sem. in die [semel in die]: once a day

semidr. [semidrachma]: half a drachm (dram)

semih. [semihora]: half an hour

sen. lat. [sensu lato]: in a broad sense

sen. str. [sensu stricto]: in a strict sense

sept. [septem]: seven

seq. [sequens]: (sing.) the following

seq. [sequitur]: it follows

seq. luce [sequenti luce]: the following day or morning

seqq. or **sqq.** [sequentia]: the following things

serv. [serva]: keep; a preserve

sesq. [sesqui]: one and one half

sesqh. or **sesquih.** [sesquihora]: an hour and a half

sesquid. [sesquidrachma]: a drachm and a half

sesquinun. [sesquinuncia]: an ounce and a half

sex. d. [sexies die]: six times a day

sex. in d. [sexies in die]: six times a day

sext. hor. [sextis horis]: every six hours

sg. or **sing.** [singularis]: singular

si dol. urg. [si dolor urgeat]: if the pain is severe

si n. val. [si non valeat]: if it does not respond

si op. sit [si opus sit]: if necessary

si vir. perm. [si vires permittant]: if strength permits

sicc. [siccus]: dry

sig. [signa]: label

sig. [signatura]: signature; a label; a direction

sig. nom. prop. [signetur nomine proprio]: label with proper name

sigill. [sigillum]: seal; signet

sign. [signetur]: let it be labeled

sin. aq. or **sine aq.** [sine aqua]: without water

sinap. [sinapis]: mustard

sing. [singulorum]: of each

sing. or **sg.** [singularis]: singular

sing. hor. [singulis horis]: every hour

sinist. [sinister]: left

Sn. [stannum]: tin

sol. or **solu.** [solutio]: a solution

sol. sat. [solutio saturata]: a saturated solution

solv. [solve]: dissolve

solv. c̄ cal. [solve cum calore]: dissolve by warming

som. [somnus]: sleep

som. hor. [somni hora]: bedtime

sp. or **spr.** or **spts.** [spiritus]: a spirit

sp. nov. [species novum]: a new species

spirit. vin. [spiritus vini]: an alcoholic spirit

s̄s̄ [semis]: one half

SS. [sanctissimi]: of the most holy

ss. [scilicet]: namely; to wit

st. [stet]: let it stand

stat. [statim]: immediately; on the spot

stern. [sterno]: to the chest

sternut. [sternutamentum]: a snuff

sub fin. coct. [sub finem coctionis]: when the boiling is nearly finished

sub. [subaudi]: to read between the lines

subind. [subinde]: frequently

subsulp. [subsulphas]: subsulphate

subt. [subtillis]: to a fine powder

subtep. [subtepidus]: lukewarm

sug. [sugatur]: let it be sucked

sum. [sumat; sume]: let him take; take

sum. [sumatur; sumantur]: let it/them be taken

sum. tal. [sumat talem]: take one such

sup. [supra]: above

sup. cit. [supra citato]: cited above

sup. gossyp. [super gossypium]: upon cotton wool

sup. lin. [super linteum]: upon linen or lint

superb. [superbibo]: to drink after

supp. or **suppos.** [suppositorium]: a suppository

sus. per col. [suspendatur per collum]: the sentence of death by hanging

syr. [syrupus]: a syrup

T

t. or **temp.** [tempore]: in the time of

t. [ter]: three times

t. or **tinct.** [tinctura]: a tincture

t.d. or **T.D.** [ter die]: three times a day

t.d.s. [ter die sumendum]: take three times a day

t.i.d. or **T.I.D.** [ter in die]: three times a day

t.o. or **tinct. op.** [tinctura opii]: tincture of opium

t.o.c. [tinctura opii camphorata]: paregoric elixir

t.q.d. [ter quaterve die]: three or four times a day

tab. [tabella]: a tablet

tal. [talis]: such; such a one

tal. dos. [tales doses]: such doses

tal. qual. [talis qualis]: such as it is

tars. ocul. [tarsis oculorum]: to the eyelids

temp. [tempore]: in the time of

tempef. [tempefactus]: made warm

tenacit. [tenacitus]: tenacity; consistency

ter in hebdom. [ter in hebdomada]: three times a week

ter quot. [ter quotidie]: three times daily

ter. [tere]: rub

ter. bene sim. [tere bene simul]: rub together well

tert. hor. [tertiis horis]: every three hours

text. rec. [textus receptus]: the received text

thorac. [thoraci]: to the chest

tinct. [tinctura]: a tincture

tot. quot. [toties quoties]: repeatedly; on each occasion

toxin. [toxinum]: a toxin

toxitabel. [toxitabella]: a poison tablet

trid. [triduum]: three days

troch. [trochiscus]: a lozenge

tunic. [tunicetur]: let it be coated

tunic. c̄ gelat. [tunicentur cum gelatino]: let them be gelatin-coated

tunic. pil. [tunicentur pilulae]: let the pills be coated

tunicat. [tunicatus]: coated

tus. [tussis]: a cough

tuss. mol. [tussis molestante or tussi molesta]: the cough being troublesome

tuss. urg. [tussi urgente]: when the cough is severe

U

u.d. [ut dictum]: as directed

u.i. [ut infra]: as stated or shown below

u.s. [ubi supra]: in the place mentioned above

u.s. [ut supra]: as stated or shown above

ult. [ultimum or ultimus]: to the last; the ultimate or extreme

ult. praesc. or **ult. praes.** [ultimo praescriptus]: last ordered or prescribed

umb. [umbilicus]: the navel

unc. [uncia]: an ounce

ung. or **ungt.** [unguentum]: an ointment

urgen. [urgente]: urgent

urgen. tus. [urgente tussi]: an urgent cough

usq. ut liq. anim. [usque ut liquerit animus]: until fainting is produced

ut dict. [ut dictum]: as directed

ut inf. [ut infra]: as stated or shown below

ut sup. [ut supra]: as stated or shown above

utri. lib. [utrius libet]: whichever he/she prefers

ux. [uxor]: wife

V

v. or **vo.** [verso]: reverse side

v. or **vs.** [versus]: against

v. [vide]: see

v.a. [vixit . . . annos]: he lived . . . years

V.D.M. [Verbi Dei Minister]: Minister of the Word of God

v.f. [vocalis fremitus]: vocal fremitus

v.g. [verbi gratia]: for example

v.i. [vide infra]: see below

v.o.s. [vitello ovi solutus]: dissolved in egg yolk

v.s. [vide supra]: see above

V.T. or **Vet. Test.** [Vetus Testamentum]: the Old Testament

v.v. or **V.V.** [vice versa]: conversely

vac. [vaccinatio]: the act of inoculation

vac. [vaccinum]: a vaccine

vac. lac [vaccinum lac]: cow's milk

vehic. [vehiculum]: a vehicle

venaes. [venaesectio]: bleeding; venesection (i.e., blood-letting)

vent. [venter or ventriculus]: stomach; belly; womb

verb. sap. [verbum sapienti]: a word to the wise

verb. sat. sap. or **verb. sat.** [verbum sat sapienti]: a word to the wise is sufficient

ves. [vesica]: bladder

ves. ur. [vesica urinaria]: urinary bladder

vesic. [vesicula]: blister

vesp. [vesper; vespere or vesperi]: evening; in the evening

vic. [vices]: time; times

vin. [vinum]: wine

vir. or **virid.** [viridis]: green

vit. or **vitr.** [vitrum]: glass

vit. ov. sol. [vitello ovi solutus]: dissolved in egg yolk

vitel. [vitellus]: egg yolk

viz. [videlicet]: that is to say; namely; to wit

vol. [volatilis]: volatile

volvend. [volvendus]: to be rolled

vom. [vomitio]: a vomiting

vom. urg. [vomitione urgente]: the vomiting becoming serious

vs. or **venaes.** [venaesectio]: bleeding; venesection (i.e., blood-letting)

vs. or **v.** [versus]: against

Z

Zn. [zincum]: zinc

zz. [zingiber]: ginger (also myrrh)

MISCELLANEOUS

THE CALENDAR YEAR
(MENSIS)

Januarius: January
Februarius: February
Martius: March
Aprilis: April
Maius or **Majus**: May
Iunius or **Junius**: June
Quinctilis or **Iulius** or **Julius** (after Julius Caesar): July
Sextilis or **Augustus** (after Augustus Caesar): August
September: September
October: October
November or **Novembris**: November
December: December

THE CALENDAR MONTH

Idus [the Ides]: the fifteenth day in March, May, July, and October; the thirteenth
  day in all other months
Kalendae or **Calendae** [the Calends]: the first day of a Roman month
Nonae [the Nones]: the seventh day in March, May, July, and October; the fifth day
  in all other months

THE DAYS OF THE WEEK
(SEPTIMANA)

Dies Dominica or **Dies Solis**: Sunday
Dies Lunae: Monday
Dies Martis: Tuesday
Dies Mercurii: Wednesday
Dies Iovis or **Dies Jovis**: Thursday
Dies Veneris: Friday
Dies Saturni: Saturday

THE DAYS OF THE WEEK
(IN PRESCRIPTIONS)

Die Soli: on Sunday
Die Lunae: on Monday
Die Martis: on Tuesday
Die Mercurii: on Wednesday
Die Jovis: on Thursday
Die Veneris: on Friday
Die Saturni: on Saturday

SOME APOTHECARY MEASURES

minimum (min.): a minim (the sixtieth part of a drachm)
scrupulus or **scrupulum (scrup.)**: a scruple (one twenty-fourth of an ounce)
drachma (drach.): drachm (also dram; one eighth of an ounce)
uncia (unc. or **oz.)**: a ounce (fluid and troy)
libra (lb.): a pound (12 ounces Roman, 16 ounces US)
semis (s̄s̄): half

COMMON METRIC MEASURES

centigramma (cg. or **cgrm.)**: a centigram
centimillilitra (centimil.): a centimilliliter
decigramma (dg. or **dgrm.)**: a decigram
decimillilitra (decimil.): a decimilliliter
gramma (grm. or **gram.)**: a gram
kilogramma (kg. or **kgrm.)**: a kilogram
milligramma (mg. or **mgrm.)**: a milligram
millilitra (mil.): milliliter

PRIMARY AND SECONDARY COLORS

albus: white
ater: dull black
caeruleus: blue
caesius: blue-gray
flavus: yellow
fulvus: brown
glaucus: green-gray

niger: black
puniceus: pink
purpureus: purple
ruber: red
viola: violet
viridis: green

169

SELECTED PREPOSITIONS AND COMMON PARTICLES

a or **ab**: from; by

ad: to; at; up to

ambo: both

ante: before

bis: twice

circa: about; near; around

circum: around or about

contra: against

coram: before; in the presence of

cui: to whom

cum: with

de: of; concerning; from

dum: while

durante: during

e or **ex**: from; out of

et: and; also

extra: without; outside of; in addition to

hac, hic, hoc: this

ibi: there

in: in; into

infra: below; beneath

inter: between; among

intra: inside; within

juxta (iuxta): near; next to; according to

ne: lest; not

nec: neither; not

nihil (or nil): nothing

nisi: unless

non: no; not

ob: for; on account of

omne (omnis): all

per: by; through

post: after

pre (prae): before

pro: for; before

propter: near; because of

qua: as

re: regarding; concerning

retro: behind; backward

semis: half; one half

semper: always

si: if; supposing that

sic: thus; so

sine: without

sub: under

super: over; above

supra: over; above

totus: all; the whole

trans: across; through

ubi: where

ultra: beyond

ut: as; so that

ROMAN NUMERALS

CARDINALS

unus (I): one
duo (II): two
tres (III): three
quattuor (IV): four
quinque (V): five
sex (VI): six
septem (VII): seven
octo (VIII): eight
novem (IX): nine
decem (X): ten
undecim (XI): eleven
duodecim (XII): twelve
tredecim (XIII): thirteen
quattuordecim (XIV): fourteen
quindecim (XV): fifteen
sedecim (XVI): sixteen
septemdecim (XVII): seventeen
duodeviginti/octodecim (XVIII):
  eighteen
undeviginti/novemdecim (XIX):
  nineteen
viginti (XX): twenty
unus et viginti (XXI): twenty-one
duoetviginti (XXII): twenty-two
duodetriginta (XXVIII): twenty-eight
undetriginta (XXIX): twenty-nine
triginta (XXX): thirty
duodequadraginta (XXXVIII):
  thirty-eight
undequadraginta (XXXIX):
  thirty-nine
quadraginta (XL): forty
duodequinquaginta (XLVIII):
  forty-eight
undequinquaginta (XLIX):
  forty-nine
quinquaginta (L): fifty
sexaginta (LX): sixty
septuaginta (LXX): seventy

ORDINALS

primus: first
secundus: second
tertius: third
quartus: fourth
quintus: fifth
sextus: sixth
septimus: seventh
octavus: eighth
nonus: ninth
decimus/decumus: tenth
undecimus: eleventh
duodecimus: twelfth
tertius decimus: thirteenth
quartus decimus: fourteenth
quintus decimus: fifteenth
sextus decimus: sixteenth
septimus decimus: seventeenth
duodevicesimus/octavusdecimus:
  eighteenth
undevicesimus/novemdecimus:
  nineteenth
vicesimus: twentieth
unetvice(n)simus: twenty-first
duoetvice(n)simus: twenty-second
duodetriginta: twenty-eighth
undetrice(n)simus: twenty-ninth
trice(n)simus: thirtieth
duodequadrage(n)simus:
  thirty-eighth
undequadrage(n)simus:
  thirty-ninth
quadrage(n)simus: fortieth
duodequinquage(n)simus:
  forty-eighth
undequinquage(n)simus:
  forty-ninth
quinquage(n)simus: fiftieth
sexage(n)simus: sixtieth
septuage(n)simus: seventieth

CARDINALS

octoginta (LXXX): eighty

nonaginta (XC): ninety

centum (C): one hundred

centum (et) unus (CI):
one hundred and one

ducenti (CC): two hundred

trecenti (CCC): three hundred

quadringenti (CD):
four hundred

quingenti (D):
five hundred

sescenti (DC): six hundred

septingenti (DCC):
seven hundred

octingenti (DCCC):
eight hundred

nongenti (DM):
nine hundred

mille (M): one thousand

duo milia/millia (MM): two thousand

ORDINALS

octoge(n)simus: eightieth

nonage(n)simus: ninetieth

centesimus: hundredth

centesimus (et) primus:
hundred and first

ducentesimus: two hundredth

trecente(n)simus: three hundredth

quadringente(n)simus:
four hundredth

quingente(n)simus:
five hundredth

sescente(n)simus: six hundredth

septingente(n)simus:
seven hundredth

octingente(n)simus:
eight hundredth

nongente(n)simus:
nine hundredth

mille(n)simus: one thousandth

bis mille(n)simus: two thousandth

ROMAN CATHOLIC LITURGY
(SELECTIONS)

THE ORDINARY OF THE LATIN MASS

1. KYRIE:

Kyrie eleison
Christe eleison
Kyrie eleison

Lord, have mercy.
Christ, have mercy.
Lord, have mercy.

2. GLORIA:

Gloria in excelsis Deo;
Et in terra pax hominibus bonae voluntatis.
Laudamus te; benedicimus te;
Adoramus te; glorificamus te.
Gratias agimus tibi propter magnam gloriam tuam,
Domine Deus, Rex coelestis, Deus Pater omnipotens.
Domine Fili unigenite Jesu Christe;
Domine Deus, Agnus Dei, Filius Patris,
Qui tollis peccata mundi,
Miserere nobis;
Qui tollis peccata mundi,
Suscipe deprecationem nostram:
Qui sedes ad dexteram Patris,
Miserere nobis.
Quoniam tu solus Sanctus: tu solus Dominus:
Tu solus Altissimus, Jesu Christe,
Cum Sancto Spiritu,
In gloria Dei Patris. Amen.

Glory to God in the highest,
And peace on earth to men of good will.

We praise you; we bless you;
We adore you; we glorify you.
We give you thanks for your great glory,
O Lord God, heavenly king, God the
Father Almighty.
O Lord Jesus Christ, the only-begotten Son:
O Lord God, Lamb of God, Son of the Father,
Who takes away the sins of the world,
Have mercy on us:
You who takes away the sins of the world,
Receive our prayers:
You who are seated at the right hand of the Father,
Have mercy on us.
For only you are holy: you alone are the Lord:
You alone, O Jesus Christ, are most high,
Together with the Holy Spirit,
In the glory of God the Father. Amen.

3. CREDO:

Credo in unum Deum, Patrem omnipotentem,
Factorem coeli et terrae,
Visibilium omnium et invisibilium.
Et in unum Dominum, Jesum Christum,
Filium Dei unigenitum,
Et ex Patre natum ante omnia saecula.
Deum de Deo; Lumen de Lumine;
Deum verum de Deo vero;
Genitum non factum;
Consubstantialem Patri,
Per quem omnia facta sunt;
Qui propter nos homines,
Et propter nostram salutem,
Descendit de coelis,
Et incarnatus est de Spiritu Sancto,
Ex Maria Virgine:
Et homo factus est.
Crucifixus etiam pro nobis:
Sub Pontio Pilato passus et sepultus est.
Et resurrexit tertia die
Secundum Scripturas;
Et ascendit in coelum,
Sedet ad dexteram Patris:

Et iterum venturus est cum gloria,
Judicare vivos et mortuos:
Cujus regni non erit finis.
Et in Spiritum Sanctum,
Dominum et vivificantem,
Qui ex Patre Filioque procedit.
Qui cum Patre et Filio
Simul adoratur et conglorificatur;
Qui locutus est per Prophetas;
Et in unam Sanctam Catholicam et Apostolicam Ecclesiam.
Confiteor unum baptisma
In remissionem peccatorum.
Et exspecto resurrectionem mortuorum;
Et vitam venturi saeculi. Amen.

I believe in one God, the Father almighty,
Maker of heaven and earth,
And of all things visible and invisible.
And in one Lord Jesus Christ,
The only-begotten Son of God,
Begotten of the Father before all ages.
God of God; Light of Light;
True God of true God;
Begotten not made;
Consubstantial with the Father,
By whom all things were made;
Who for us men,
And for our salvation,
Came down from heaven
And was incarnate by the Holy Spirit
Of the Virgin Mary;
And was made man.
He was crucified also for us,
Suffered under Pontius Pilate, [died], and was buried.
And the third day he rose again
According to the Scriptures;
And ascended into heaven
And is seated at the right hand of the Father:
And he will come again with glory,
To judge the living and the dead:
Of whose kingdom there shall be no end.
And I believe in the Holy Spirit,
The Lord and Giver of life.

Who proceeds from the Father and from the Son;
Who together with the Father and the Son
Is worshipped and glorified;
Who has spoken by the Prophets.
And in one holy Catholic and Apostolic Church.
I confess one baptism
For the remission of sins,
And I look for the resurrection of the dead;
And the life of the world to come. Amen.

4. SANCTUS:

Sanctus, Sanctus, Sanctus,
Dominus Deus Sabaoth.
Pleni sunt coeli et terra gloria tua.
Osanna in excelsis.
Benedictus qui venit in nomine Domini.
Osanna in excelsis.

Holy, Holy, Holy,
Lord God of Hosts.
Heaven and earth are full of your glory.
Hosanna in the highest.
Blessed is he who comes in the name of the Lord.
Hosanna in the highest.

5. AGNUS DEI:

Agnus Dei, qui tollis peccata mundi,
Miserere nobis.
Agnus Dei, qui tollis peccata mundi,
Miserere nobis.
Agnus Dei, qui tollis peccata mundi,
Dona nobis pacem.

Lamb of God, who takes away the sins of the world,
Have mercy upon us.
Lamb of God, who takes away the sins of the world,
Have mercy upon us.
Lamb of God, who takes away the sins of the world,
Grant us thy peace.

GENERAL-USE PRAYERS

IN NOMINE

In nomine Patris, et Filii, et Spiritus Sancti. Amen.

In the name of the Father, and of the Son, and of the Holy Spirit. Amen.

GLORIA PATRI

Gloria Patri et Filio et Spiritui Sancto.
Sicut erat in principio, et nunc et semper, et in saecula saeculorum. Amen.

Glory be to the Father and to the Son and to the Holy Spirit.
As it was in the beginning, is now and ever shall be, world without end. Amen.

BENEDICAT

Benedicat vos omnipotens Deus, Pater, et Filius, et Spiritus Sanctus. Amen.

May God Almighty, the Father, Son, and Holy Spirit, bless you. Amen.

PATER NOSTER

Pater noster, qui es in caelis, sanctificetur nomen tuum.
Adveniat regnum tuum;
Fiat voluntas tua sicut in caelo et in terra.
Panem nostrum quotidianum da nobis hodie.
Et dimitte nobis debita nostra,
Sicut et nos dimittimus debitoribus nostris.
Et ne nos inducas in tentationem,
Sed libera nos a malo. Amen.

Our Father, who art in Heaven, hallowed be Thy name.
Thy kingdom come;
Thy will be done on earth as it is in heaven.
Give us this day our daily bread.
And forgive us our trepasses,
As we forgive those who trepass against us.
And lead us not into temptation,
But deliver us from evil. Amen.

AVE MARIA

Ave Maria, gratia plena;
Dominus tecum;
Benedicta tu in mulieribus,
Et benedictus fructus ventris tui, Jesus.
Sancta Maria,
Mater Dei,
Ora pro nobis peccatoribus,
Nunc et in hora mortis nostrae. Amen.

Hail Mary, full of grace;
The Lord is with you;
Blessed are you among women,
And blessed is the fruit of your womb, Jesus.
Holy Mary,
Mother of God,
Pray for us sinners,
Now and in the hour of our death. Amen.

ENGLISH–LATIN INDEX

A

abbess: **abbatissa**

abbey: **abbatia**

abbot: **abbas**

about: **circa** or **circum**

above: **supra**

abridgment: **compendium**

absence of justice: **jus nullum**

abundance: **copia**

according to: **juxta (iuxta)** or **secundum**

according to custom: **ad usum**

according to practice: **de praxi**

according to taste: **ad gustum**

according to the circumstances: **pro re nata**

according to the rate: **juxta ratam**

according to the value: **ad valorem** or **in valorem**

accursed: **maledicus**

accused person: **homo reus**

Achilles tendon: **tendo calcaneus** or **tendo Achillis**

acid: **acidum** or **acidus**

acolyte: **acolythus**

acquittal: **liberatio**

acre: **ager**

act: **actus**

act of God: **actus Dei**

additional postscript: **post postscriptum**

adolescence: **juventus**

aforementioned: **praedictus**

after birth: **post partum**

after death: **post mortem** or **post obitum**

after meals: **post cibum**

after noon: **post meridiem**

after the fact: **ex post facto** or **post facto**

against: **contra** or **(ad)versus**

against the law: **contra legem**

against the peace: **contra pacem**

age: **aetas**

agreement: **pactum**

aid: **auxilium**

air: **aer**

alias: **alias** or **alias dictus**

all: **omnis**

all-powerful: **omnipotens**

Almighty God: **Omnipotentia Dei**

alms: **eleemosyna**

alone: **solus**

altar: **ara** or **mensa**

altogether: **in toto**

always: **semper**

among equals: **inter pares**

among friends: **inter amicos**

among other persons: **inter alios**

among other things: **inter alia**

among ourselves: **inter nos**

among the people: **in populo**

ancient: **antiquus**

and so forth: **et cetera**

and spouse: **et conjunx**

and the following: **et sequens**

and what follows: **et sequentia**

and wife: **et uxor**

angel: **angelus**

angelic: **angelicus**

ankle: **talus**

annual: **annuus**

annually: **per annum**

annuity: **annua pecunia**

anointing: **inunctio** or **unctio**

anonymous: **sine nomine**

anthology: **collectanea**

aorta: **arteria magna**

aperture: **foramen**

apostle: **apostolus**

apostolic: **apostolicus**

Apostolic See: **Sedes Apostolica**

apple: **malum**

argument: **argumentum**

arm: **bracchium (brachium)**

armed: **cum telo**

armpit: **axilla**

armpit odor: **hircismus**

around: **circa** or **circum**

as: **qua**

as a gift: **ex dono**

as a matter of form: **pro forma**

as a matter of law: **ex lege**

as directed: **more dicto** or **ut dictum**

as far as I know: **quantum scio** or **quod sciam**

as if said: **quasi dictum**

as matters stand: **e re nata**

as soon as possible: **quamprimum**

as stated above: **ut supra**

as stated below: **ut infra**

ashes: **cinis**

asleep: **per somnum**

asphalt: **bitumen**

at bedtime: **decubitus hora** or **hora decubitus** or **hora somni**

at chambers: **in camera**

at Compline: **ad completorium**

at court: **ad curiam**

at first light: **prima luce**

at full length: **in extenso**

at home: **domi**

at Lauds: **ad laudes**

at length: **ad longum** or **per extensum** or **tandem**

at my own risk: **meo periculo**

at night: **nocte**

at None: **ad nonam**

at once: **statim**

at one's own risk: **suo periculo**

at pleasure: **ad libitum**

at Prime: **ad primam**

at Sext: **ad sextam**

at Terce: **ad tertiam**

at the beginning: **ad initium**

at the day: **ad diem**

at the point of death: **in extremis**

at the public expense: **sumptibus publicis** or **sumptu publico**

at the same time: **uno tempore**

at the suit of: **ad sectam**

at this place: **ad hunc locum**

at this word: **ad hanc vocem**

at Vespers: **ad vesperas**

at will: **ad arbitrium**

B

back: **dorsum**

bad: **malum** or **malus**

bad conscience: **conscientia mala**

bad credit: **mala creditus**

baked: **coctilis**

bald: **calvus**

bandage: **fascia**

banishment: **exilium (exsilium)**

banquet: **convivium**

baptism: **baptisma** or **baptismus**

baptistry: **baptistarium**

bare: **nudus**

bark: **cortex**

barley: **hordeum**

base: **turpis**

bastard son: **filius populi**

bath: **balneum**

beak: **rostrum**

beard: **barba**

beat of the heart: **pulsus cordis**

bedroom: **cubiculum**

bee: **apis**

beer: **cerevisia**

beeswax: **cera flava**

before: **coram** (in space) or **ante** (in time)

before a judge: **coram judice**

before childbirth: **ante partum** (**antepartum**)

before Christ: **ante Christum**

before daybreak: **ante lucem**

before death: **ante mortem**

before meals: **ante cibum**

before noon: **ante meridiem** or **ante meridianus**

before the court: **in facie curiae**

before the judge: **pro tribunali**

before the war: **ante bellum**

beggar: **mendicus**

beginning point: **terminus a quo**

begotten: **genitus**

behind: **a tergo**

behind closed doors: **januis clausis**

behold the Lamb of God: **ecce Agnus Dei**

behold the man: **ecce homo**

behold the sign: **ecce signum**

belching: **ructus**

belly: **gaster** or **venter** or **ventriculus**

beside the point: **nihil ad rem**

betrayer: **traditor**

better: **melior**

between friends: **inter amicos**

between meals: **inter cibum** or **inter cibos**

between ourselves: **inter nos**

beware of danger: **in cauda venenum**

beware of the dog: **cave canem**

beyond belief: **ultra fidem**

beyond legal authority: **ultra vires**

beyond measure: **ultra mensuram**

beyond one's power: **ultra vires** or **supra vires**

beyond the law: **praeter jus**

beyond the legal limit: **ultra licitum**

beyond the powers of: **extra vires**

beyond the value: **ultra valorem**

Bible: **Biblia**

biblical: **biblicus**

big toe: **digitus pollex** or **pollex** or **hallex**

bile: **fel**

bill: **libellus**

birth: **partus**

birthday: **dies natalis**

bishop: **episcopus**

bitter: **acerbus** or **amarus**

bitterness: **amarities**

blackened: **attinctus** or **denigratus**

bladder: **vesica**

blank slate: **tabula rasa**

blessed: **beatus**

blind: **caecus**

blistering: **epispasticus**

blood: **sanguis**

bloodshot: **sanguine suffusus**

bloodthirsty: **sanguinarius**

bodily: **corporalis** or **corporeus**

body: **corpus**

Body of Christ: **Corpus Christi**

boiled: **coctus**

boiling: **bulliens** or **coctio** or **fervens**

boiling hot: **fervidus**

bond of marriage: **vinculum matrimonii**

bone: **os**

bony: **osseus**

book: **codex** or **liber**

book of judgment: **liber judiciarum**

born: **natus**

both: **ambo**

boundary: **terminus**

bowels: **alvus**

box: **scatula**

boy: **puer**

brain: **cerebrum**

brave: **fortis**

bread: **panis**

bread crumb: **mica panis**

breakfast: **ientaculum** or **jentaculum**
breast: **mamma** or **pectus**
breastplate: **thorax**
breath: **halitus**
brief: **breve** or **brevis**
broken: **fractus**
broth: **brodium**
brother: **frater**
brotherhood: **fraternitas**
brothers and sisters: **fratres**
bruised: **contusus**
brush: **peniculus**
built: **aedificatus**
burden of proof: **onus probandi**
burial: **sepultura**
buried: **sepultus**
burnt offering: **holocaustum**
butter: **butyrum**
buyer: **emptor**
buying and selling: **emptio et venditio**
by accident: **per accidens**
by all: **per omnes**
by birth: **natu**
by chance: **per accidens**
by command: **jussu (iussu)**
by common consent: **communi consensu**
by default: **per defaltam**
by degrees: **gradatim**
by divine right: **jure divino**
by families: **per stirpes**
by favor: **de gratia**
by foot: **pedibus**
by force: **manu forti**
by hearsay: **ex auditu**
by heart: **ex memoria** or **memoriter**
by itself: **per se**
by land: **pedibus**
by moonlight: **ad lunam**
by mouth: **per os**
by my fault: **per meam culpam**
by name: **per nomen**
by oath: **juramento (iuramento)**

by one's peers: **per pares**
by oral examination: **viva voce**
by order: **jussu (iussu)**
by pledge: **per plegium** or **per vadium**
by proxy: **per procurationem**
by representation: **per stirpes**
by retaliation: **per vices**
by special favor: **speciali gratia**
by stealth: **furtim**
by that very fact: **ipso facto**
by that very law: **ipso jure**
by the day: **per diem**
by the entire court: **per totam curiam**
by the grace of God: **Dei gratia** or **gratia Dei**
by the head: **capitatim** or **per capita**
by the hundred: **per centum**
by the light of day: **de claro die**
by the month: **per mensem**
by the thousand: **per mille**
by turns: **invicem**
by virtue of office: **virtute officii**
by way of: **per viam**
by way of example: **in rei exemplum**
by ways and means: **viis et modis**
by weight: **ad pensam** or **pondere**
by what means?: **quo modo? (quomodo?)**
by what right?: **quo jure?**
by witnesses: **per testes**
by word of mouth: **ore tenus** or **viva voce**

C

camel-hair brush: **peniculum camelinum**
canon law: **jus canonicum** or **lex canonica**
capital punishment: **judicium capitale**
care: **cura**
carnal: **carnalis**
carpenter: **carpentarius** or **lignarius**
cask: **cadus**

catacomb: **arenaria**

cataract: **caligo lentis**

catholic: **catholicus**

catnip: **nepeta cataria**

caution: **caveat**

celibacy: **coelibatus**

censer: **incensarium** or **thuribulum**

censor of books: **censor librorum**

censor of morals: **censor morum**

center: **centrum**

centerpoint: **umbilicus**

certainly: **certo**

chair: **sedes**

chalice: **calix**

chalk: **creta**

change: **immutatio**

chapel: **capella**

chaplet: **frons**

charity: **caritas (charitas)**

charter: **carta (charta)**

cheap: **vilis**

cheek: **bucca** or **gena**

chest: **pectus** or **sternum** or **thorax**

chicken pox: **varicella**

chilly: **frigidus** or **frigus**

chin: **mentum**

choir: **chorus**

chosen: **electus**

Christ: **Christus**

Christian: **christianus**

church: **ecclesia**

circular reasoning: **circulus vitiosus**

circumlocution: **circuitus verborum**

citizen: **civis**

city: **civitas** or **urbs**

City of Earth: **Civitas Terrena**

City of God: **Civitas Dei**

civil case: **causa privata**

civil law: **jus civile**

clarified: **despumatus**

claw: **unguis** or **ungula**

clay: **lutum**

cleric: **clericus**

clock: **horologium**

cloister: **claustrum**

close by: **juxta (iuxta)**

cloth: **pannus**

cloud: **nimbus**

club: **clava**

coated: **tunicatus**

codliver oil: **morrhuae oleum**

coffee: **caffea**

coin: **nummus**

cold: **frigidus** or **frigus** or **gelidus**

cold shivers: **horridus**

collaterally: **ex latere**

command: **mandatum**

commercial: **venalis**

common: **communis** or **vulgaris**

common good: **bonum publicum** or **commune bonum**

common law: **jus commune** or **lex communis**

common opinion: **communis opinio**

commonwealth: **respublica**

communion: **communio**

communion of the saints: **communio sanctorum**

community: **communitas**

compassion: **misericordia**

completed: **consummatus**

concave: **cavus**

concealed: **reconditus**

concerning: **in re** or **re**

condemned: **damnatus**

condition: **status**

cone: **conus**

confidentially: **sub rosa**

confined: **restrictus**

connection: **nexus**

consecrated: **sacer** or **sacra** or **sanctus**

consecrated oil: **chrisma**

consent of the nations: **consensus gentium**

consider the result: **respice finem**

constable: **comes stabuli**

contemplation of flight: **meditatio fugae**

continuance: **dies datus partibus**

contract: **pactum**

contrary to good morals: **contra bonos mores** or **adversus bonos mores**

conversely: **e converso** or **vice versa**

cooked: **coctus**

cooking: **coctio**

cooling: **refrigerans**

copper: **cuprum**

cork: **suber**

coroner: **coronator**

corporal punishment: **poena corporalis**

corporeal: **corporalis** or **corporeus**

corpse: **cadaver**

cough: **tussis**

council: **synodus**

country: **patria**

courageous: **ferox**

court of justice: **curia**

cow: **vacca**

cow's milk: **vaccinum lac**

crab louse: **pediculus pubis**

cream: **cremor**

creed: **credo**

criminal act: **actus reus**

criminal case: **causa publica**

crocodile tears: **lacrimae simulatae**

cross: **crux** or **lignum**

croup: **angina trachealis**

crown: **corona**

crozier: **baculus pastoralis**

crucifixion: **crucis supplicium**

crumb: **mica**

crushed: **contusus**

cultivated: **sativus**

cultivated land: **terra culta**

cup: **poculum**

cure: **remedium**

cure-all: **panacea**

curfew bell: **ignitegium**

curled: **crispus**

curse: **exsecratio** or **maledictio**

cursed: **maledicus**

custodian of morals: **custos morum**

custody: **gardia**

custom: **mos**

customs: **mores**

D

daily: **cotidianus (cotidie)** or **diurnus** or **in dies (indies)** or **quotidianus (quotidie)**

damned: **damnatus**

dandelion: **leontodon teraxacum** or **taraxacum dens-leonis**

dandruff: **porrigo**

danger: **periculum**

darkness: **tenebrae**

daughter: **filia**

dawn: **aurora**

day: **dies**

day by day: **per singulos dies**

Day of Judgment: **Dies Irae**

daybreak: **diluculum**

days of grace: **dies gratiae**

deacon: **diaconus**

dead: **defunctus** or **mortuus**

deadly nightshade: **belladonna**

deaf: **surdus**

deafness: **surditas**

dear: **carus**

death: **mors**

death penalty: **ultimum supplicium**

debris: **rudera**

deceased: **defunctus** or **demortuus**

deceit: **dolus**

deception: **fraus**

decided: **adjudicata**

decree: **edictum**

deed: **actus** or **factum**

deed: **carta (charta)**

deeds: **res gestae**

defendant: **reus**
degree: **gradus**
deity: **deitas**
delight: **gaudium** or **gaudimonium**
demon: **daemonium**
demon-possessed: **daemoniacus**
den of iniquity: **colluvies vitiorum**
denied: **negatum**
desertion: **transfugium**
devil: **diabolus**
devil's advocate: **advocatus diaboli**
diabolical: **diabolicus**
digestive: **pepticus**
digression: **excursus**
dinner: **prandium**
disease: **morbus**
dissolved: **solutus**
distilled: **destillatus**
district: **vicus**
ditch: **fossa**
divine law: **jus divinum**
Divine Office: **Divinum Officium** or **Opus Dei**
divine soul: **anima divina**
divine will: **numen**
diviner: **auspex**
divinity: **deitas** or **divinitas**
division: **schisma**
dizziness: **vertigo**
doctrine: **doctrina**
Domesday book: **liber judiciarum**
domestic court: **forum domesticum**
done: **factum**
door: **ostium**
dose: **dosis**
double right: **duplicatum jus**
dove: **columba**
dower: **dos**
dowry: **dos**
dozen: **duodecim**
draught: **haustus**
dregs: **faex**
dregs of society: **faex populi**

dried: **exsiccatus**
droit droit: **duplicatum jus**
drop by drop: **guttatim**
drops: **guttae**
dropsy: **aqua intercus**
drowsiness: **stupor**
drug: **medicamentum**
drug store: **apotheca**
drunk: **ebrius**
dry: **siccus**
dry land: **terra firma**
during: **durante**
during the night: **inter noctem**
dust: **pulvis**
dying: **moribundus**

E

each: **ana** or **quaque (quaeque)**
eagle: **aquila**
ear: **auris**
ear drops: **auristillae**
ear wax: **cerumen**
early in the morning: **prima luce**
earth: **terra**
east: **oriens**
easy: **facilis**
ecclesiastical court: **forum ecclesiasticum**
egg: **ovum**
egg white: **ovi albumen**
egg yolk: **ovi vitellus** or **vitellus**
elbow: **cubitum**
elder: **senex**
elders: **majores**
elected: **electus**
embroidery: **acupictura**
empty: **inanis**
empty threat: **fulmen brutum**
enclosure: **claustrum**
end: **finis**
ending point: **terminus ad quem**

enemy: **hostis**

enough: **satis**

entrance: **ostium**

entreaty: **precatio**

envy: **invidia**

epilepsy: **morbus caducas** or **sacer morbis**

episcopal: **episcopalis**

epistle: **epistola** or **epistula**

equal: **aequalis** or **aequus** or **par**

equal parts: **partes aequales**

equality: **aequalitas**

equitable: **justus (iustus)**

equity: **aequitas**

error: **erratum** or **lapsus**

esoteric: **arcanus**

eternal: **aeternus**

eternal darkness: **tenebrae aeternae**

eternally: **in aeternum**

eternity: **aeternitas**

ethereal: **aethereus**

eucharistic: **eucharisticus**

eunuch: **eunuchus**

evening: **vesper**

evergreen: **sempervirens**

everlasting glory: **sempiterna gloria**

every: **quaque (quaeque)**

every day: **per singulos dies**

every hour: **quaque hora**

every morning: **quaque mane**

every night: **quaque nocte**

everyday: **cotidianus (cotidie)** or **quotidianus (quotidie)**

everyone: **nemo non**

everything: **nihil non**

evil: **malum** or **malus**

evil intent: **malo animo**

evil spirit: **daemonium**

example: **specimen**

excrement: **merda**

executioner: **carnifex**

exempt: **immunis**

exile: **exilium (exsilium)**

exorcism: **exorcismus**

eye: **oculus**

eye for an eye: **lex talionis**

eye ointment: **oculentum**

eyebrow: **supercilium**

eyewitness: **oculatus testis**

F

face: **facies**

fact: **factum**

faith: **fides**

faith alone: **sola fide**

faithful: **fidelis**

false: **falsus**

family: **familia**

family name: **cognomen**

famine: **fames**

far and wide: **longe lateque**

farewell: **bene vale**

farmer: **agricola**

fat: **pinguis**

fate: **fas**

father: **genitor** or **pater**

father of a family: **paterfamilias**

father of the nation: **pater patriae**

fatherly: **paternus**

fault: **culpa**

fear not: **noli timere** or **nolite timere**

fearful: **timidus**

feast: **festum**

feather: **pluma**

fellowship: **communitas**

female: **femina**

feminine: **femininum**

festivity: **festivitas**

fever: **febris**

few: **paucus**

fierce: **ferox**

fight: **pugna**

finally: **ad finem**

finger: **digitus**

fingernail: **unguiculus**
finish: **finis**
fire: **ignis**
first: **prima** or **primus**
first among equals: **prima inter pares**
first impression: **prima facie**
first of all: **imprimis**
firstborn: **primogenitus**
fish: **piscis**
flame: **flamma**
flatulence: **flatus**
flood: **diluvium**
flour: **farina**
flourished: **floruit**
flower: **flos**
fluid: **fluidus**
fly: **musca**
foliage: **frons**
food: **alimentum** or **pabulum**
food of the gods: **ambrosia**
fool(ish): **stultus**
foot: **pes** or **pedis**
foot bath: **pedilavium**
foot-washing: **pedilavium**
for a day: **in diem**
for a time: **in tempus**
for and against: **pro et contra**
for better or for worse: **de bono et malo**
for breach of faith: **pro laesione fidei**
for eternal life: **ad vitam aeternam**
for example: **verbi gratia**
for external use: **pro usu externo**
for instance: **exempli causa** or **exempli gratia** or **verbi causa**
for life: **ad vitam**
for many years: **ad multus annos**
for my part: **pro mea parte**
for now: **pro nunc**
for one's country: **pro patria**
for political reasons: **rei publicae causa**
for the public good: **pro bono publico** or **pro bono**
for the time being: **pro tempore**

for this occasion only: **pro hac vice**
for this purpose: **ad hoc**
forbidden: **nefastus**
force: **vis**
forearm: **cubitus**
forefathers: **majores**
forefinger: **index**
forehead: **frons**
foremost: **primus**
forever: **ad perpetuitatem** or **imperpetuum** or **in perpetuum** or **in saecula**
forever and ever: **in saecula saeculorum**
forfeited: **forisfactum**
forgiveness: **indulgentia**
fork: **furca**
forthwith: **quamprimum**
fortunate: **felix**
foul: **turpis**
fountain: **fons**
fraud: **dolus**
free: **liber**
free from pain: **indolentia**
free will: **liberum arbitrium**
freedom: **libertas**
freely: **gratis**
freeperson: **homo liber**
freewill: **voluntas**
fresh: **recens**
friend: **amicus**
from a distance: **ex longinquo**
from afar: **a longe**
from all evil: **ab omni malo**
from all sin: **ab omni peccato**
from boyhood: **a pueris** or **a puero**
from childhood: **a teneris annis** or **ab incunabulis** or **ex pueris**
from day to day: **de die in diem**
from everlasting to everlasting: **in aeternum**
from hearsay: **de auditu**
from memory: **ex capite** or **ex memoria** or **memoriter**

from the absurd: **ab absurdo**

from the beginning: **a principio** or **ab initio** or **ab origine** or **ab ovo**

from the cradle: **ab incunabulis**

from the egg: **ab ovo**

from the first: **a primo**

from the heart: **ex animo**

from the inside: **ab intra**

from the outside: **ab extra**

from the side: **a latere** or **ex latere**

from the start: **ab initio**

from within: **ab intra**

from without: **ab extra**

from words to blows: **a verbis ad verbera**

front: **frontis**

frozen: **congelatus**

fruit: **fructus**

fruitful: **fertilis**

furnace: **fornax**

G

gall bladder: **fel**

gallon: **congius**

gallows: **arbor infelix** or **furca**

game warden: **custos ferarum**

gap: **lacuna**

garlic: **alium (allium)**

gasp: **singultus**

gate: **porta**

gauze: **carbasus**

gelatin: **gelatinum**

gender: **sexus**

gentile: **gentilis**

gentle: **lenis**

genuine: **verus**

genuinely: **bona fide**

gift: **donum**

ginger: **zingiber**

girl: **puella**

given as a gift: **dono dedit**

gland: **glandula**

glass: **vitrum**

Glory be to the Father: **Gloria Patri**

go in peace: **vade in pacem**

god: **deus**

God be with you: **Deus vobiscum**

God forbid!: **Deus avertat!**

God the Father: **Genitor**

God the Mother: **Genetrix (Genitrix)**

God the Son: **Genitus**

God willing: **Deo volente** or **volente Deo**

goddess: **dea**

godly: **pius**

gold: **aurum**

gold leaf: **auri lamina**

golden: **aureus**

good: **bonus**

good citizen: **civis bonus**

good conscience: **conscientia recta**

good deeds: **bene facta**

goods: **bona** or **merx**

goose bumps: **cutis anserina**

Gospel: **evangelium**

grace: **gratia**

grace alone: **sola gratia**

gradually: **gradatim**

Grant us peace: **Dona Nobis Pacem**

granulated: **granulatus**

grave: **sepulchrum**

great: **magnus**

greater: **major**

greatest: **maximus** or **summus**

gray: **cinereus**

grief: **luctus**

grinding of the teeth: **brygmus**

gross ignorance: **crassa ignorantia**

gross negligence: **crassa neglegentia** or **crassa negligentia**

grove: **lucus**

guardian: **tutor** or **tutrix**

guardians of the peace: **custodes pacis**

gum: **gingiva**

gum: **gummi**

H

habitually: **de more**

Hail Mary: **Ave Maria**

hair: **capillus** or **crinis** or **pilus**

hairy: **capillatus** or **pilosus**

half an hour: **semihora**

half-dead: **seminex**

halo: **aureola** or **nimbus**

hammer: **malleus**

hand: **manus**

handful: **manipulus**

handkerchief: **sudarium**

hangman: **carnifex**

happiness: **felicitas** or **laetitia**

happy: **felix**

hard: **durus**

hardened: **induratus**

harlot: **meretrix**

harmless: **innocuus** or **innoxius**

harmony: **concordia**

hatred: **invidia** or **odium**

have mercy on me: **miserere mei**

have mercy on us: **miserere nobis**

head: **caput**

head of a household: **paterfamilias**

head of hair: **capillus**

headache: **cephalagia**

healing: **cura** or **curatio**

healing power: **medicinalis operatio** or **vis medicatrix**

health: **salus** or **sanitas**

healthy: **sanus**

hearsay: **oratio obliqua**

heart: **cor**

heartburn: **ardor ventriculi**

heat: **aestus** or **calor**

heathen: **ethnicus**

heavenly: **caelestis** or **coelestis**

heavy: **ponderosus**

heel: **calcaneum** or **calx**

heir: **heres (haeres)**

help: **auxilium**

helpless: **inops**

hemp: **cannabis**

here and now: **hic et nunc**

here and there: **passim** or **sparsium**

here is the proof: **ecce signum**

here lies (buried): **hic jacet (sepultus)**

heroic: **heroicus**

hiccup: **singultus**

hidden: **absconditus** or **occultus** or **reconditus**

high: **celsus**

high priest: **pontifex** or **pontifex maximus**

high treason: **laesa majestas**

highest: **summus**

highest good: **summum bonum**

highest law: **summum jus**

highway: **alta via** or **via alta**

hip: **coxa**

hip-bone: **ilium**

hoarseness: **raucitas**

hole: **foramen**

hollow: **cavus**

holy: **sacer** or **sacra** or **sanctus**

holy bread: **panem sanctum**

holy day: **dies festus**

holy of holies: **sanctum sanctorum**

Holy Orders: **Sacrae Ordines**

holy sacrifice: **sanctum sacrificium**

Holy Scriptures: **Scripturis Sanctis**

homeless: **domo carens**

honey: **mel**

honey bee: **apis mellifica**

honeycomb: **favus**

honorary: **honorificus** or **honoris gratia**

hoof: **unguis** or **ungula**

hope: **spes**

horn of salvation: **cornu salutis**

horned: **cornutus**

horseradish: **armoracia**

host: **hospes**

hot: **calidus** or **fervens**

hour: **hora**

hour and a half: **sesquihora**

hourly: **in horas**

house: **domus**

house arrest: **custodia libera**

human: **humanus**

human being: **homo**

human body: **corpus humanum**

human soul: **anima humana**

humanity: **humanitas**

humility: **humilitas**

hump: **gibbus**

hunger: **fames**

husband and wife: **vir et uxor**

hymn: **hymnus**

hypocrisy: **hypocrisis**

hypocrite: **hypocrita**

I

I: **ego**

I myself: **ego ipse**

ice: **glacies**

icy: **glacialis**

idolator: **idolatra**

idolatry: **idolatria** or **idololatria**

if: **si**

if all did thus: **si sic omnes**

if necessary: **si opus sit**

ill will: **malevolentia**

illegal: **illicitus (inlicitus)**

illegitimate son: **filius nullius** or **nullius filius**

image: **imago**

image of God: **imago Dei**

imitation of God: **imitatio Dei**

immediately: **illico** or **statim**

immortality: **immortalitas**

implied: **tacitus**

impunity: **impunitas**

in a bad sense: **sensu malo**

in a bottle: **in phiala**

in a box: **in scatula**

in a broad sense: **lato sensu** or **sensu lato**

in a cool place: **in loco frigido**

in a glass: **in vitro**

in a good sense: **sensu bono**

in a nutshell: **in nuce**

in a series: **seriatim**

in a similar case: **in pari causa**

in a state of nature: **in naturalibus**

in a strict sense: **sensu stricto**

in a test tube: **in vitro**

in a vacuum: **in vacuo** or **vacuo**

in a word: **uno verbo**

in absence: **in absentia**

in all respects: **in omnibus**

in an analogous case: **in pari materia**

in bad faith: **in mala fide** or **mala fide**

in Christ's name: **in Christi nomine**

in common: **in communi**

in contemplation of flight: **in meditatione fugae**

in contempt of court: **in contumaciam**

in default: **in mora**

in delay: **in mora**

in different ways: **alius aliter**

in divided doses: **partitis vicibus**

in doubt: **in dubio**

in due time: **ad tempus**

in episcopal robes: **in pontificalibus**

in equal parts: **partes aequales**

in equilibrium: **in equilibrio**

in every respect: **omnibus rebus** or **toto genere**

in exchange: **in excambio**

in exile: **in exilium (in exsilium)**

in fact: **in facto** or **re vera (revera)**

in full: **in pleno**

in full court: **in banco** or **in pleno**

in good faith: **bona fide** or **ex bona fide**

in hand: **in manu**

in hymns and songs: **in hymnis et canticis**

in its proper place: **suo loco**

in itself: **in se** or **per se**

in jest: **per jocum**

in lieu of: **in loco**

in little pieces: **frustillatim**

in manner and form: **modo et forma**

in memory of: **in memoriam**

in my absence: **me absente**

in my judgment: **meo judicio**

in my opinion: **me judice**

in number: **numero**

in one's own right: **suo jure**

in open court: **in curia**

in part: **partim** or **pro parte**

in person: **in persona**

in place of: **in loco**

in place of a guardian: **loco tutoris**

in place of a parent: **loco parentis**

in plain words: **nudis verbis**

in pledge: **in vadio**

in pontificals: **in pontificalibus**

in possession: **in manu**

in prison: **in carcerem**

in private: **in privato**

in proportion: **pro portione**

in public view: **in oculis civium**

in reserve: **in pectore**

in sacred matters: **in sacris**

in secret: **in pectore** or **januis clausis**

in short: **ad summam**

in similar conditions: **in pari causa**

in so many words: **totidem verbis**

in suspense: **in suspenso**

in the absence of fever: **absente febre**

in the back: **in dorso**

in the beginning: **in principio**

in the custody of the law: **in custodia legis** or **custodia legis**

in the dark: **in tenebris**

in the essentials: **in essentialibus**

in the field: **in campo**

in the first place: **ante omnia** or **imprimis** or **in primis** or **primo loco**

in the future: **in posterum**

in the Golden Age: **in illo tempore**

in the highest: **in excelsis**

in the last place: **ultimo loco**

in the living organism: **in vivo**

in the matter of: **in re** or **re**

in the meantime: **ad interim** or **interim** or **per interim**

in the name of: **in nomine**

in the name of God: **in Dei nomine**

in the nature of things: **in rerum natura**

in the night: **in tenebris**

in the nude: **in naturalibus**

in the place cited: **in loco citato** or **loco citato**

in the place of a parent: **in loco parentis**

in the presence of: **coram**

in the presence of fever: **adstante febre**

in the presence of the court: **in facie curiae**

in the rear: **a tergo**

in the same matter: **in pari materia**

in the same place: **ibidem**

in the very act: **in flagrante delicto**

in the womb: **in utero**

in the work cited: **opere citato**

in this month: **hoc mense**

in this name: **hoc nomine**

in this place: **hoc loco**

in this sense: **hoc sensu**

in this year: **hoc anno**

in time of war: **in bello**

in transit: **in transitu**

in truth: **re vera (revera)**

in vain: **frustra** or **in vanum**

in what way?: **quo modo? (quomodo?)**

inauspicious: **nefastus**

incense: **tus (thus)**

incense burner: **thuribulum** or **incensarium**

inch: **digitus** or **pollex**

incidentally: **obiter**

incorporeal: **incorporeus**

incredible: **ultra fidem**

incurable: **insanabilis**

indispensible condition: **sine qua non**

indispensible person: **sine quo non**

indisputably: **sine controversia**

indulgence: **indulgentia**

infant: **infans**

inferior: **vilis**

inflamed: **inflammatus**

informal remark: **obiter dictum**

inheritance: **hereditas (haereditas)** or **res familiaris**

inherited property: **patrimonium**

injury: **injuria** or **vulnus**

insanity: **dementia**

instead of: **ad vicem** or **instar**

instruction: **catechesis** or **doctrina**

insurance premium: **pretium periculi**

intermarriage: **connubium**

internal: **internus**

international law: **jus gentium**

interwoven: **intertextus**

intrinsically: **per se** or **in se**

it does not follow: **non sequitur**

it follows: **sequitur**

it is finished: **consummatum est**

it is proven: **probatum est**

J

jaundice: **icterus**

jaundiced: **ictericus**

jealous: **zelotypus**

Jew: **Judaeus**

Jewish: **Judaicus**

joint: **artus**

jointly and severally: **conjunctim et divisim**

journey: **peregrinatio**

joy: **gaudium** or **gaudimonium** or **laetitia**

judge: **judex (iudex)**

judgment: **arbitrium** or **judicium**

judgment of God: **Dei judicium** or **judicium Dei**

juice: **succus**

juiceless: **exsucidus**

juicy: **sucidus**

jurors: **juratores**

jury: **duodena** or **jurata**

just: **justus (iustus)**

justice: **justitia (iustitia)**

justice for all: **justitia omnibus**

K

key: **clavis**

kidneys: **renes**

king: **rex**

kingdom: **regnum**

Kingdom of God: **Regnum Dei**

kiss: **osculum**

kiss of peace: **osculum pacis**

knee: **genu**

kneecap: **geniculum** or **patella**

kneeling: **genu flexo**

knot: **nodus**

know thyself: **nosce te ipsum (nosce teipsum)** or **te nosce**

knowledge: **scientia**

L

lamb: **agnus**

Lamb of God: **Agnus Dei**

lameness: **clauditas**

lamentation: **lamentatio**

land: **ager**

language: **lingua**

lapse: **lapsus**

lard: **adeps** or **axungia**

large: **magnus**

larger: **major**

Last Supper: **Cena Novissima (Coena Novissima)**
last will: **testamentum**
late at night: **multa nocte**
Latin Vulgate: **Editio Vulgata**
law: **jus (ius)** or **lex**
law of retaliation: **lex talionis**
law of the land: **lex terrae**
lawful: **licitus**
lawless: **inlex**
laws: **jures**
layperson: **laicus**
lead: **plumbum**
leaf: **folium**
leap year: **annus bisextus**
learned: **doctus** or **literatus (litteratus)**
learning: **scientia**
leech: **hirudo**
left: **laevus** or **sinister**
left eye: **oculus sinister**
leg: **crus**
legal act: **actus legitimus**
legal action: **lis**
Lent: **Quadragesima**
leprosy: **lepra**
leprous: **leprosus**
lesbian: **lesbius**
less: **minus**
let it stand: **stet**
let the buyer beware: **caveat emptor**
let the seller beware: **caveat venditor**
let the traveler beware: **caveat viator**
let there be light: **fiat lux**
let us pray: **oremus**
letter: **epistola** or **epistula**
liberty: **libertas**
licorice: **glycyrrhiza**
lie: **mendacium**
life: **vita**
life force: **vis vitae**
life principle: **aura vitalis**
life span: **summa vita** or **vitae summa**
lifeless: **inanimus**

lifelike: **ad vivum**
light: **lumen** or **lux**
light of faith: **lumen fidei**
light of grace: **lumen gratiae**
light of the world: **lux mundi**
light weight: **levis**
light-headedness: **vertigo**
lily: **lilium**
limb: **membrum**
limb by limb: **membratim**
lime: **calx**
limitless: **ad infinitum**
lion: **leo**
lip(s): **labia** or **labium**
liquid: **fluidus**
liquified: **liquefactus**
literally: **ad literam (ad litteram)** or **ad verbum** or **de verbo in verbum (de verbo)** or **pro verbo**
liver: **hepar** or **iecur (jecur)**
living: **vivus**
living voice: **viva vox**
loan: **pecunia mutua**
location: **situs**
long: **longus**
loophole: **fenestra**
lord: **dominus**
Lord, have mercy: **Kyrie eleison**
Lord's Supper: **Cena Domini (Coena Domini)**
loss and injury: **damnum et injuria**
lotion: **lotio**
louse: **pediculus**
love: **amor** or **caritas (charitas)**
love of money: **amor nummi**
love potion: **philtrum**
lozenge: **rotula** or **trochiscus**
lukewarm: **tepidus**
lunatic: **furiosus**
lunch: **prandium**
lung: **pulmo**
lust: **libido**
lying down: **decubitus**

M

madness: **furor**

magical: **magicus**

magician: **magus**

maiden: **virgo**

majesty: **majestas**

majority: **major pars**

Maker of the World: **Orbis Factor**

male: **masculus**

malice: **malevolentia**

malignant: **malignus**

mallet: **malleus**

malpractice: **mala praxis**

man: **homo** or **vir**

manger: **praesepe** or **praesepium**

manuscript: **manuscriptum**

many: **multus**

market: **mercatum**

marriage: **connubium** or **nuptiae**

marriage partner: **conjunx (conjux)**

married: **nupta**

marrow: **medulla**

martyrdom: **martyrium**

marvelous: **mirabilis**

masculine: **masculinum**

Mass: **Missa**

Mass for the dead: **requiem**

master: **dominus** or **magister**

masterpiece: **magnum opus** or **opus magnum**

material: **materia**

Matins: **Matutinum**

matter: **materia**

meal: **cibus**

measles: **morbilli** or **rubeola**

medical: **medicus**

medicated: **medicatus**

medicinal: **medicinalis**

medicine: **medicamentum** or **medicina**

meek: **mitis**

memory: **memoria**

merchandise: **merx**

merciful: **misericors**

mercury: **argentum vivum** or **hydragyrum**

mercy: **miseratio** or **misericordia**

messenger: **nuncius (nuntius)**

metaphysics: **metaphysica**

midwife: **obstetrix**

mild: **mitis**

milk: **lac**

mind: **mens**

mine: **meus**

mine and thine: **meum et tuum**

ministry: **ministerium**

mint: **mentha**

miracle: **miraculum**

mirror: **speculum**

miscellany: **collectanea**

mist: **nebula**

mistake: **erratum**

mix: **misce**

mixed: **mixtus**

mixture: **mistura**

monastery: **coenobium**

money: **nummus**

month: **mensis**

monthly: **menstruus** or **per mensem**

more: **plus**

morning: **mane**

morning and night: **mane et nocte**

morsel: **mica**

mortgage: **mortuum vadium** or **vadium mortuum**

mortification: **maceratio**

most blessed: **beatissimus**

mother: **genetrix (genitrix)** or **mater**

Mother of God: **Mater Dei**

mourning: **luctus**

mouse: **mus**

mouth: **os**

mouthwash: **collutorium**

movable: **mobilis**

much: **multus**

mumps: **angina parotydea**

murder: **homicidium**

muscle: **musculus**

muscle spasms: **angina pectoris**

mustard: **sinapis**

mutual consent: **mutuus consensus**

mutually: **inter nos**

my: **meus**

my fault: **mea culpa**

mystery: **mysterium**

mystic: **mysticus**

mystical union: **unio mystica**

N

nail: **clavus**

nail: **unguis** or **ungula**

naked: **nudus**

naked body: **nudatum corpus**

name: **nomen**

namely: **scilicet** or **videlicet**

narrow: **angustis**

native land: **patria**

native soil: **natale solum**

natural: **naturalis**

natural law: **jus naturae** or **jus naturale**

natural world: **rerum natura**

nautical: **navalis**

naval: **navalis**

navel: **umbilicus**

near: **circa** or **juxta (iuxta)**

neck: **collum** or **collus**

needle: **acus**

needy: **inops**

negligence: **culpa**

neighbor(ing): **vicinus**

nephew: **nepos**

new: **novus**

newly born: **neonatus**

next to: **juxta (iuxta)**

night: **nox**

night and morning: **nocte et mane**
    or **nocte maneque**

night watch: **matutinum**

nipple: **papilla**

no: **non**

nocturnal: **nocturnus**

none: **nullus**

noon: **meridies**

nose: **nasus**

nostril: **nares (naris)**

not guilty: **non culpabilis**

not of sound mind: **non compos mentis**

not permitted: **non licet**

not pleasing: **non libet** or **non placet**

not proven: **non liquet**

not without cause: **non sine causa**

notary public: **registrarius**

note well: **nota bene**

nothing: **nihil** or **nil**

notwithstanding: **non obstante**

nourishment: **victus**

number: **numerus**

nut: **nux**

nutmeg: **myristica**

O

oath: **jusjurandum (iusiurandum)**
    or **sacramentum**

oatmeal: **avenae farina**

odorless: **inodorus**

of blessed memory: **beatae memoriae**

of course: **de cursu**

of each: **ana**

of sound mind: **sanae mentis**

of the faith: **de fide**

office of Compline: **Completorium**

officially: **ex cathedra**

oil: **oleum**

ointment: **unguentum**

old: **antiquus** or **vetus**

older: **senior**

olive oil: **oleum olivae** or **olivum**

omen: **auspicium**

on all points: **in omnibus**

on bail: **per plegium**

on equal terms: **ex aequo** or **in aequo**

on the back: **in dorso**

on the contrary: **e contra** or **e converso** or **ex contrario**

on the death bed: **in lecto**

on the left: **a sinistra** or **a sinistris**

on the morrow: **in crastino**

on the right: **a dextra** or **a dextris**

on the spot: **statim**

on the way: **in transitu**

on the whole: **ad summam** or **ex toto** or **in summa** or **in toto**

once: **semel**

once for all: **semel pro semper**

one and one half: **sesqui**

one by one: **membratim**

one heart, one way: **cor unum, via una**

one of a kind: **sui generis**

one half: **dimidius**

only: **solus**

only-begotten: **unigena** or **unigenitus**

opened: **apertus**

opening: **foramen** or **os**

opinion: **sententia**

optical illusion: **deceptio visus**

oracle: **oraculum**

orange: **aurantium**

origin of evil: **origo mali**

other things being equal: **ceteris paribus (caeteris paribus)**

Our Father: **Pater Noster (Paternoster)**

ours: **nostrum**

out of court: **ex curia** or **extra judicium**

out of date: **obsoletus**

out of the depths: **de profundis**

out of the way: **extra viam**

outside the law: **exlex**

oven: **fornax**

over: **supra**

ox gall: **fel bovinum**

P

pact: **pactum**

pain: **dolor**

painful: **dolens**

painless: **sine dolore**

palimpsest: **codex rescriptus**

palpitation of the heart: **cardiopalmus** or **cardiotromus**

papacy: **pontificium**

papal encyclical: **bulla**

paper: **charta**

parable: **parabola**

parent: **parens**

part: **pars**

part for the whole: **pars pro toto**

party: **pars**

paste: **pasta**

patient: **aeger** or **patiens**

patrimony: **heredium (haeredium)**

patriot: **civis bonus**

patronage: **patrocinium**

peace: **pax**

peace be with you: **pax vobiscum**

Peace of God: **Pax Dei**

peace offering: **pacificum**

peaceful: **pacificus**

peel: **cortex**

peeled: **decorticatus**

penal: **poenalis**

penance: **poenitentia**

pending the suit: **pendente lite**

penis: **membrum virile**

people: **gens** or **plebs** or **populus**

pepper: **piper**

peppermint: **mentha piperita**

peril: **periculum**

permitted: **licitus**

person: **persona**

petition: **libellus**

pharmacist: **medicamentarius**

physical: **corporalis** or **corporeus**

physician: **medicus**

piecemeal: **membratim**
pierced: **foratus** or **perforatus**
pig: **porcus**
pilgrimage: **peregrinatio sacra**
pill: **pilula**
pillar: **columna**
pillbox: **pyxis**
pimple: **papula**
pint: **octarius** or **sextarius**
pious: **pius**
pit: **nucleus**
pitchfork: **furca**
pith: **medulla**
pity: **commiseratio**
place: **locus**
place of the seal: **locus sigilli**
plague: **lues**
plaster: **emplastrum**
plastic: **ductilis**
plenty: **copia**
point: **punctum**
point for point: **punctatim**
poison: **toxicum** or **venenum**
poison ivy: **rhus radicans**
poisonous: **venenosus** or **venificus**
polluted: **foedata**
pope: **pontifex maximus**
popular: **popularis**
position: **status**
posse: **posse comitatus**
postscript: **postscriptum**
poultice: **cataplasma**
pound: **libra**
poverty: **impotentia** or **inopia**
powder: **charta** or **pulvis**
power: **potentia** or **potestas** or **vis**
powerless: **impotens**
practice: **praxis**
praise be to God: **laus Deo**
praiseworthy: **laudatus**
pray for us: **ora pro nobis**
prayer: **oratio** or **precatio** or **prex**
preacher: **praedicator**

preaching: **praedicatio**
precious: **carus** or **pretiosus**
premature: **praecox**
prepared: **paratus** or **praeparatus**
prescription: **prescriptio (praescriptio)**
previous: **prius**
priest: **pontifex** or **presbyter** or
　sacerdos
prime of life: **juventus**
prince: **princeps**
prison: **carcer**
privately: **privatim**
prodigy: **prodigium**
profit: **lucrum**
prohibition: **interdictum**
proper: **proprius**
property: **bona** or **pecunia**
prophecy: **prophetia**
proportion: **quota**
proxy: **procurator**
pruning hook: **falx** or **falcis**
psaltery: **psalterium**
pubescent: **pubescens**
public: **publicus**
public affairs: **negotia publica**
public archives: **tabulae publicae**
public enemy: **inimicus**
public opinion: **vulgi opinio**
public property: **res publicae**
publicly: **publice**
pulley: **trochlea**
pulse: **pulsus**
pumice: **pumex**
punishment: **poena**
pure: **purus**
purified: **depuratus** or **purificatus**
purple: **ostrinus**
putrid: **putris**

Q

quack medicine: **nostrum**
quantity: **quantitas**

quart: **duo sextarii**
queen: **regina**
query: **quaere**
question: **quaere**
question of fact: **quaestio facti**
question of intention: **quaestio voluntatis**
question of law: **quaestio juris**
quicklime: **calx viva**
quickly: **cito**
quicksilver: **argentum vivum**
quota: **numerus clausus**

R

rape: **raptus**
rate: **rata**
raw: **incoctus**
reason: **ratio**
received text: **textus receptus**
reciprocally: **per vices**
red: **ruber**
redeemer: **redemptor**
refuge: **refugium**
refugee: **domo profugus**
regarding: **in re** or **re**
related by blood: **consanguinitas**
relics: **reliquiae**
religious: **religiosus**
remainder: **reliquum** or **reliquus**
remedy: **remedium**
repentance: **poenitentia**
republic: **respublica**
rest: **requies**
restless: **inquietus**
retroactive: **nunc pro tunc**
rib: **costa**
right eye: **oculus dexter**
ring: **annulus (anulus)**
ringworm: **herpes circinatus** or **porrigo**
risk: **periculum**

river: **flumen** or **fluvius**
robbery: **furtum** or **rapina**
robe: **stola**
rock: **petra** or **saxum**
root: **radix**
rosary: **corona** or **rosarium**
rotten: **putris**
rough: **durus**
royal: **regalis** or **regius**
rub well: **tere bene**
rubbish: **rudera**
rule: **regula**
rural and urban: **rustica et urbana**
rye: **secale**

S

sac: **bursa** or **diverticulum**
sacrament: **sacramentum**
sacred: **sacer** or **sacra**
sacred law: **jus sacrum**
sacred mysteries: **sacra mysteria**
sacred places: **numen loci**
sacrifice: **sacrificium**
sacrificial animal: **hostia**
sacrilege: **sacrilegium**
sacrosanct: **sacrosanctus**
sad: **tristis**
safe: **tuta**
safety: **salus**
said and done: **dictum factum**
saint: **beatus**
salt: **sal**
salt of the earth: **sal terrae**
same as above: **idem**
sample: **specimen**
sanction: **sanctio**
sanctuary: **asylum**
sane: **sanus**
sanity: **sanitas**
savior: **soter**
scales: **libra**

scalp: **cutis capitis** or **epicranium**
scaly: **squamatus**
scarlet fever: **scarlatina**
scattered about: **sparsium**
scene of the crime: **locus criminis** or **locus delicti**
school: **schola**
scissors: **forfex**
scourge: **flagellum** or **flagrum**
scribe: **scriba**
scripture alone: **sola scriptura**
scurvy: **scorbutus**
scythe: **falx** or **falcis**
sea: **mare**
seal: **sigillum** or **signum**
season: **tempus**
seaweed: **alga**
second to none: **nulli secundus**
second-hand report: **oratio obliqua**
secret: **arcanum** or **occultus**
secretarial matters: **ab epistulis**
secular: **saecularis**
secular court: **forum seculare**
secure: **tuta**
see: **vide**
see above: **vide supra**
see and believe: **vide et crede**
see below: **vide infra**
seed: **semen**
seriousness: **gravitas**
sermon: **praedicatio** or **sermo**
sex: **sexus**
sex organs: **naturalia**
sexual desire: **libido**
sexual union: **coitus (coetus)**
shade: **umbra**
shadow: **umbra**
shaggy: **villosus**
shake: **agita**
share: **quota**
sheep: **ovis**
shepherd: **pastor**
sheriff: **comes stabuli** or **vicecomes**

sherry: **vinum xericum** or **xericus**
shin-bone: **crus** or **tibia**
ship: **navigium** or **navis**
short: **brevis**
shoulder: **humerus (umerus)**
shoulder blade: **scapula**
shredded: **rasus**
sick: **aeger**
sickle: **falx** or **falcis**
sickly: **infirmus**
sickness: **infirmitas** or **morbus**
sieve: **colum** or **cribrum**
sifted: **cribratus**
sign: **index**
signature: **signatura** or **subscriptum**
signet: **signum**
silent: **tacens** or **tacitus**
silver: **argentum**
simple: **simplex**
simplicity: **simplicitas**
sin: **delictum**
sincerely: **ex animo** or **ex bona fide**
singer: **cantor**
sinner: **peccator**
sinus: **fossa**
sister: **soror**
situation: **situs**
skeleton: **ossa**
skimmed: **despumatus**
skin: **cutis**
skull: **calvaria**
skull-cap: **galerum** or **galericulum**
slate: **tabula**
sleep: **somnus**
sleepless: **ex somnis** or **insomnis**
sleeplessness: **insomnia**
sleepy: **somnolentus**
slip of the memory: **lapsus memoriae**
slip of the tongue: **lapsus linguae**
slippery: **lubricus**
slippery elm: **ulmus fulva**
slow: **tardus**
slowly: **lente**

small: **parvus**

smallpox: **variola**

smoke: **fumus**

smooth: **levis**

snout: **rostrum**

snuff: **sternutamentum** or **sternutatorium**

so help me God: **medius fidius** or **sicut me Deus adjuvet**

so it is: **ita est**

so ordered: **ordinatum est**

soap: **sapo**

soapy: **saponarius**

sodium: **natrium**

soft: **mollis**

soil: **solum**

solemn: **solemnis**

solid: **solidus**

solid earth: **terra firma**

soluble: **solubilis**

solution: **solutio** or **solutum**

son: **filius**

song: **carmen** or **cantus**

soon: **mox**

soothsayer: **augur**

soothing: **leniens**

sorceress: **pharmaceutria**

sorrowful: **lacrimosus** or **tristis**

soul: **anima** or **animus**

sound: **sonus**

sound of mind: **compos mentis**

sour: **acerbus**

source: **fons**

spearmint: **mentha viridis**

speech: **lingua**

speech: **sermo**

speech impediment: **haesitantia linguae**

spinal column: **columna vertebralis**

spinal cord: **medulla spinalis**

spirit: **numen** or **spiritus**

Spirit of Christ: **Anima Christi**

spirit of the law: **mens legis** or **voluntas legis**

spirits of the dead: **manes**

spiritual food: **manna**

spiritual gift(s): **chrisma(ta)**

spittle: **sputum**

spoken: **locutus**

sponge: **peniculus** or **spongia**

spontaneously: **sponte**

spoonful: **cochleare**

spot: **punctum**

spotless: **sine maculis**

spotted: **maculatus** or **maculis distinctus**

spouse: **sponsus** or **sponsa**

sprinkling: **aspersio**

star: **stella**

starch: **amylum**

statute: **lex**

statute law: **lex scripta**

steam bath: **balneum vaporis**

step: **gradus**

step by step: **gradatim**

sterilized: **sterilisatus**

sticky: **glutineus**

stomach: **gaster** or **stomachus**

stone: **lapis** or **saxum**

stool: **sedes**

stopper: **epistomium**

straight: **rectus**

strained: **colatus**

strainer: **colum**

stranger: **hospes**

strength: **potentia** or **virtus** or **vis**

strong: **fortis**

stronger: **fortior**

strongest: **fortissimus**

struck by lightning: **fulmine ictus**

subpoena: **subpoena duces tecum** or **duces tecum**

such as it is: **talis qualis**

suddenly: **subito**

sugar: **saccharum**

sugar-coated: **saccharatus**

suicide: **felo-de-se**

suit: **lis**

suitable: **proprius**

summary: **compendium**

sunflower: **helianthus annuus**

sunstroke: **ictus solis**

supper: **cena** (**coena**)

supposing that: **si**

surgeon: **chirurgus**

surgical: **chirurgicalis** or **chirurgicus**

surname: **cognomen**

suture: **chorda**

sweat: **sudor** or **dulcis**

sweet: **dulcis**

sweetened: **edulcoratus**

swelling: **tuber**

swift: **celer**

swine: **sus**

swollen: **tumidus**

sword: **gladius**

symptom: **indicium**

synagogue: **synagoga**

syphilis: **lues** or **lues venerea**

syringe: **sipho**

syrup: **syrupus**

T

table: **mensa**

tablet: **tabella** or **tabula**

take notice: **nota bene**

talon: **unguis** or **ungula**

tapeworm: **taenia**

taste: **gustus**

tasteless: **insipidus**

tax: **tributum**

taxation: **tributum**

teacher: **magister**

teaching: **doctrina**

tear: **lacrima**

tear ducts: **viae lachrymalis**

tearful: **lacrimosus**

tears: **lacrimae**

teat: **papilla**

temporarily: **ad interim** or **in tempus** or **pro tempore**

Ten Commandments: **Decalogus**

tenth: **decimus**

that is to say: **id est**

the best: **optimus**

the blessed life: **vita beata**

the following (things): **sequens** or **sequentia**

the heavens: **caelum** (**coelum**)

the like: **ejusdem**

the Lord be with you: **Dominus vobiscum**

the rest is lacking: **cetera desunt** (**caetera desunt**)

the same: **idem**

the state: **res publica** (**respublica**)

the whole: **totum**

theft: **furtum**

then: **tunc**

there and then: **ibi**

therefore: **ergo** or **igitur**

thick: **spissus**

thickened: **spissatus**

thief: **fur**

thigh: **femur**

thirst: **sitis**

this is my body: **hoc est corpus meum**

thorn: **spina**

threshold: **limen**

throat: **guttur** or **jugulum** (**iugulum**)

throne: **thronus**

thumb: **digitus pollex** or **pollex** or **hallex**

thus: **sic**

Thy will be done: **fiat voluntas tua**

time: **tempus**

tin: **plumbum album** or **stannum**

tissue: **tela**

to err is human: **errare humanum est** or **humanum est errare**

to have and to hold: **habendum et tenedum**

to infinity: **ad infinitum**

to the end: **ad extremum**

to the extreme: **ad extremum**

to the highest authority: **ad limina**

to the last: **ad ultimum**

to wit: **scilicet** or **videlicet**

today: **hodie**

toe: **digitus pedis** or **pedis digitus**

toenail: **unguiculus**

together: **simul**

together with: **simul cum** or **una cum**

tomb: **sepulchrum**

tomorrow: **cras**

tongs: **forceps**

tongue: **glossa** or **lingua**

tonight: **hac nocte**

tonsillitis: **angina tonsillaris**

tonsils: **amygdalae**

tooth: **dens**

toothache: **odontalgia**

touch: **tactus**

towel: **sudarium**

treasure: **thesaurus**

tree: **arbor**

trench: **fossa**

trial: **judicium**

trial by duel: **lex manifesta**

trial by fire: **ignis judicium**

trial by jury: **judicium parium**

trial by ordeal: **Dei judicium** or **judicium Dei** or **lex manifesta**

trifles: **de minimis**

trough: **praesepe** or **praesepium**

true: **verus**

true bill: **billa vera**

truth: **veritas**

twelve: **duodena**

twice: **bis**

twice a day: **bis in die**

twins: **gemini**

typewritten: **typographum**

typhus fever: **typhusus**

U

unabridged: **in extenso**

unaided: **sine auxilio**

unanimous(ly): **omnes ad unum** or **ad unum omnes** or **uno consensu** or **uno ore**

unburied: **inhumatus**

unconstitutional: **non legitimus**

uncooked: **incoctus**

under age: **infra aetatem**

under oath: **juratus (iuratus)**

under penalty: **sub poena (subpoena)**

under seal: **sub pede sigilli**

under the present circumstances: **e re nata**

under the skin: **intercus**

undeveloped: **in ovo**

unfaithful: **infidelis**

unique: **sui generis**

unity: **unitas**

universal: **catholicus**

universal consent: **consensus omnium**

unjust: **injustus**

unknown: **ignotus**

unknown region: **terra incognita**

unlawful: **nefas**

unleavened: **azymus**

unlimited: **infinitum**

unmarried: **caelebs (caelibis)**

unmedicated: **immedicatus**

unprepared: **imparatus**

unprovoked: **non laccessitus**

unripe: **immaturus**

unspoken: **tacitus**

unthankful: **male gratus**

until: **donec**

untilled earth: **terra non secta**

unwelcome person: **persona non grata**

upper arm: **humerus (umerus)**

use: **usus**

usefulness: **utilitas**

utility: **utilitas**

uvula: **columna oris**

V

vacuum: **vacuum**

vain: **vanus**

vapor: **nebula**

vein: **vena**

venom: **venenum**

verbally: **ore tenus**

vessel: **vas**

vestment: **stola**

veteran: **emeritus**

veterinarian: **veterinarius**

victim: **hostia**

victory: **victoria**

vigil: **pervigilium**

vinegar: **acetum**

virgin: **virgo**

virginity: **virginitas**

virtue: **virtus**

voice: **vox**

voice of the people: **vox populi**

W

wall: **murus**

want: **inopia**

war: **bellum**

warm: **calidus**

warmed: **calefactus**

warmth: **calor**

warning: **caveat**

wart: **verruca**

watch and pray: **vigilate et orate**

watchful: **vigil**

water: **aqua**

watery: **aquosus**

wax: **cera**

way: **via**

wayfarer: **viator**

wealth: **pecunia**

wedge: **cuneus**

week: **hebdomada** or **septimana**

weekday: **feria**

weeping: **lamentatio**

weight: **pondus**

weighty: **gravitas** or **ponderosus**

well: **bene**

wet: **humidus**

wheat: **triticum**

wheel: **rota**

which is: **quod est**

which see: **quae vide** or **quod vide**

whip: **flagellum** or **flagrum**

whole: **totus**

wholeness: **sanitas**

whooping cough: **pertussis** or **tussis convulsiva**

wicked: **malum** or **malus** or **nefarius**

wife: **uxor**

wild: **ferus**

will: **arbitrium** or **voluntas**

willow: **salix**

willy-nilly: **nolens volens**

wind: **ventus**

window: **fenestra**

windpipe: **arteria aspera**

wine: **vinum**

winter: **hiems**

winter solstice: **bruma**

wisdom: **sapientia** or **sophia**

witch hazel: **hamamelis**

with: **cum**

with a grain of salt: **cum grano salis**

with aid and counsel: **ope et consilio**

with authority: **ex cathedra**

with full right: **optimo jure**

with good reason: **non sine causa**

with greater force: **a fortiori**

with me: **mecum**

with one mind: **uno animo**

with one voice: **una voce**

with reservation: **cum grano salis**

with water: **cum aqua**

with wife and child: **cum uxoribus et liberis**

within the court: **infra curtem**

within the law: **intra legem**

within the limits: **infra metas**

within the metes and bounds: **infra metas et divisas**

within the realm: **infra regnum**

without: **sine**

without care: **sine cura**

without counsel: **inops consilii**

without deceit: **sine fraude**

without delay: **sine mora**

without doubt: **sine dubio**

without end: **infinitum**

without injury: **absque injuria**

without issue: **sine prole**

without jesting: **sine joco**

without partiality: **pari passu**

without smell: **inolens**

without stain: **sine maculis**

without water: **sine aqua**

witness: **testis**

wizard: **magus**

wolf: **lupus**

woman: **femina** or **mulier**

womb: **uterus**

wonderful: **mirabilis**

wood: **lignum**

wool: **lana**

word for word: **ad verbum** or **de verbo in verbum (de verbo)**

word to the wise: **verbum sapienti**

words: **verba**

work: **opus**

work of God: **Opus Dei**

world: **mundus** or **orbis terrae** or **orbis**

worm: **lumbricus** or **vermis** or **vermiculus**

worn out: **obsoletus**

worship: **cultus**

worthless: **vilis**

worthy: **dignus**

wound: **vulnus**

wrath: **ira**

wrath of god: **ira deorum**

wrist: **carpus**

writ: **breve**

writ of inquiry: **scire fieri**

writer's cramp: **chorea scriptorum**

written: **scriptus**

Y

year: **annus**

yeast: **fermentum**

yes: **certo**

yesterday: **heri**

yoke: **jugum**

younger: **junior**

your: **vester**

youth: **adolescens** or **juventus**

youthful: **juvenilis**

Z

zealot: **zelotes**

zinc: **zincum**

zodiac: **zodiacus**